MARCH OR DIE

MARCH OR DIE

PHILIP D. CHINNERY

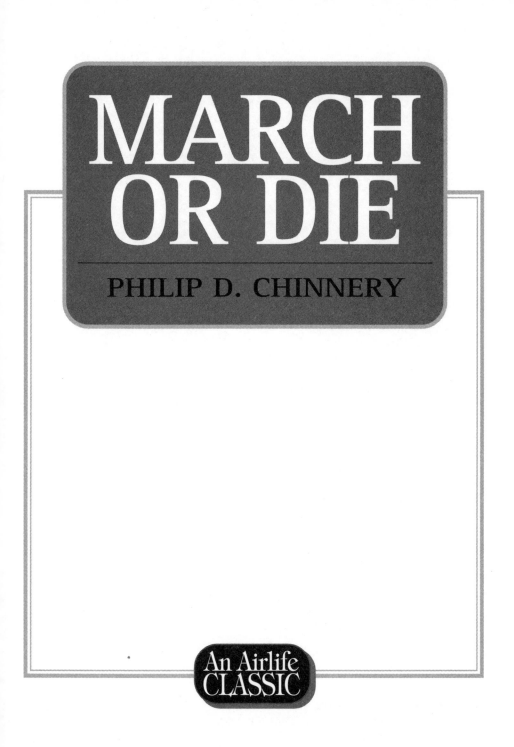

An Airlife
CLASSIC

First published in the UK in 1997
by Airlife Publishing Ltd

This edition published 2001

British Library Cataloguing-in-Publication Data
  A catalogue record for this book
  is available from the British Library

ISBN 1 84037 289 3

Printed in England by St Edmundsbury Press Ltd, Bury St Edmunds, Suffolk

Airlife Publishing Ltd
101 Longden Road, Shrewsbury, SY3 9EB, England
E-mail: airlife@airlifebooks.com
Website: www.airlifebooks.com

Foreword

I was especially pleased to be asked to write the foreword to this book. The author has taken the trouble to find and interview many of my old Chindit comrades and hear their stories at first hand. It also gave me great pleasure to talk about Orde Wingate, our leader and my good friend.

I first met Wingate during the dark days of 1942 when our Army was retreating from Burma to India. Morale was low and the Japs seemed invincible. However, Wingate knew better and so did I. He was chosen by Wavell to find a way to defeat the Japs and was given a brigade with which to try out his ideas in action. I was proud to command one of his columns in that brigade and in 1943 we crossed the Chindwin to wreak havoc behind the Jap lines.

Eventually, deep inside Burma and vastly outnumbered, we dispersed and found our way back to India. Wingate had proved his theories and, by a stroke of luck, won the patronage of the Prime Minister. Winston Churchill was nobody's fool and always seized upon signs of unorthodox genius; he sent Wingate back to India with the rank of Major-General and instructions to raise a division of men to fight behind the Jap lines, using his own methods of Long-Range Penetration.

On the 5th of March 1944, I led Wingate's old brigade back into Burma. This time we flew in by glider, courtesy of the Americans who also believed in Wingate and provided him with an Air Commando Group to support us. Five more brigades followed us into battle.

Disaster struck on the 24th of March when Wingate was killed in a flying accident. Overall control of the Chindits was passed to the American General 'Vinegar Joe' Stilwell, who had little liking for the limeys and even less idea how to use the Chindits as Wingate had planned. We were kept in the jungle behind enemy lines for four months, much longer than Wingate had ever intended and we were used to fight battles for which we were not equipped. We fought the monsoon weather, the jungle and the best troops the enemy could throw against us. When we finally marched out of the jungle, we left many brave men behind. The men of my brigade were awarded three Victoria Crosses, two of them posthumously.

Philip Chinnery's book tells of the conditions in which we fought and the reasons why we did so. It is a very good effort and I happily recommend it to everyone as a memorial to the very brave men who were the Chindits.

Brigadier Michael Calvert, DSO.
London, January 1997

'To those who remained,
on the paths, on the hills.'

from *The Road Past Mandalay* by Jack Masters

Contents

Acknowledgements

The author would like to thank the following for their help with the research for this book;

77 BRIGADE – 1943
Private Charles Aves, 7 Column
Lance Corporal George Bell, 2 Group HQ
CQMS Duncan Bett, 2 Group HQ
Major George Bromhead, 4 Column
Private Denis Brown, 8 Column
Major Mike Calvert, 3 Column
Captain John Carroll, 8 Column
Private John Cartner, 8 Column
Major George Dunlop, 1 Column
Private Leon Frank, 7 Column
Lieutenant Alec Gibson, 3 Column
Private Roger Hamer, 8 Column
Sergeant Eric Hutchins, Brigade HQ
Lieutenant Harold James, 3 Column
Private Fred Morgan, 7 Column
Lieutenant Nick Neill, 8 Column
Captain Ray Scott, 4 Column Burma Rifles
Sergeant John Thornburrow, 5 Column
Signaller Byron White, 5 Column
Lieutenant Allen Wilding, Brigade HQ
Sergeant Arthur Willshaw RAF, Brigade HQ

1944 – SPECIAL FORCE

3rd WEST AFRICAN BRIGADE: Denis Arnold 7NR, Charles Carfrae 7NR, Kenneth Kerin 6NR, R. St John Walsh 6NR, Maurice Stanion 6NR, Dr Leslie A. Wilson, Cyril Hall 12NR.

14 BRIGADE: Percy Bowles 2nd YL, Robert Boyd 1st BH, Bill Lark 2nd BW, Frank Luxa 2nd YL, Jim Perry 1st BH, Ken Robertson RE, John Salazar 1st BH, Arthur Shadbolt 2nd BW.

16 BRIGADE: Joe Adamse 2nd QU, Cyril Baldock 45th RR, Roger Brewer 45th RR, George Grossmith RE/2nd RL, John Hesketh RA, George Hill 2nd QU, George King RA, John Knowles RAF/2nd QU, Robin Needham RA, Jim Paines 45th RR, James Randall 45th RR, Ernie Rogers 45th RR, Philip Sharpe 45th RR, Peter Taylor 45th RR, Roy Vine 45th RR, Jimmy White 45th RR, Roddy Wilkins 45th RR, Jack Wilkinson 2nd RL, Arthur Withey 45th RR.

23 BRIGADE: Frank Billyeald 1st EX, Stan Hutson RA, Charles Tinsley 4th BR.

77 BRIGADE: Joe Bate 1st SS, Ken Battey 1st SS, Brigadier Mike Calvert, Dr John Chesshire 1st SS, Ron Degg 1st SS, Norman Durant 1st SS, Fred Freeman 1st KL, Bert Gilmore 1st LF, Paul Griffin 3/6GR, Arthur House 1st KL, John Lucas 3/6GR, John Mattinson 1st LF, Bill Merchant 1st LF, Hugh Patterson 1st LF, John De Quidt 1st LF, David Wilcox 1st SS, Bill Williams 1st SS.

111 BRIGADE: Norman Campbell 1st CA, Ken Davenport 1st KL, Chesty Jennings RAF, John Long 1st KL, George MacKenzie 1st CA, Joe Milner 1st KL, Maubahadur Rai 3/9GR, Brian Soppitt 1st CA, Geoffrey Straight 1st CA, Bill Towill 3/9th GR, Fred Tyhurst 2nd KO, David Wardle RSigs, Dr Desmond Whyte.

MORRIS FORCE/DAH FORCE: Bill Howe SOE, Donald McCutcheon 3/4GR, Pat O'Brien RAF, Bert Reeves RSigs, Ian Simpson 3/4GR.

SPECIAL FORCE HEADQUARTERS: Claude Fairweather RSigs.

BLADET FORCE: Stewart Binnie; **1st Air Commando Group, USAAF**: Frank Merchant, B-25 captain.

The author would also like to thank Carol Mason, Archivist, Gurkha Museum; and Lt-Col the Revd Guy Armstrong, OBE, Isle of Wight Burma Star Association.

Note: Ranks have been omitted in the 1944 credits as many men were promoted during the campaign, some more than once. Men who served with both 77 and 111 Brigades have been listed with the brigade where they served the longest. Unit names have been abbreviated, such as 1st KL – 1st Battalion, The King's (Liverpool) Regiment.

Introduction

In 1941 and 1942 the Japanese Army seemed invincible. Hong Kong, Malaya and Singapore had fallen and the British Army in Burma was retreating towards India, hotly pursued by fanatical Japanese troops who moved through the jungle like ghosts, outflanking and outfighting all who stood before them. These were dark days, and when General Archibald Wavell sent for a little known Lieutenant-Colonel in the Royal Artillery, no one would have guessed it would make such a difference to the war in Burma.

Orde C. Wingate was an expert in guerrilla warfare, a skill learnt in Palestine and Abyssinia. He came to Burma with a DSO and a reputation for the unorthodox. His trademarks were a battered Wolseley helmet and a beard, and bitter contempt for the officers of the stiff-necked Indian Army. Wingate raised and trained a brigade of 3,000 men and led them back into Burma in February 1943. Employing his revolutionary methods of long-range penetration the brigade used the jungle to its advantage, and it was supplied by Royal Air Force planes summoned by another innovation: RAF officers and NCOs equipped with wireless sets and attached to the brigade. They fought the Japanese at their own game, ambushing the jungle tracks and destroying railway bridges until they found themselves deep inside Burma, surrounded and outnumbered. Wingate dispersed his brigade into small groups and told them to make their own way back to India. Only two-thirds of them made it, but they had learnt much about jungle fighting. Prime Minister Winston Churchill was impressed and summoned Wingate to London. At last, someone had emerged who could defeat the Japanese. To the chagrin of the armchair Generals in India, Wingate was sent back, promoted to Major-General and given a whole division of six brigades to train in his methods. On 5 March his jungle fighters, now known as Chindits, flew back into Burma by glider to establish strongholds in the heart of the Japanese occupied countryside. Operation 'Thursday', the Chindit invasion of Burma, had begun.

Sadly, Wingate was killed in an air crash three weeks after his second campaign had begun. Command of the Chindits fell to the American General 'Vinegar Joe' Stilwell, whose dislike of anything British was well known. He kept the Chindits in the jungle long after the monsoon began, ignoring Wingate's dictum that the men must be taken out after ninety days behind the lines. It was five months before the survivors, debilitated by disease and malnutrition, were flown back to India. No other unit in the Second World War was kept in the field, deprived of relief or recuperation, for any length of time approaching that of the Chindits.

Fighting deep behind Japanese lines, the men who were wounded or fell sick could not be allowed to slow down the columns. While the American 1st Air Commando Group and their light planes could be relied upon to evacuate casualties during the dry months of March to May 1944, they were not available during the first expedition in 1943, nor during the monsoon season from May to August 1944. More often than not, sick or wounded Chindits had but one option, to keep up with their comrades or fall by the wayside; to march or die.

Fifty years on, their ranks have thinned considerably, but they still lead the march-past at the Cenotaph every November. Look for the men wearing the blue and yellow 'Chinthe' badge on their blazers and shake their hands. Pray, also, when the forces of evil again threaten to break down the walls of peace that men like Orde Wingate and his Chindits come forward to stand against them. Ninety Chindits, who took part in Wingate's first expedition into Burma in 1943 and the larger Chindit invasion of Burma in 1944, have spoken to the author about their experiences. From Wingate's right-hand man, Brigadier 'Mad Mike' Calvert, to the lowliest Private, these surviving Chindits describe their war in the jungle against sickness, disease, and the best that the Imperial Japanese Army could throw against them.

Part One

The First Wingate Expedition to Burma, 1943

General Wavell visiting 77 Brigade just before they set off on the first expedition to Burma in 1943. Brigadier Wingate is at the extreme right and Major Fergusson is nearest the camera wearing the rucksack. Note the censor has obliterated the Black Watch badge on his hat.

The landing area discovered by Major Scott and 8 Column as they trekked back towards India. They marked out a landing strip running from the finger of jungle at top left, towards the clear area in the top right of the picture. The area was known as 'Piccadilly' in the 1944 campaign

Inside the rescue plane, seventeen of Major Scott's men head for safety. The party comprised one Gurkha, one Burma Rifleman, fourteen men of 13th King's and Lt-Col Sam Cooke.

Signaller Eric Hutchins was in the seventh and last boat of Wingate's party attempting to recross the Irrawaddy. Left behind, only four of the seven in the boat made it back to India.

Two men of the 13th King's and a Gurkha comrade show their relief at being rescued after they marked out PLANE LAND HERE NOW in a clearing in the jungle. Note the deep jungle sores on the left arm of the man on the right.

Chapter 1

Declaration of War

Monday, 8 December 1941 was the day which altered the whole course of the Second World War. For two years Great Britain had been at war with Nazi Germany and most of mainland Europe had fallen to the armies of the Wehrmacht. Fortunately the expected invasion of Great Britain had been called off and the might of the German armies was now being directed against the Soviet Union. The 4th Army stood at the gates of Moscow, while the Russians desperately prepared to counter-attack along a 500-mile front.

In the Far East, another force of evil was readying itself to wreak death and destruction on its neighbours. Japan had already occupied Korea and its troops had been fighting in China for five years. In 1940 Vichy France had agreed that the Japanese could station five thousand troops in French Indo-China. As 1941 came to an end the Japanese had such military might in the area that it was reasonable for the people of the East Indies, Malaya, Thailand and the Philippines to fear attack. On 6 December, President of the United States Theodore Roosevelt sent an urgent note to Emperor Hirohito, the 'Son of God', in an attempt to dispel the clouds of war gathering on the horizon. It was a futile gesture. Six Japanese aircraft carriers were already steaming across the Pacific Ocean towards the Hawaiian Islands and Pearl Harbor, where the American Pacific Fleet lay at anchor. At 7.55 a.m. on 8 December the first Japanese dive-bombers began their bombing runs against the airfields and the eighty-six ships spread out beneath them. Within two hours nineteen warships had been damaged or sunk, including four of the seven giant battleships in the fleet; 350 aircraft were damaged or destroyed and 2,403 men were dead, including 1,000 of the crew of the battleship *Arizona* which blew up and sank at its moorings. It was, as President Roosevelt declared, 'a day that will live in infamy'. That evening the United States declared war on Japan and the sleeping American giant began to stir.

Great Britain had planned to announce its own declaration of war the same evening, after the United States, but news arrived that Japanese troops had begun landing in Malaya, so the Cabinet approved the declaration at once and it was delivered to the Japanese envoy at one p.m. Within a week, Japanese troops were fighting British, Indian and

Australian forces in Malaya and Hong Kong, and Japanese Marines were storming ashore on the main Philippine island of Luzon. The United States had few planes in the area with which to stop them. On 11 December the British battleships HMS *Repulse* and *Prince of Wales* were attacked by waves of Japanese dive-bombers as they headed for the base of Singapore, on the southern tip of Malaya. Within two hours they had been sunk and 840 crew had been killed. On the fifteenth, troops from the Japanese 15th Army advanced westwards from Thailand into Burma, capturing three key southern airfields. Their objective was to take Rangoon and then cut the main Allied supply line to General Chiang Kai-shek's Chinese Nationalists already fighting the Japanese in their vast country. The Japanese Army could also make good use of the twelve million acres of rice under cultivation in Burma, together with its natural resources such as oil and manganese. Burma would also provide a springboard for the invasion of India, the largest British possession in the East.

The early months of 1942 saw one defeat after another inflicted upon the Allied forces. On 15 February Singapore fell and 130,000 British, Indian and Australian troops were taken prisoner. It was the greatest military defeat in the history of the British Empire. Five days later the northern Australian port of Darwin was attacked by Japanese naval aircraft and that country began to prepare for invasion. In Burma, the airfield and town of Moulmein had fallen and the Japanese continued their advance towards Rangoon. The important Sittang Bridge was blown up too soon by the defenders on 23 February, marooning thousands of British and Indian troops on the east side of the river, in the path of the advancing Japanese. Hundreds died as they tried to swim across. On 8 March Rangoon was abandoned and the British defenders under General Alexander began their long retreat northwards to India. Two days later the first reports reached the British government of Japanese atrocities in Hong Kong and Malaya, including the cold-blooded murder by bayoneting or beheading of hundreds of prisoners of war, including wounded men, civilians and nurses. The true nature of the enemy was now becoming apparent.

On 19 March Lt-General William Slim took command of the two depleted divisions retreating through Burma, the 17th Indian Division and the 1st Burma Division. As they made their way up the Irrawaddy valley they destroyed the largest oil field in the Far East at Yenangyaung, to prevent the wells falling into Japanese hands. On 29 April the Japanese captured Lashio, cutting the Burma road to China, and at midnight the next day the men of Burcorps blew up the Ava Bridge across the Irrawaddy River and turned towards India. They had two weeks of hard marching ahead of them; 13,463 British, Indian, Burmese and Gurkha troops lost their lives during the 900-mile retreat, together with three-quarters of a million refugees. By 20 May all of Burma was in Japanese hands.

One of the men trying desperately to fight a rearguard action against the seemingly invincible Japanese was Major Mike Calvert, the commander of the Bush Warfare School at Maymyo. Together with instructors from the school and whatever stragglers he could conscript he had been operating behind the retreat, getting in the Japanese troops' way whenever possible and picking up anyone left behind. One night in April he received a message from a loyal Burmese that there were some Gurkhas in the next village who were lost and wanted to be put back on the right road to India. They were in a longhouse that stood on stilts and a faint light shone through cracks in the badly-fitting door as Calvert and two of his men approached. 'They may think we are Japs so we'll talk loudly in English as we get near the door,' he told his Corporal. 'I knocked on the door, lifted the latch and walked in. The house consisted of one long room and in the middle stood a table with nine or ten chairs around it. I already had a smile of greeting on my face, but there were no answering smiles from the occupants of the chairs. They were all Jap officers. I stopped abruptly two paces inside the doorway, but my Corporal and Private, having no idea that anything was wrong, bumped into me and pushed me further into the room before they too came to a halt when they saw the yellow faces. For what seemed like hours we stared at each other. They seemed too stunned to think of shooting. We certainly were. Suddenly I realised that there was only one thing to do. I said quickly, "Excuse me gentlemen. Good night." Then I turned, grabbed my men by the arms and bundled them out through the door and down the steps. Then we ran like hell for the jungle.'

Not long afterwards, Calvert and a dozen of his men reached a tributary of the Chindwin River. They had not seen the enemy for a couple of days and the temptation was too hard to resist. They stripped off for a badly needed bath. Calvert wandered around a little headland and dived in. He was naked except for his boots, one item of clothing never taken off in the jungle. It was fortunate that he stuck to his rule and still wore them. A Japanese officer had also decided to bathe in the same small cove and he advanced towards Calvert, determined to kill him in hand to hand combat. Around the other side of the cove, a party of Japanese soldiers was also splashing and shouting. The Japanese officer had also heard Calvert's men, but did not know their strength. If the alarm was raised they might have outnumbered the score of men in his own patrol, so he decided to tackle Calvert with his own bare hands. It was a great mistake. Calvert recalled: 'He knew his ju-jitsu and the water on his body made him as slippery as an eel, but I was bigger and stronger. It is extraordinarily difficult to keep balance or move quickly in two or three feet of water. The Jap got more vicious as he jabbed his fingers at my face in an attempt to blind me. He was putting up a tremendous show and I was hard put to it, to hold him. I pulled myself together. I had to kill him, or he would kill me. I managed to grab the Jap's wrist and force his arm behind his back. I buried my face in his chest to stop him clawing my eyes out, then as he lashed out with his left arm and both feet, I forced him gradually under water. My boots gave me a firm grip and I shut my eyes and held him under the surface. Eventually he went limp and his body floated away downstream.' There was no time to lose. Calvert staggered around the headland and alerted his men. 'Japs, in the next cove but one. They don't know we're here but they will do in a moment. I killed their officer. Get after them now.' They grabbed their guns and found about twenty Japanese and killed them all. They only just made it: soon after they reached the cove the body of the officer floated past.

Weeks would pass before Mike Calvert and his men arrived safely in India. On the way he would have plenty of time to recall his first meeting in February 1942 with a man who would change his life forever. That particular day had not started well. Calvert had been recalled seventy miles to Prome, while in the middle of a successful waterborne raid down the Irrawaddy to Henzada, only to find himself on the receiving end of a sharp rebuke for commandeering a riverboat belonging to the Irrawaddy Flotilla Company and damaging property of the Burmah Oil Company during his demolition operations. The fact that the property would have fallen into the hands of the Japanese anyway was ignored by the stiff-necked staff officer. (Years later Field Marshal Viscount Slim would refer to Calvert's 'daring raid by river on Henzada' in his memoirs.) Pretty fed up, he made his way back to the Bush Warfare School only to find a Brigadier sitting in his office, behind his desk. 'Who are you?' Calvert glared at the stranger. He was quite calm and composed. 'Wingate' he replied. 'Who are you?' 'Calvert. Excuse me, but that's my desk.' 'I'm sorry,' said the Brigadier and he moved aside at once to let Calvert sit down. Calvert later recalled: 'I was impressed. He showed no resentment at this somewhat disrespectful treatment by a major. He began talking quietly, asking questions about the showboat raid. And to my surprise they were the right sort of questions. Tired as I was, I soon began to realise that this was a man I could work for and follow. Clearly he knew all that I knew about unconventional warfare and a lot more; he was streets ahead of anyone else I had spoken to. Suddenly I no longer felt tired. For even at that first meeting something of the driving inspiration inside Orde Wingate transferred itself to me.'

Wingate did indeed know what he was talking about. From 1928 to 1933 he had served with the Sudan Defence Force, during which time he had become fluent in Arabic and gained his profound knowledge of the Middle East. Because of this he was sent for when groups of Arab rebels starting raiding Jewish settlements and damaging oil installations in Palestine and Transjordan in 1936. Wingate raised, trained and led a force of what became known as 'Night Squads', Jewish volunteers who fought and defeated the Arabs at their own game, using Wingate's guerrilla tactics. This achievement earned Wingate the DSO and the undying gratitude of the Jews, who would very possibly have chosen him to lead their own army when they fought to establish the state of Israel in 1948. Wingate's next exploit was to command a force of guerrillas against the Italians in Abyssinia, which gave him more experience and a chance to try out his theories on mobile, free-moving columns of troops, operating behind enemy lines. During some of these exploits Wingate had served under General Wavell, who was impressed with the man and his methods, and when he was appointed Supreme Commander Southwest Pacific, which put him in overall command of Burma, he sent for Wingate and ordered him to take charge of all guerrilla activities there.

It soon became clear that in the summer of 1942, nothing could be done to stop the advance of the Japanese to the Indian border. All Wingate could do was study the land and the people and the tactics of the Japanese troops. He stayed at Maymyo for a while and he and Calvert walked for miles and talked for hours. 'My conviction grew that this was a man I could fight for.' Calvert took Wingate to see General Slim, the commander of Burma Corps, and left them together. On the way back to Maymyo Wingate said he was very impressed with Slim. 'Best man, bar Wavell, east of Suez.' Wingate continued his tour of Burma, using Maymyo as a base, and in March met the Chinese General Chiang Kai-shek, some of whose troops had crossed the border into northern Burma to carry on the fight against the Japanese under the command of American General 'Vinegar Joe' Stilwell, who had been appointed Chiang's chief of staff. He wanted the views of Chiang, experienced as he was in fighting the Japanese, on the idea of a long-range penetration force to be used in the Burmese jungle. Soon Wingate was recalled to Delhi to write a full paper on what he wanted and what he planned to do if he got it. The report was submitted to General Wavell and Wingate was destined to spend weeks waiting in Maidens Hotel, Delhi while it was being considered.

While Wingate cooled his heels in Delhi, Mike Calvert continued to operate behind the Japanese advance. By the time he and the remains of his Bush Warfare School men arrived in India, sick and emaciated, two months had passed and Wingate's report had finally been accepted. He had been ordered by Wavell to form a long-range penetration brigade and was looking for volunteers to join him. Although Calvert had lost a third of his body weight due to the conditions under which he had been fighting and his good friend Captain George Dunlop was in hospital suffering from cholera, they both said yes. Instructed to get well again before reporting for duty, Calvert once again had a purpose in life. A full brigade of troops was to be trained to fight the Japanese at their own game and Wingate would lead them.

Chapter 2

77 Brigade

Wingate described his theory of long-range penetration thus: 'Granted the power to maintain forces by air and direct them by wireless, it is possible to operate regular ground forces for indefinite periods in the heart of enemy-occupied territory to the peril of his war machine.' It sounded simple enough, but it was a radical concept. The British Army fought its battles with a long logistic lifeline behind it; trucks would bring supplies and reinforcements to the front and take casualties away to the rear areas. Wingate's proposal did away with this long established system and replaced it with an aerial logistic lifeline. Once behind enemy lines, his men would be supplied by air. Their supplies, food and ammunition would be dropped by parachute into clearings in the jungle. The aircraft would be summoned by wireless, instructed which supplies to drop and told where and when. The men would collect their supplies and melt away into the jungle to continue their task. Wireless could also be used to direct air attacks on targets of opportunity if any were found in the enemy rear areas.

If Wingate's method of resupply was innovative, so indeed was the manner in which his men would move and fight. The brigade would be split into eight columns 'big enough to deliver blows of the necessary weight while small enough to slip through the enemy's net'. Four columns would comprise mainly British troops and four mainly Gurkhas (see details of column composition opposite).

One criterion for the successful employment of long-range penetration troops was that they should be used in conjunction with a main force offensive, which would occupy the enemy front-line troops while the LRP forces wreaked havoc in their rear areas. Failure to achieve this would allow the enemy to concentrate all of his forces on the destruction of the invaders. As time went by, however, it became apparent that there would be no attempt to retake Burma in 1943 and it was only with reluctance that Wavell gave Wingate permission to launch Operation 'Longcloth'. The object of the operation was firstly to demonstrate the correctness or incorrectness of Wingate's LRP theory. The second object was to test the revolt potential of the Burmese, especially the hill tribes, and to make arrangements and plans that would assist the eventual reconquest of Burma. Thirdly, the purely military object was to disrupt the Mandalay–Myitkyina line of communications, exploiting the result-ing situation and, if it seemed worthwhile, to march on across the Irrawaddy to operate against the main Japanese communications to the north and east, Maymyo–Lashio–Bhamo (see map pages 40–41). Wavell must have been convinced at an early stage that Wingate's ideas were viable, because after 77 Brigade entered Burma he ordered a second LRP unit, 111 Brigade, to be formed.

Organisation of a British Column

Unit	Number of Personnel
Column headquarters	8
RAF section	5
Medical section	5
Regimental signallers	6
Royal Corp of Signals detachment	5
Sabotage Group (Commandos)	29
Burma Rifles Platoon (Reconnaissance)	45
Infantry Company	115
Support Group	31
2nd Line Transport	57
Total	306

Notes
a)   A Gurkha column comprised 369 men as their infantry company and support group were larger, at 166 and 41 respectively. This was because they took their first reinforcements into the field with them.
b)   Each infantry company would carry four Boyes anti-tank rifles and nine light machine-guns (Brens). Two more LMGs were carried by the 2nd Line Transport for anti-aircraft duties.
c)   Each support group would carry two three-inch mortars and two Vickers machine-guns.
d)   Fifteen horses and 100 mules were allowed in each column. There were fifty-one first-line mules and forty-nine second-line.

In June 1942 Wingate was allocated the following resources from which to form his columns: 13th Battalion, The King's (Liverpool) Regiment; 3rd Battalion, 2nd King Edward VII's Own Gurkha Rifles; 142 Commando Company; 2nd Battalion Burma Rifles (composed of Karens, Kachins and Chins, the Karens from the Delta, the other two from the hills); a number of RAF sections commanded by Flight Lieutenants with recent fighting experience; a Brigade Signal Section from the Royal Corps of Signals; and a Mule Transport Company. Neither the mules nor the muleteers to lead them were readily available. It was decided that the majority of the muleteers would be Gurkhas, an unwise decision as it later transpired.

In nearly every case the troops allotted were chosen because they were the only ones available at the time. India Command was at that time very badly off for British troops and those available were unseasoned. The 13th

King's was a garrison battalion with a high proportion of middle-aged and married men and forty per cent would be weeded out and replaced with infantry drafts from Deolali before the operation commenced. Wingate stated that 'There are three elements which go to make up a good soldier: physical toughness, training (in which are included intelligence and education, which alone ensure adaptability and grasp), and courage. The last, which is the most important, may be defined as the power to endure present evil for the sake of ultimate good. A hard, well-trained soldier needs far less courage than a soft and ignorant one.' Wingate set out to mould his men into a tough, well-trained force. As for courage, they would need all they could find before the operation was over. Private John Cartner recalled the feelings of the men when they were told that they were to be commanded by Wingate: 'When we were told that he had picked us because he wanted North Country men for the job, there were the usual comments such as "What did he want to pick on us for, we were quite comfy doing garrison duties." I personally got to speak to him once, when we were resting during a training exercise. I was sat with our Labrador dog Judy when he came by. He stopped and asked me what I thought of her and I replied that she had been very impressive during her training. She was a very intelligent dog, well-trained, and her job was to convey messages between sections. On one occasion I had to go on patrol and left Judy with another soldier. Unfortunately he lost her and we never saw her again.'

The 3/2nd Gurkhas was an average wartime Gurkha rifle battalion. Only one of its officers had seen service in any war and few of the junior officers could speak Gurkhali. It was not unheard of for a battalion commander to communicate directly with the Gurkha officers and NCOs and then brief his British officers, who would command the men in battle. Soon, 200 of the 750 Gurkhas in the 3rd Battalion were weeded out and 1,200 more arrived direct from the Regimental Centre to fill the spaces in the battalion and provide muleteers for the columns. They arrived only a few weeks before the end of training and Wingate admitted in his after-action report that 'most of the Gurkhas entered Burma insufficiently trained'.

142 Commando Company was originally supposed to have been a battalion, but there were not enough trained men available. Its function was to provide each column with a squad of fighting saboteurs. They were trained by Mike Calvert and soon became experts at blowing up railway lines and bridges and laying booby-traps. Calvert was a Royal Engineer officer whose knowledge of explosives had been put to good use in Norway during the retreat of the British Expeditionary Force, and in southern England when plans were being made to resist a possible German invasion. He gained notoriety together with Captain Peter Fleming when they blew up General Montgomery's flowerpots while testing security at Monty's headquarters.

The Mule Transport Company suffered from the late arrival of both men and animals and the lack of trained personnel in the art of mule tending. Gurkhas are at their best in their traditional family unit; the battalion and the parcelling out of men as muleteers to British columns was not a good idea. However, the men themselves were physically fit, having just arrived from the Regimental Centre. This was essential as Wingate was of the opinion that 'the physical effort of mule leading is such that double pay for muleteers is underpayment'. The problem facing Wingate, of course, was 'the great difficulty in the British Army of finding the indispensable minimum of persons who could tell one end of an animal from the other'. Sadly only one or two of the mules would ever see India again. Most would be killed, eaten or set free behind the Japanese lines.

The 2nd Battalion Burma Rifles comprised native Burmese troops led by British officers, most of whom were already working in Burma when war broke out. They knew the countryside and they spoke the language of their men. Wingate later stated that they were the finest men that he had ever had under his command in the field. Their forte was reconnaissance. Carrying out patrols in enemy territory, gathering local intelligence, handling boats and living off the countryside were all tasks at which the Burmese hillmen excelled. They were also very loyal to their officers and a bond existed between officers and men that has no comparison in the British Army regimental system. Their commander was Lieutenant-Colonel L. G. Wheeler, who would be posthumously awarded the DSO after being killed by a sniper some months later, on the way back to India. The battalion would win two DSOs, one MBE, one Order of Burma, seven Military Crosses, twenty-one Burma Gallantry Medals (equivalent to the Distinguished Conduct Medal or the Indian Order of Merit) and twenty-seven Mentions in Despatches. Towards the end of the operation, after Wingate ordered his brigade to disperse and return in small groups to India, the 'Burrifs' came into their own, scouting for the enemy, walking alone into villages in search of food and seeking out boats with which to cross the Irrawaddy and Chindwin Rivers.

Wingate's brigade would be divided into two Groups. The Northern Group consisted of the following elements: Brigade Headquarters commanded by Wingate (250 all ranks); Burma Rifles Headquarters commanded by Wheeler (150 all ranks); Headquarters 2 Group (120 all ranks); 3, 4, 5, 7 and 8 Columns, each of 330 all ranks (total strength 2,200 men, 850 animals). The Southern Group comprised Headquarters 1 Group, plus 1 and 2 Columns, and had a total of almost 1,000 men and 250 animals.

Wingate's plan was to take his brigade across the Chindwin River at Tonhe and over the south–north Zibyu Taungdan Escarpment just west of the line between Pinbon and Pinlebu (see map pages 40–41). The Mu River would then be crossed and the Mangin mountain range climbed before reaching the main Japanese south–north supply line, the

Mandalay–Myitkyina railway. The line would be demolished at various points and then, continuing eastwards, the Irrawaddy River could be crossed. Thereafter the whole force could continue to harass the enemy, with support from friendly tribes in the area. Perhaps the force could sit out the monsoon in the hills, supplied by air, or maybe they could continue eastwards into China and thence back to India. It was an ambitious plan.

Order of Battle: 77th Indian Infantry Brigade

Commander:	Brigadier Orde C.Wingate, DSO, late Royal Artillery
Brigade Major:	Major R. B. G. Bromhead, Royal Berkshire Regiment, later
	Major G. M. Anderson, Highland Light Infantry
Staff Captain:	Captain H. J. Lord, Border Regiment

NUMBER 1 (SOUTHERN) GROUP

Commander:	Lt-Colonel Alexander, 3/2nd Gurkha Rifles
Adjutant:	Captain Birtwhistle, 3/2nd Gurkha Rifles
No 1 Column:	Major G. Dunlop, MC, Royal Scots
No 2 Column:	Major A. Emmett, 3/2nd Gurkha Rifles

NUMBER 2 (NORTHERN) GROUP

Commander:	Lt-Colonel S. A. Cooke, The Lincolnshire Regiment, attached the King's Regiment
Adjutant:	Captain D. Hastings, The King's Regiment
No 3 Column:	Major J. M. Calvert, Royal Engineers
No 4 Column:	Major Conron, 3/2nd Gurkha Rifles, later Major R. B. G. Bromhead, Royal Berkshire Regiment
No 5 Column:	Major B. E. Fergusson, The Black Watch
No 7 Column:	Major K. D. Gilkes, The King's Regiment
No 8 Column:	Major W. P. Scott, The King's Regiment

2ND BATTALION, THE BURMA RIFLES

Commander:	Lt-Colonel L. G. Wheeler, Burma Rifles
Adjutant:	Captain P. C. Buchanan, Burma Rifles

The dividing line between the Japanese forces in Burma and the British forces in India was the Chindwin River. Wingate's problem was how to get his 3,000 men and 1,000 animals through the corps front and across the river and walk some 150 miles to the railway without interception. All main roads, rivers and railway lines in Burma run from south to north, forming a series of hurdles for the men to cross during the course of the expedition. Careful planning was the key. No one knew whether the Japanese would be waiting on the far bank of the Chindwin, and if they were not and the crossing was successful, would they be found in force around the Zibyu Taungdan Escarpment, the first obstacle to climb? In order to confuse the enemy as to the intention of the brigade, a diversionary force of 1,000 men and 250 animals would cross the Chindwin further south. 1 (Southern) Group, consisting of a Headquarters plus 1 and 2 Gurkha Rifle Columns, would cross at Auktaung, just south of Sittaung. A small force led by Major Jeffries, commander of 142 Commando Company, would accompany them. Jeffries would wear the uniform of a Brigadier to convince the enemy that Wingate was with them. As soon as the group was across, its commander, Lieutenant-Colonel Alexander, had orders to slip away unobserved over the mountains to the east, proceed at speed to the railway near Kyaikthin, attack it in passing and then cross the Irrawaddy at Tagaung, and continue on to the mountains around Mongmit to await the arrival of the main force or further orders. It would mean a march of 250 miles through enemy-occupied territory (see map pages 40–41).

The monsoon was in full swing when Major Mike Calvert joined Wingate's new brigade at Saugor in central India and in typical fashion Wingate had chosen the camp site many miles from the nearest road, right in the thick of the jungle. He later recalled: 'Training with this human dynamo was tough but stimulating. After marching for miles and fighting mock battles in the thick bush we would strip to the waist in the steamy rain and sit round an eighth-century well, part of an ancient temple now in ruins, listening to Wingate propound his new lore of the jungle.' During the evenings the officers would sit around trying to think what to call themselves. They were known as the Long-Range Penetration Brigade and later as Special Force, but they wanted something better that would sum up in one word what they were trying to be and to do. After training was completed and the brigade was staging through Tamu, on the Assam–Burma border, prior to crossing the Chindwin, Wingate found the answer. He asked Aung Thin, one of the Burmese officers, what was the national creature of Burma. He suggested the peacock, but had to think again as Wingate considered a peacock to be un-warlike, so Aung Thin suggested the Chinthe, the mythical beast, half-lion and half-eagle, statues of which guard the entrances to many Burmese temples. Wingate thought the Chinthe symbolised the close co-operation between ground and air that was necessary for successful behind the-lines fighting. The name soon became 'Chindit' although it was not really established until after the expedition.

Wingate always contended that any ordinary soldier could be trained to operate behind the enemy lines. There was no formal selection system as used in modern times by regiments such as the Special Air Service. However, the unfit were weeded out as the training progressed and in fact 6 Column had to be broken up as those without the mental or physical abilities to survive in the jungle were sent to other units. As the word got around that a special force was being formed, officers and men from other units came forward to volunteer. We will now meet some of them.

Major George Bromhead was one of three of the original seven column commanders still alive in 1996. He knew Wingate well.

'I first knew Wingate in 1936 during the Palestine rebellion. I was an intelligence officer and as the rebellion continued and units were added to the brigade we began to look like a division. (In those days a Brigade Headquarters had four staff officers!) Eventually a Division HQ was sent from England to take over and Wingate was the intelligence staff officer.

'The next time we met was in New Delhi six years later. I was doing a temporary staff job at GHQ. One day down a passage came a slightly untidy figure wearing a Wolseley helmet instead of the more normal topee. This I later knew was Wingate's trademark . The figure greeted me with "Just the sort of chap I am looking for, I need a Brigade Major." My temporary staff job was nearly complete, so my boss let me go and there I was. Wingate explained that he had been running guerrilla operations behind Italian lines in Ethiopia, now finished since the enemy had packed in. Wavell had sent for him to do a similar job behind Jap lines in the jungle. Thus was 77 Indian Infantry Brigade formed. A British battalion raised for defence in the United Kingdom and sent to India for peacekeeping and, on average, rather old for their new role. So we had the unenviable task of sorting out the older members. A Gurkha battalion rather too young. There are no birth certificates in Nepal! Lastly a Burmese battalion which had previous experience in the retreat through Burma. One of their Majors, who was left out because of age, I met in a hotel in Delhi. "What are you doing here?" I said "A bit of leave before I go back to Rangoon. Yes, I walk. You see I am working for intelligence and every few weeks I have to walk across Burma to report and I take a spot of leave in a comfortable hotel." And we left him out for reason of age!

'Two incidents stand out in my mind during jungle training. First, an early monsoon was drumming on my office tent and the flies were sagging. Approaching through the mud came a pair of bare feet; as they came nearer a pair of naked knees appeared, and then some more naked body and finally Wingate crouched under the tent flies – wearing his Wolseley helmet and nothing else! Second, the river where the Gurkha unit was camped started to rise and we were out of touch. Nothing for it, I had to swim through the flooded water to make contact. It was a nightmare. Every animal which could swim was in the water with me. I could rest by holding the branches of trees which was what the snakes were doing. An alligator gave me a dirty look. But it ended happily. The Gurkhas had taken to the trees and were safe if not happy, and the water went down quite quickly.

'Wingate had a convenient theory about official correspondence: if left in the pending tray, most of it answered itself. If really important a reminder would follow and that was the time to reply. Sponsored by Wavell, he had of course the ear of all the heads of department in Delhi. However, he didn't understand the Indian bureaucracy and didn't want to, so every time he visited Delhi I had to nip up next day to get the results in black and white and signed. I didn't mind, I knew the system and had a girlfriend there.

'Perhaps the most important aspect during training was to work out supply by air. We had an RAF officer volunteer with each column, but there was no radio in those days to enable us to speak to the pilot from the ground. The method of marking the dropping zone was with fires in a recognisable pattern and the pilot had to rely on his fellow on the ground. Working out the rations caused many a headache. They had to be compact enough for each man to carry six days on his back and within the resources of India to produce, not to mention acceptable to the religions concerned.'

Two of the most important innovations to be tried out by Wingate's men were the use of long-range radio communication and the dropping of supplies to the men in the field by the Royal Air Force. Wingate took the unusual but very sensible decision to take Royal Air Force personnel with him to co-ordinate the air drops. Who better to talk to a pilot in the air than a pilot on the ground? In April 1942 a message was received at Headquarters 222 Group, RAF in Colombo, Ceylon: 'Volunteers are required for a special mission – officers who have knowledge of Japanese aircraft and wireless operators who have a thorough knowledge of ground to air communication.' Arthur Willshaw, a wireless operator, received the message in code. An alleged friend in the Orderly Room told him the rumour was that a captured Japanese aircraft in India was wanted for examination in the UK – a pilot to fly it and a wireless operator to work signal stations on the route. 'This was just up my street,' Arthur recalled.

'I had been a wireless operator in Singapore from 1939 until it fell and I had worked every wireless and signals station from Singapore to the UK during this time. I wanted to fly and above all I wanted to get home to take an eagerly awaited chance at "Aircrew". After an interview with my Commanding Officer a signal was received from Headquarters at New Delhi instructing me to report for an interview with the AOC-in-C. It was on Colombo railway station that I met up with my first two compatriots, a Flight Lieutenant Longmore and a Sergeant Davies, who knew no more than I did – except a rumour. Their rumour very nicely agreed with mine – little did we know!

'During the journey from Ceylon, across India to Delhi, we got to know each other. Arthur Longmore was an ex-rubber planter from Malaya, the first man, he told me, ever to loop a glider. Cliff Davies was an Australian, quiet, studious, wanting anything except a nice secure desk job. And so to Headquarters, New Delhi. Marble staircases, a very ornate office and a personal interview with Air Vice-Marshal D'Albiac. His questions rather puzzled me. What were my teeth like? Could I live on hard biscuits for a few weeks? And finally, the truth! A senior Army officer was going behind the Japanese lines in Burma. We had to try to get on to a Japanese airfield where we would take some photographs, probably even throw a few grenades, and then a quick return to India. He assured us that this would be all over in a matter of weeks. The clinching argument came: "How long have you been overseas?" "Two and a half years, Sir" "Hm – well by the time you have done this job we should be able to see you home immediately afterwards." Twelve months later, having walked some 1,500 miles over some of the most difficult country in the world, in the company of some of the world's finest soldiers, the Air Vice-Marshal kept his word!

'In those twelve months I had enough adventures to last me a dozen lifetimes. We were ordered to report to a Long-Range Penetration Group, training in the central provinces at Jhansi in India. Our RAF element had now been joined by Flight Sergeant Allan Fidler and we arrived at Jhansi in best uniform – tailored gabardine – in the middle of the monsoon. Getting off our train we were told that the brigade we were to join was in camp at Malthone some ten miles away in the jungle. On asking for transport we were none too politely told there was none available and that orders were "all personnel joining the brigade were to walk it". Leaving our suitcases behind, walk we did, the first few miles along a reasonable road and then a plunge on to a jungle track which we followed to our destination. Most of the track was signposted with the odd Army noticeboard and for the last few miles it was completely under water. Wet, miserable, bedraggled we reached the Brigade Headquarters – just a few tents in a jungle clearing. All around, people seemed to be living in trees and the surrounding water was deep enough in places to swim in. Tired, weary and fed up with life in general, I found myself having to make a bed in the forks of a large tree and then, dreaming of wild animals, especially snakes, I dropped off to sleep.

'And so began three months of hard and bitter experience. How I hated it – used to the comforts of barrack life, it became a fight for existence. We were paraded before daybreak, plunged into icy cold rivers, taught how to build bridges, how to cross lakes and fast-flowing rivers, how to shoot, how to handle explosives, how to be amateur Tarzans swinging on ropes from tree to tree, how to travel in the jungle and, above all, how to live off the jungle. The explosives tent was always open – take what you want and learn how to use it. Woe betide the careless! March, march, march ten, fifteen, twenty miles from camp along the only track in existence. We were then turned off the track into the jungle and told to find our way back to Headquarters. Added information was that the track we had come down was mined and that anyone found on it was likely to be shot. It was – and they were! Soon we began to be exactly what Brigadier Wingate, the brigade commander, required – an efficient jungle warfare force.

'We lived off the jungle, no food except biscuits – if we wanted food we foraged for it. We ate snakes, frogs, lizards, fish, roots, leaves, in fact we tried everything at least once! Pigeons were a great favourite, but there isn't much left of a pigeon that's been shot with a .303 from short range. Six pigeons just about made a meal. Stuffed with broken biscuit and served with young bamboo shoots – I can still taste them. But, of course, as we foraged, game became scarcer. Peacocks, which were plentiful to start with (they taste very much like sweet turkey), soon left the area and most of the other bigger game too. This meant foraging further and further afield into the jungle in order to get food, in order to live. We learned by experience which leaves, when dried, made tobacco substitute and which leaves to use for other vital necessities. One of my most painful recollections was the time when, somewhat in a hurry, I picked the largest leaf handy, only to find, too late, that it was covered with small hairs that, when crushed, caused a nasty itchy rash. I never made that mistake again! And so after three months of this type of living we had toughened up considerably. Flabby flesh had disappeared, chests had filled out, muscles developed where only outlines had existed before and we began to glory in a new feeling of self-reliance that was to be so important in the coming task.

'I found myself allocated to the Headquarters column together with Flight Sergeant Allan Fidler and Squadron Leader (now promoted) Longmore. Our main job was to co-ordinate the requirements of all columns, the RAF element of each being an RAF officer and two NCOs. These teams would recce for a suitable area for an air supply drop, co-ordinate the requirements of all columns and pass the information to the Brigade HQ column via the RAF wireless set. They would then go out, light flare paths in a line with the dropping zone and supervise the drop from the ground. My job on HQ column was to keep wireless contact with all the columns and also with RAF HQ New Delhi who planned and put into execution the requirement for the air supply drops. We were to carry our wireless equipment on mules and learning how to look after and cope with these obstinate animals became part of our daily life. Together with these mules we marched many, many miles on exercises in the central provinces of India.

'Our wireless equipment was the best then available, but still formed quite a cumbersome load which was carried in two leather panniers – one on each side of a mule's back. Ensuring that we had the best equipment caused quite a stir. I was instructed to proceed to Karachi to the Maintenance Unit at Drigh Road and to take what we needed from the shelves of the depot, then to bring the whole lot of equipment back by rail to Jhansi. I was assured that everything had been arranged and that I would be expected. I travelled by train from Jhansi to Gwalior, thence by BOAC Sunderland flying boat across India to Karachi. I was anything but expected, but put yourselves in their shoes: here was an NCO, with only an identification card, saying that he was authorised to take what he pleased of your scarce and important stocks. In next to no time I found myself in custody in the guardroom, and it was only when a disbelieving officer placed a telephone call directly to Air Headquarters, New Delhi and spoke to Air Vice-Marshal D'Albiac – who, on being given a situation report, requested the call be transferred to the Commanding Officer of the depot – did things start to happen my way. I found myself walking around the radio spares section saying, "Ten of those, twelve of these, all of those", while a very worried equipment officer was wondering how on earth he was to get replacements. All the items were packed on the spot and, together with a Corporal Stonelake, two truck loads of equipment were escorted across India by rail back to Jhansi. I will always remember the look on Corporal Stonelake's face, whom I am certain had been specially chosen to ensure that the precious equipment reached a service destination, when he saw our jungle home, and I know that an audible sigh of relief passed his lips when he escaped back to a normal RAF existence.

'Another three months followed, getting prepared, getting fitter, experimenting, breaking down the myth that the Japanese were the world's finest jungle fighters. It was drummed into our heads that the jungle was like the sea – boundless – in which men could move around for weeks, even months on end, within rifle shot of the enemy but without ever encountering him. We were taught to regard the jungle as our environment, and as a friend.

'Halfway through our training the sickness rate became very high and Wingate had to put his foot down. "Everyone is taught to be doctor minded," he said. "Although it is all right in normal civilian life, where ample medical facilities are available, it will not apply to us in the jungle. You have to diagnose your own complaints and then cure yourselves. When we go into action and you are sick, it will be just too bad. We shall not stop for you, for our very lives may be jeopardised by waiting for stragglers. If you are sick you are of no use to us – you become an unwanted liability, we shall leave you to effect your own salvation." Attending sick parades without good cause became a punishable offence and doctors only gave treatment to the seriously injured and really ill. We were all given our own small dispensary – quinine and atebrin for malaria, sulfaguanadin for dysentery, and other sulphur drugs for infectious wounds. We learned lessons that were to prove invaluable during our months behind the Japanese lines.

'Individual training progressed to platoon training, platoon to column, column to group, and group would exercise against group. Problems arose on all sides, signals, ciphers, transport, demolitions, all having to be solved and solved quickly. Exercises got stiffer, those that were considered unfit were weeded out. Soldiers were made NCOs and NCOs were made soldiers and had to prove themselves worthy of the leadership that would be required of them before either being ousted or re-admitted to the fold.

'And so in January 1943 we moved as a brigade by rail from Jhansi to Dimapur, which was a railhead on the road which leads via Imphal and Tamu to the Chindwin and Burma. It was here that we heard of our new name – "The Chindits". I still have a great sense of pride in knowing that I was one of them, and even more so in the fact that I was one of the very few "RAF Chindits". At the Dimapur camp our first real air droppings were successfully carried out, and then followed a 130-mile march to Imphal. We marched by night and slept by day, taking six days to do the stretch. By the first week in February 1943 we were all set to go, but the General Staff in India, even at this late hour, were worried about the advisability of turning this crazy Brigadier and his travelling circus loose behind the Japanese lines. But, on 7 February 1943, 3,000 men and 1,000 animals marched towards the Burmese border, the Chindwin and the invincible, until then, Japanese Army.'

Lieutenant R. Allen Wilding was sent to India on an officers' draft in May 1942. Much against his will he was sent on a cipher course in the November. Determined to join a fighting unit, he was rewarded for coming second in his class with a posting to 77 Indian Infantry Brigade. He detrained at Lalitpur, dressed in immaculate bush shirt and slacks fairly creaking with starch, shoes brilliantly polished and revolver clean, bright and slightly oiled. A three-tonner arrived and transported him to the brigade location.

'There I found a camp fire in the middle of the jungle with some rather scruffy officers sitting round it. Everyone was most welcoming and I was handed a soft drink. I later found out that Brigadier Wingate preferred us not to drink. Talk was resumed. It was about the terminal velocity of bombs of all things. When bedtime was upon us, the Brigade Major indicated a bush and said: "Under that if you like." So I slept there not at all disturbed by the information that this was splendid tiger country.

'I got to know the other officers at Brigade Headquarters, with whom I was to work. The intelligence officer Captain Hosegood was a very nice chap who gave me lots of help. The signals officer Lieutenant Spurlock was quite brilliant at his job and a very good chap; we remain in touch. There were also two delightful Burmese officers named Major Po and Captain Aung Thin. I gathered that our task, briefly, was to march into Burma, create such havoc as we could and then return to India. The Brigadier's idea was that, as long as we had good signal communications and reasonable air superiority, we could do without conventional lines of communication. This may sound pretty obvious now – it wasn't then. The top brass, except for Wavell, were to put it mildly sceptical. It was up to us to prove them wrong. We expected to be seriously outnumbered and the Brigadier evolved the 'dispersal' procedure.

'The whole brigade was split up into "dispersal groups" each of approximately platoon strength. On 'First Dispersal' signalled by four Gs on the bugle, each dispersal group commander was to get his group into cover, arrange all-round defence, and await orders. The "Second Dispersal" was signalled by the "alarm" on the bugle. On hearing this, each dispersal group "broke trail" and proceeded to an RV previously arranged. Everyone was supposed to know this and it was always a) forwards, rather than back the way we had come, and b) a line of some sort, i.e. a stream, so that if you missed the exact spot you could scout up and down until you found it. I got all this information from Graham Hosegood who added cheerfully that we should expect fifty per cent casualties.

'Wingate was, most certainly, a great man. A lot of little men have done their best to denigrate him. They would have been better employed trying to help him. He had great physical and moral courage and possessed a will of iron. I have been fortunate in that I have spent most of my life in the company of very intelligent people, so I am some sort of judge of intelligence. His was a blazing intelligence. He was a great reader of the Old Testament. I suppose he was possibly the last of the "Sword and Bible Generals". Of course he had his faults; he could or would not suffer fools gladly, he could be rather rude and he was ruthless. Ruthlessness is, I fear, something that all commanders must have. He never threw a life away, but you always felt that he realised that his life and the life of each of us was expendable if it was necessary. I remember, when things were very bad, sitting under a bush with my Sergeant trying to decipher a more than usually corrupt signal and hearing him ask the MO, "How long can Wilding last? The MO said, "About a week I think. The Brigadier's reply was, "I only want him for another two days." Of course neither of them knew I was within earshot and were taken aback by my not very respectful interjection, "After that I suppose you will have me shot like the bloody mules." But he was also very kind. One day I had been working very hard and, having lost my spectacles, had developed a raging headache. The Brigadier was passing and stopped to ask how I was. When I explained that I had a cracking headache, he sat down and started to tell me some hilarious stories about the liberation of Abyssinia, in which he took a prominent part. His description of his entry into Addis Ababa on a most photogenic white horse sticks in my memory. When he had finished he put his hand on my head and went away. My headache had gone.

'About ten days after I joined the brigade, we set out for Saugor. It was about 100 miles and we took four days to do it. We arrived on 4 December 1942 and set out for Jhansi on the ninth, my thirty-second birthday. The march, which was mainly at night, took nine days and the distance was between 150 and 160 miles. I used to go to sleep on the march, and, as my normal gait was quicker than that of the column, I often found myself marching alongside the Brigadier who was leading. At first he asked if there was anything wrong, but later he got used to me and merely said, "Wake up Wilding." Sleeping on the march is a useful knack, but should not be used in enemy country!'

TOP LEFT: Signaller Byron White was one of 74 men from 5 Column who crossed the chest-deep, fast-running Schweli River at night, after treacherous Burmese marooned them on an island in the river. Forty-six others either drowned or refused to cross and were captured by the Japanese in the morning.

TOP RIGHT: Lieutenant Allen Wilding, the 77 Brigade Cipher Officer on the first Wingate expedition. Captured by the Japanese on the way back to India, he was one of the few Chindits to survive two years in Rangoon jail.

BOTTOM LEFT: Lieutenant Nick Neill, twelve months after successfully reaching India with Lt Tag Sprague and their party. He still has the Tommy gun that he acquired on the way out and used it to good effect a few days after this picture was taken. His patrol ambushed and killed 30 Japs without loss.

BOTTOM RIGHT: Sergeant John Thornburrow of 5 Column, who took over Lt Stibbe's platoon after he was wounded at Hintha. He was later awarded the Military Medal.

Lance-Corporal George Bell, from Headquarters Northern Group, escaped back to India with Lieutenant Pearce's party after Wingate dispersed his brigade.

Photographed at Secunderabad before the first Wingate expedition, 7 Column members Charles Aves *(centre)* with Leon Frank on his left. Frank was captured whilst trying to escape to China and was one of the few Chindits to survive two years as a prisoner in Rangoon jail.

Brigadier Wingate *(right)* and George Bromhead his Brigade Major, plan 77 Brigade's expedition into Burma in early 1943. Bromhead later took over command of 4 Column a day or so before it was scattered by a Jap ambush.

Private Roger Hamer of the 13th King's trekked out of Burma with Major Scott's party from 8 Column. After one ambush, whilst in bivouac by a river, he found himself in a group of 22 men, of which only two had rifles.

Chapter 3

Operation 'Longcloth'

A s the brigade was formed, the size of headquarters increased until it was nearly as large as a column. With the exception of the Gurkha Defence Platoon, it was not a coherent fighting force. Apart from staff officers, their orderlies and grooms, there was an intelligence section, a small cipher section, an RAF signals section, the senior medical officer and his orderlies and a propaganda section, complete with loudspeakers. All these, with their respective mules, horses, bullocks and those animals' attendants, came to about 200 people. Allen Wilding was allocated half of a mule, to carry his cipher tables.

Just before the brigade set off for the Chindwin River, a group of journalists arrived. Wilding recalls:

> 'They much appreciated the Brigadier who talked to them for three-quarters of an hour without losing their attention. When we set off they came with us, for about, I think, two days' march over the Chindwin. Then they went home. On the march to the Chindwin one of them gave his camera to one of the Burma Rifles to carry, which was a liberty. The Burrif (short for Burma Rifles) was wheeling a bicycle – heaven knows why – and he strapped the camera to the luggage grid. Clearly the path was unsuitable for cycles so the Burrif cast it down the khudside, camera and all. The journalist was not amused. I once described the crossing of the Chindwin as resembling a boat race between Colney Hatch and Bedlam, but we got away with it. Sadly one of the British muleteers was drowned – our first casualty. Over the next six weeks we covered about 600 miles. Our usual day's march must have been about twenty miles and this would have been a piece of cake had we received proper rations and if water had not been such a problem. The brigade's ration scale was designed for use by paratroops and for a trip of four to five days. We lived on them for ten weeks, and averaged, according to my reckoning, only one third of the proper ration per day.'

Brigadier Wingate's first expedition crossed the Chindwin River into Burma on 13 February 1943. They were not to know that almost one third of them would never see India again. The main body crossed the Chindwin at Tonhe, where the river is only 400 yards wide. The diversionary force crossed over further south. Wingate had forecast that their chances of survival were fifty-fifty and warned that any wounded who were unable to

33

walk would have to be abandoned. The thoughts of the men, as they trod their first steps on Japanese occupied soil, can be imagined. Luck was with Wingate as he led his brigade into Burma. Japanese patrols had been positioned at several important points on trails crossing the Zibyu Taung-dan Escarpment. In addition, two companies of Japanese infantry had been despatched to reconnoitre the situation along the Chindwin River and were in fact still on their way when Wingate crossed over. Whether by luck or design, 77 Brigade was advancing along the operational boundary between the 18th and 33rd Japanese Divisions. The Japanese plan at that time was purely defensive as far as India was concerned, while they reorganised and tightened their grip on Burma. However, Wingate's expedition would change all that – he would well and truly put the cat amongst the pigeons.

ORDER OF THE DAY
Issued to the columns as they crossed the Chindwin, 13 to 17 February 1943

Today we stand on the threshold of battle. The time of preparation is over, and we are moving on the enemy to prove ourselves and our methods. At this moment we stand beside the soldiers of the United Nations in the front-line trenches throughout the world. It is always a minority that occupies the front-line. It is a still smaller minority that accepts with a good heart tasks like this that we have chosen to carry out. We need not, therefore, as we go forward into the conflict, suspect ourselves of selfish or interested motives. We have all had the opportunity of withdrawing and we are here because we have chosen to be here; that is, we have chosen to bear the burden and heat of the day. Men who make this choice are above the average in courage. We need therefore have no fear for the staunchness and guts of our comrades.

The motive which has led each and all of us to devote ourselves to what lies ahead cannot conceivably have been a bad motive. Comfort and security are not sacrificed voluntarily for the sake of other by ill-disposed people. Our motive, therefore, may be taken to be the desire to serve our day and generation in the way that seems nearest to our hand. The battle is not always to the strong nor the race to the swift. Victory in war cannot be counted upon, but what can be counted upon is that we shall go forward determined to do what we can to bring this war to an end, which we believe best for our friends and comrades in arms, without boastfulness or forgetting our duty, resolved to do the right so far as we can see the right.

Our aim is to make possible a government of the world in which all men can live at peace and with equal opportunity of service.

Finally, knowing the vanity of man's effort and the confusion of his purpose, let us pray that God may accept our services and direct our endeavours, so that when we shall have done all we shall see the fruit of our labours and be satisfied.

O.C. WINGATE, Commander,
77th Indian Infantry Brigade

Each of the five columns in the main Northern Group was given specific tasks as they advanced into Burma. 3 Column under the command of Major Mike Calvert, and 5 Column led by Major Bernard Fergusson, a volunteer from the Black Watch, would head for the railway with the aim of cutting the line in as many places as possible. While those two columns made for the railway line, laden with explosives and demolition equipment, the other three columns would seek out and engage the enemy. Lance-Corporal George Bell, a section commander in the 13th King's was with Northern Group Headquarters, under Colonel Sam Cooke. He recalled the start of the great adventure, in particular the approach march from the railhead to the Chindwin:

'All regimental and battalion flashes were removed, and we walked only by night in silence; secrecy was the order of the day. I do, however, remember the glorious sunrises. Finally down to the plains and Imphal. The mules arrived a few days later, but there were insufficient Gurkhas to act as muleteers. By the usual Army style of volunteering, "You, you and you", I was given a mule to look after. As a townie, I hadn't a clue, but after a few errors of judgement initially, I really enjoyed the experience. The mules were obstinate, awkward, occasionally playful, but I soon found that, as with most animals, if you were kind to them they reciprocated. I was rather sorry to lose "Daisy Bell" when the remaining Gurkhas arrived. We stayed at Imphal for a while, and on 7 February we were inspected by General Wavell. My mule did not appreciate the occasion and was very awkward as he approached.

'All the columns set off, the first hazard being the crossing of the Chindwin. On the way we crossed the Burmese border, which is to the west of the river. We were told to throw away any unnecessary articles to reduce the load we had to carry. My first error of judgement was discarding one half of my mess tin. It caused me great inconvenience during the next few months. I threw away all my shaving kit and eventually sported quite a beard – Victorian style with "mutton chop" whiskers. An officer had thrown away a copy of *For Whom the Bell Tolls* and I read it in the next few days in the periodic breaks, then slung it.

'Our last-minute instructions were, "Do not stray away from the main party. You are in Nagaland and some of the natives were recently headhunters!" Actually, they were very friendly people. The order of the day was, "The River Chindwin is your river of Jordan. Once over, there is no return except via Rangoon." I wonder if Wingate really meant that – it seemed a long way to walk!

'Most of the lads had no idea what was the purpose of our expedition, other than vague ideas: "To overcome the fallacies that British troops are inferior to the Japs in jungle fighting." We were excited about where we were going, but what would happen when we arrived there was a mystery.

35

Did the top brass know? Nevertheless, we plodded on until we finally reached the Chindwin and the columns crossed at different places. I crossed late in the afternoon on a large raft with about ten others. There were no problems generally, apart from some awkward mules who insisted on going back.

'On guard that night I was concerned that the Japs might attack and realised how noisy the jungle was. As we pushed on, we reached the first village. There had been a supply drop before we got there, enough for five days' rations per man. Our mail had, however, gone astray – rumour had it that it had fallen into Jap hands and despite all our secrecy they knew almost everyone in our columns. One day's rations consisted of three packets of hard biscuits, four in each pack; one tin of cheese for two days; milk powder; raisins and nuts; three tea bags; one bar of chocolate or acid drops; sugar; twenty cigarettes and one box of matches. Our menu for the next few weeks consisted of one packet of biscuits for each meal, broken up and boiled in the mess tin, mixed with cheese, chocolate or nuts and raisins. As we had a limited time to prepare these delicacies, my loss of half of my mess tin mentioned earlier, meant that at times I had to forgo the tea. If the Japs were around, fires were not allowed and the biscuits had to be eaten cold. They were almost as hard as dog biscuits. In retrospect, this was a serious error of judgement by Wingate. Those rations I felt were only suitable for a short raid, e.g. Dieppe, and not for a campaign of a few months. The problem became even worse when at times we received five days' rations every eight or ten days, and as we proceeded further east no droppings were possible on some occasions. We relied then on rice from the villages. Bearing in mind that on most days we were walking twenty miles or more, with a temperature of over 100 degrees, the conditions of some of the men, especially those about thirty years of age, deteriorated quicker than expected. This obviously affected their fighting abilities.

'In the first village, a girl complained about the behaviour of one of our lads and we were given a strict warning direct from the top that if anyone interfered with a Burmese girl, Wingate would personally shoot him in front of the assembled villagers. As he pointed out, our lives were dependent on these villagers being on our side.

'Reports came in that there were Jap troops at Sinlamaung and a party under Colonel Cooke and Major Scott, the commander of 8 Column, including myself, marched all day and night only to find the Japs had fled. For the first time I thought we were going to see action and was apprehensive, but not frightened. We went deeper into Burma and had a further supply drop at Tonmakeng. Apart from rations, I received eight letters from home. One air letter card had only taken about two weeks. Surely this was air mail at its best!

'We then crossed the Zibyu Taungdan Range by a little known path which had been used by British troops and civilians the previous year, during the retreat to India. Quite a few skeletons at the side of the track of those who did not make it. Occasionally met lads of other columns who had had several skirmishes with the Japs. The position at that time was one of aggression in that orders were given to attack Japs wherever possible or feasible. Much different to the orders given later when we were coming out.'

On 19 February, probably as a result of translating the mail that had been inadvertently dropped near to a Japanese outpost on 15 February, the enemy began drawing in its patrols and by the twenty-fourth had evacuated all posts between the Chindwin and the Mu Valley, including Sinlamaung. It was later discovered that one of the pilots taking part in the supply drop had arrived over the DZ just as a thunderstorm began and he failed to find the flare path. Not wishing to attempt the return flight over high mountains with icing occurring with a full load, he jettisoned the load on a sandbank within a mile or two of a Japanese outpost. The Japanese immediately collected the supplies, including the mail, and were soon aware of the British Order of Battle. However, it may have been providential that this occurred, because if the enemy had not pulled back and battle had been joined at Tonmakeng and Sinlamaung, the force would not have been able to reach the railway.

On 1 March, the main group dropped down the Zibyu Taungdan Escarpment into the Chaunggyi Valley and bivouacked not far from Pinbon. Wingate sent 3 and 5 Columns ahead towards the railway and directed 7 and 8 Columns towards Pinlebu and Pinbon, while 4 Column moved towards Indaw. Early reports of British troops east of the Chindwin were not taken too seriously by the Generals commanding the 18th and 33rd Japanese Divisions and the commander of 15th Army, Lieutenant General Renya Mutaguchi (after 26 March). They judged them to be small intelligence units and left counter-measures in the hands of local regimental or battalion commanders. It was not until 1 Column started bridge demolitions between Kawlin and Kyaikthin around 20 February that they revised their estimates of the British strength and plans. Clearly greater steps had to be taken to counter them. Both 18th and 33rd Divisions were ordered to cut the enemy ground lines of communication, not knowing at the time that the Chindits were being supplied by air. General Sakurai, 33rd Division commander, sent his 215th Infantry Regiment to Kyaikthin to mop up the enemy there. However, they were ambushed by 1 Column and Major Nasu, the commander of their 2nd Battalion, was killed. The manoeuvring of 4, 7 and 8 Columns caused the Japanese to move troops up from the area of the railway to counter the threat in the Mu Valley, allowing Calvert's and Fergusson's columns to slip through unobserved to the railway.

However, 4 Column's days were numbered. 4 Column was the first of the seven to break up and return to India. It had been led from the start by Major Conron of 3/2nd Gurkhas and had reached the brigade rendezvous at Tonmakeng on 24 February. Thereafter it was tasked to protect a brigade supply dropping and then to reconnoitre and improve Castens Trail, the secret track of the Zibyu Taungdan Escarpment. It was hard work clearing the route, but necessary to avoid the Japanese. As the columns descended they saw a deep valley, in reality the head-waters of two: the Chaunggyi or Great Stream, which went northward for a few miles before turning abruptly to the west to break through the Zibyu Taungdan in a deep gorge; and the Mu Valley proper. Across the valley rose the hills of the Mangin range, running up to 3,700 feet of the Kalat Taung opposite. Beyond the hills was the Meza Valley and beyond that, the railway and the important communications centre of Indaw. As the columns reached the valley floor, Major Fergusson noted that 'Wingate was not in the best of tempers. He was annoyed with 4 Column for some sin of omission.' That day, 1 March, Wingate relieved Major Conron of his command and replaced him with Major Bromhead, his Brigade Major. The official reason for such a drastic step is hard to fathom. The change of command was not mentioned in Wingate's after-action report. Bromhead himself told the author: 'We were halfway across Burma when 4 Column commander lost his nerve. He could not stand the sound of a battery charging engine and so his radios failed. Wingate withdrew him to Brigade HQ and I took his place. We managed after a day or two to get the main radio working and set off to follow Brigade HQ, now way ahead.' Conron was never able to tell his side of the story. After Wingate later ordered the dispersal of the columns he was last seen near the Shweli River in command of a group from Brigade Headquarters. According to an eyewitness account he was drowned through the treachery of Burmese boatmen while attempting to cross that river.

On 2 March, the day after Bromhead took over command, the Burrif reconnaissance detachment bumped a group of Japanese soldiers near Pinbon and one man was lost. A fighting patrol out searching for the missing man encountered another Japanese patrol and shot dead an NCO. In the meantime Wingate had decided to shift his attack on the railway from the Indaw area to the Wuntho-Bonchaung area, thirty-five miles further south. He instructed 4 Column to rejoin the main group without delay. During the morning of 4 March, while the column was marching south-east along the base of the mountains, all hell broke loose. The column was in the usual single-file 'snake' formation and strung out over 1,000 yards when the undergrowth came alive with enemy small arms fire. Half of the formation had already crossed a small stream, when a shower of enemy mortar bombs began to fall on the ford, preventing the rest from crossing. The column had walked into a trap. While a rearguard platoon held the enemy at the stream, Lieutenants Stewart-Jones and Green and Subedar Tikajit led 135 men and thirty mules away to the north. The remainder of the column that had already crossed the stream dispersed in small groups and headed for the pre-arranged rendezvous twenty miles to the south. Bromhead's group comprised about fifteen souls, including Captain Ray Scott of the Burma Rifles, whose knowledge of the countryside would help to get them home. However, their radios were finished. Bromhead recalled:

'We met a Jap patrol and although we beat them off our only radio got a bullet. Since the Japs used soft-nosed bullets it was the end of that radio. The column was split by the encounter, but all reached the RV that evening and we sat down to consider our situation. No communications, little food and no way of getting more except courtesy of the locals, and the British officers of the Gurkha column reported very poor morale. What to do?

'We could not influence the war, so I decided to turn back. At this point our luck changed a bit. A villager told me that at the top of a steep hill behind the village there started a forest boundary trail, going, roughly, the right way. The hill was certainly steep, but the Gurkhas with their kukris cut steps for the mules and we all reached the top. And there was a well marked trail and I could recognise the forest blazes. We managed to buy enough rice and had an uneventful march back to the Chindwin. I mapped the route and by coincidence a battalion of my regiment used most of it later when Burma was invaded. On the way back my main worry was that we might be mistaken for the enemy by our own forces. Fortunately we spotted a British patrol east of the Chindwin before they saw us and made contact. We crossed the river where a battalion of a state force held the front. Jaipur I think. Memorable because the CO said, "I expect you could do with a bath", and his men dug a hole, lined it with ground sheets and filled it with hot water. The best bath I can remember.

I had written a series of non-committal "air grams" before we went into Burma and left them back at air base to be posted weekly. Thus it was that my mother got a brief letter saying that all was quite routine at the same time as she opened her morning paper to see my ugly mug spread across the front page.

'I went back to Imphal and set up shop at the Army HQ. My tummy rebelled in a big way at the rich food and I realised that when the brigade got back some hospital checks would be necessary. Eventually Wingate and the columns returned but, alas, with many a gap. The Gurkhas to their own centres and the British to Bombay. Wingate and I visited Simla, the summer capital, to report. Finally he started raising the next year's

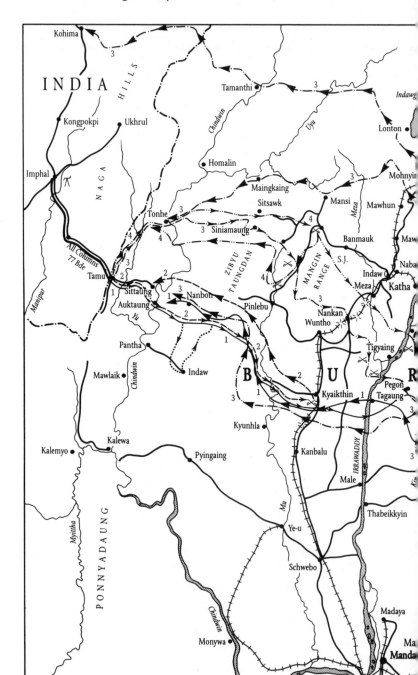

The movements of 1, 2, 3 and 4 columns during the 1943 campaign

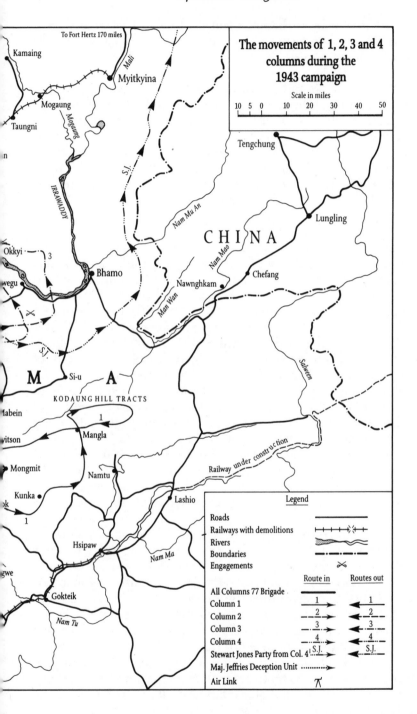

The movements of 1, 2, 3 and 4 columns during the 1943 campaign

Scale in miles

10	5	0	10	20	30	40	50

Legend

Roads	
Railways with demolitions	
Rivers	
Boundaries	
Engagements	✕

	Route in	Routes out
All Columns 77 Brigade		
Column 1	1	1
Column 2	2	2
Column 3	3	3
Column 4	4	4
Stewart Jones Party from Col. 4	S.J.	S.J.
Maj. Jeffries Deception Unit		
Air Link	大	

force. At that moment the Army sent me to Staff College at Quetta, presumably to learn how it should be done. Next year I was in New Guinea with the Aussies.'

As for Lieutenant Stewart-Jones, his troubles were only just beginning. On the evening of the ambush he led his men north in an effort to contact the other columns. After two days he handed over command to Captain Findlay of the commando detachment and went ahead with eight others. Six days later, out of food and near collapse, they made contact with 8 Column. In the meantime Captain Findlay and his party had turned back for India, menaced by starvation. Weeks later, Stewart-Jones and his four faithful Gurkha riflemen reached safety in Fort Hertz, a British outpost on the border with China.

After Lieutenant-Colonel Alexander's Southern Group crossed the Chindwin fifty miles south of the main body, Group Headquarters and 1 Column pressed ahead. 2 Column, under Major Emmett, followed at a distance and on 20 February, while passing the village of Ywaitha, it was learned that a Japanese unit which had recently bumped into 1 Column had just passed through, carrying a number of wounded. Over the next seven days the column climbed the escarpment and slowly descended to the plain below. Alexander gave 2 Column the task of destroying Kyaikthin railway station, forty miles to the east. The period of concealment was over. The group would now move openly in order to attract enemy forces away from the area to which Wingate's group was heading. Scouts halted in villages to convey misleading information that might reach the ears of the Japanese, while Major John B. Jefferies in his Brigadier's uniform and accompanied by his deception group, held court in various villages before hurrying to catch up with Major Emmett's column. They finally joined them on 2 March, three miles from Kyaikthin. That night the column was scheduled to blow up the railway station.

While 2 Column bivouacked in the Wild Life Sanctuary Forest a couple of miles west of the station, Burma Rifle scouts reported that two trains had arrived during the afternoon. Unbeknown to Major Emmett, they were full of Japanese soldiers from the 215th Infantry Regiment. At 2200 hours Major Emmett formed up his column and marched down the line of the narrow gauge railway. No sooner had the advance begun than a fusillade of firing began from the front and both flanks. They had walked into an ambush. Men dived to the ground as salvoes of mortar bombs began to land among the laden mules, causing a stampede. Emmett ordered his men to try to break through the ambush, but it was impossible. As individual fire fights continued along the length of the column the dispersal call was sounded. Those that were able broke away from the railway line and into the jungle. Jemadar Manbahadur Gurung covered the withdrawal with his platoon, accounting for many Japanese. Wingate's decoy uniform was discovered by the Japanese at the site of the ambush and for a while they thought they had destroyed the main force and announced this fact in a printed broadsheet which they took the trouble to drop on 5 Column as it crossed the Irrawaddy at Tigyaing, a week later. Major Emmett and other groups marched through the darkness towards the rendezvous. Half of the column eventually joined him there and took stock of their situation. They were without signal equipment, medical stores or reserve ammunition and could neither contact Wingate or ask for resupply by air. Harassed by the enemy, Emmett turned his men around and headed back towards the Chindwin and India. Wingate was later damning in his comments on 2 Column's lack of success. He charged that their movement had been too slow, the bivouac near Kyaikthin too obvious. In addition, during the fighting, Emmett had changed the rendezvous point to one in the rear, replacing the original rendezvous at Taunguan, twelve miles east of Kyaikthin and fifteen miles from the scene of the ambush. As a result the column split in different directions. Whether or not Wingate's comments were justified, the result was to be expected. The column had been ordered to lay a plain trail and attract the enemy to them, and they did just that.*

Many of the dispersed groups continued towards the east and the rendezvous at Taunguan. Subedar Major Siblal Thapa spent the night in the area of the ambush, collecting men and equipment. He arrived at the RV together with four young British officers, seventy Gurkha other ranks, sixty-five mules, four machine-guns and a quantity of ammunition. He had also found the bodies of seven Gurkhas and delivered two seriously wounded riflemen into the safety of the nearest village. On 5 March the remnants of 2 Column and Group Headquarters joined forces with Major George Dunlop's 1 Column which had successfully destroyed a railway bridge eighteen miles north of Kyaikthin and had continued towards the Irrawaddy. Because all the ciphers of Southern Group and 2 Column had been lost in the ambush, Alexander decided not to use 1 Column's radio to contact Wingate. He was mistaken in this, because they were using one-time cipher pads and in fact no ciphers were carried which could have compromised others if they fell into enemy hands. However, for four days the remains of Southern Group struggled through dense jungle to throw the enemy off their trail, while

* One puzzling aspect of this ambush is the whereabouts of Lieutenant-Colonel Alexander, the Southern Group commander, when 2 Column was ambushed. Wingate's report on the expedition states that he was with 2 Column at Kyaikthin and George Dunlop confirmed to the author that he was not travelling with 1 Column at that time. However, the few published reports of the ambush and dispersal of this column do not mention Alexander at all. As the senior officer present and the group commander, surely the responsibility for 2 Column and its fate was in his hands, rather than Emmett's?

Wingate waited for word from them. On 9 March, Alexander led his men across the Irrawaddy.

While Southern Group remained out of contact, Mike Calvert's 3 Column reached the area around Nankan railway station on 6 March. His target was some bridges over chaungs (streams) with forty-five foot banks, together with the railway line itself. Calvert divided his column into two demolition parties, three covering sections and a transport and headquarters group, the latter to remain hidden in the jungle. With Lieutenant Harold James and his platoon of Gurkhas as escort, Calvert advanced along the railway line, dropping off some of his commandos to start cutting the line at 100-yard intervals with one-pound slabs of gun-cotton. At Milestone 555 they came to a box girder bridge with a hundred-foot span and a long drop to the chaung below. Calvert, Sergeant-Major Blain and his party set to work fixing the charges and connecting the fuses. Calvert was almost ready when the distant boom of an explosion reached his ears. Lieutenant Jeffrey Lockett of the commandos had brought down his bridge, a three-span steel girder bridge with stone abutments stretching 120 feet over a deep chaung. Harold James later recalled: 'The next moment Calvert was running towards me, shouting for everyone to take cover behind a bank. We scrambled over and not long afterwards there was a great roar as the bridge went up, pieces of metal flew in all directions, and a large section passed low over our heads like a fighter aircraft, screaming past to embed itself in a tree-trunk with the noise of a large drum.'

While Calvert and his men were preparing to blow their bridge, Gurkha Subedar Kumba Sing Gurung was crouched behind a Boyes anti-tank rifle, squinting through the sights at the first of two Japanese trucks which had come into view on the road to the north of the station. He slowly squeezed the trigger and the truck burst into flames and veered out of control into the jungle. His Bren gunner opened fire on the Japanese leaping from the second truck and the riflemen of his small section joined in too. They were outnumbered three to one and a brisk fight ensued. Captain Taffy Griffiths, the column Burma Rifles officer, and his Karens ran over from the east of the station to join in, as more trucks appeared with Japanese reinforcements. A runner was sent to Calvert at the bridge. Leaving Blain and his commandos to continue cutting the railway line, Calvert, with Harold James and his platoon ran towards the firing. Suddenly a bearded face appeared in their path. It was Captain Erik Pedersen, a free Dane, and two platoons who had been separated from 7 Column and were following the tracks of 3 Column in the hope of catching up. 'You are just in time for a bit of action, if you wish,' said Calvert. 'I think we would like that,' replied the Dane, and Calvert led them forward. The King's men from 7 Column soon dealt with an armoured truck which came into view and the Gurkhas' mortars blew another truck to pieces. Other enemy soldiers were shot down as they tried to cross open ground to outflank the Chindits. As the firing petered out and darkness approached, Calvert and his men withdrew to their rendezvous.

That night Calvert sat beside a fire in the jungle, surrounded by sleeping Gurkhas and produced a bar of chocolate, half of which he gave to Second Lieutenant Harold James. 'It's my birthday and I have reached the ripe old age of thirty.' 'If I had known I would have brought you a present,' James replied. Calvert grinned. 'I had my present today. How many people can say they celebrated their birthday by blowing up a bridge!' It had been a good day. Apart from destroying the bridges they had cut the railway line in seventy places and killed a score of Japanese, for no loss to themselves. Taffy Griffiths was later awarded the Military Cross for this action and others during the expedition. Kumba Sing received the Indian Distinguished Service Medal. And Pedersen the Dane? He rejoined 7 Column, but was later wounded in the head. After Wingate dispersed the columns his men tied him to a horse and brought him out with them to China.

The same day that 3 Column carried out their attack on the railway at Nankan, Major Fergusson's 5 Column reached their target a few miles away. The railway bridge at Bonchaung was blown at 2100 hours and the forty-foot centre span dropped into the river. Other demolitions in the nearby gorge brought thousands of tons of rock down onto the rails. Sadly, there had been casualties. One party of forty men under Captain Roberts had been sent towards Nankan to deal with any enemy there, but had bumped a truck full of Japanese in the village of Kyaukin. Within a quarter of an hour fifteen of the enemy had been killed and, assuming they had accounted for all of them, Roberts gave orders to return to the column. As Lieutenant Kerr formed up his platoon, an enemy machine-gun opened fire and killed four of the men and wounded six others, including the Lieutenant. By the time Fergusson reached the scene, there was little he could do. Lieutenant Kerr and four other wounded were left in the deserted village with some food and water, in the hope that friendly Burmese might find and take care of them. Sadly it was not to be. Two of the men died on the spot, another was found and murdered by Burmese, the fourth died after capture on the way to Rangoon. Kerr himself was tortured by the Japanese to divulge Fergusson's plans, but managed to hold out until it no longer mattered. Fergusson was soon aware that the Japanese were rushing reinforcements to the general area and even drawing troops away from their operations in the Fort Hertz area. He hurried his column on towards the Irrawaddy.

During this time, 6 to 11 March, Wingate reconsidered his options. 4

Column had returned to India and there was no sign of, or sound from the Southern Group. He debated whether the four remaining columns could take to the impassable mountains north of Wuntho, form a Permanent Rendezvous for the columns where they could be supplied by air, and launch them forth to attack the roads and railway. The Japanese had never followed a column into dense jungle and would therefore avoid a mountain stronghold. Once established the columns could do the job they had been trained for, laying ambushes rather than avoiding them and carrying out hit and run raids. The problem with this idea was that the columns were then operating over an area of ten thousand square miles and it may have proven difficult for 3 and 5 Columns to rejoin 7 and 8 and Brigade Headquarters.

Finally, Wingate received news that in compliance with his orders, Southern Group had crossed the Irrawaddy. It had not been an easy task. Major Dunlop told the author:

> 'Jefferies, Edmunds, Weatherall and I were on the bank looking across this vast river. Someone, Jefferies I think, remarked, "And how do we get over that?" Edmunds retorted at once, "Call up the old man. He'll tell you how Jesus Christ did it!" This comment was not without its bit of irony. Wingate's HQ had constantly refused to take our radio calls. Perhaps he thought that the Japs were putting out bogus calls, using ciphers captured from 2 Column at Kyaikthin. In the whole operation I received only two radio messages after reporting the success of our first encounter. These were both the two biblical ones telling us to take to the mountains and not turn back the way we had come.'

Calvert and Fergusson now requested permission to cross the river and this was given. Wingate decided to follow suit and take the rest of his brigade across the wide river. The decision was not made lightly. To those who suggest that Wingate should have remained on the west side of the river, to form a bridgehead if the other columns should need to return, I quote his reasons for crossing, direct from his post-expedition report:

> 'Had I not crossed the Irrawaddy I should have learned nothing real about crossing wide and swift streams, nor about opposed crossings. It is this want of real as opposed to second-hand, book-derived or related experience that leads to so many mistakes by commanders in war. Further, although it is easy to be wise after the event, I had at this time every reason to believe that we would find conditions far easier on the east bank. I did not know the difficulty of the country between the Irrawaddy and the Shweli from our point of view at that time of the year. It is true to say that had I throughout known all that I know now, I could have done almost anything, including the generous use of Emergency Landing

Grounds and irruption into China. But I did not know one tenth part of what I know now. Neither did anyone else.'

Wingate signalled Calvert to take command of both 3 Column and Fergusson's 5 Column and move towards the Gokteik gorge on the Maymyo–Lashio road. During the 1942 retreat to India Calvert had spent a week at Gokteik awaiting orders to destroy the huge viaduct that straddled the gorge. The order never came, but when Calvert later reported to General Alexander the first thing the General asked was, 'Did you blow up the viaduct?' When Calvert replied that he asked for permission half a dozen times, but was told to leave it alone, Alexander looked rather put out. He explained that the order could not be given for political reasons, but he had sent Calvert there because he had been told that he was the most likely person to disobey orders! Now, a year later, he would do the job properly. Wingate directed Southern Group to move towards Mongmit for a rendezvous at the end of March with Captain 'Fish' Herring of the Burma Rifles and his Kachin guerrilla platoon. Herring had been despatched in advance of the brigade to cross the Irrawaddy with the intention of raising the hill tribes in revolt against the Japanese. He found many supporters of the British cause but was hampered by Wingate's refusal to give him a long-range radio with which to report his success. The only way Herring could signal Wingate would be after a planned rendezvous with 7 Column at the end of March. However, Southern Group was despatched to the area instead, and by the time they arrived the area was crawling with Japanese troops.

Chapter 4

A River Too Far

On 18 March, Wingate and his Northern Group reached the Irrawaddy near the village of Hlwebo and crossed over. Here the river was between seven and eight hundred yards wide and swift flowing. Wingate discovered that given country boats with skilled native paddlers, the process of loading, crossing, unloading and returning occupied one hour. The RAF circular dinghies holding 1,500 pounds net weight could be towed across by a country boat, but were quite unmanoeuvrable alone. He made a note for the future that each column would need at least forty men skilled in handling boats and at least eighty per cent of the men should be able to swim. At that time the great majority could hardly swim at all.

The crossing began during the afternoon and was completed by daylight. Fortunately the Japanese kept away, as did the local members of the enemy-sponsored Burma Defence Army based at Inywa on the East Bank. The village itself was raided by the Headquarters Defence Platoon and a number of boats and a large junk were commandeered to assist in the crossing. 5 Column had crossed at Tigyaing with the cheerful assistance of the villagers. The Japanese arrived just as Major Fergusson made the crossing in the last boat. He was the last man into the overloaded boat and had to kneel on the stern with his head under the canopy and his rear in the air. Fortunately the Japanese were poor shots and Fergusson later remarked 'I am the first British officer to have crossed the Irrawaddy on all fours.' Calvert's column played a game of hide and seek with the Japanese on the way to the river, leaving booby-traps behind them as they moved. A Japanese force caught up with them as they prepared to cross over just south of Tigyaing, but a rearguard held the enemy at bay while the bulk of the column got across. There were a few casualties and many animals had to be abandoned, but disaster was avoided.

After 4 and then 2 Column suffered their reverses in early March, Headquarters 15th Army believed the main force of the enemy had been destroyed and some staff officers estimated that the enemy had already retreated to the west. However, troops from the 55th Infantry Regiment reported that the enemy was in fact crossing the Irrawaddy and soon after realised that they were being supplied by air. It was troops from this

regiment that had attacked 3 Column as it crossed the river. Consequently 18th and 56th Divisions were ordered to locate and destroy the
enemy. It was easier said than done. Lance-Corporal George Bell, still
with the Northern Group Headquarters, takes up the story:

'We had several skirmishes as we eventually crossed the railway and
reached the Irrawaddy River. We hid in the hills overlooking Wuntho for
five days as Wingate contemplated attacking the garrison there, but he
decided against it. We crossed the Irrawaddy by boat late in the afternoon
with the CO, Lieutenant-Colonel Cooke. At the time, several of the
officers still had bedding rolls carried on their chargers. Most of the lads
by then had nothing, we kipped down on the ground. The CO was one of
those officers and it annoyed some of the lads; to me it was typical of
Army life. When we arrived at the far side of the river the CO's bedding
roll had disappeared. He was very annoyed and asked his batman and me
to find it. The lads told me that it had been thrown into the Irrawaddy by
some disillusioned soldiers who didn't see why the CO should have such
privileges. I daren't tell the CO.

'For some time I had been what can only be described as the CO's
bodyguard. On occasions either Wingate or the column commander
wished to rendezvous with the CO. I would walk ahead of him down the
tracks towards the agreed RV with rifle cocked, on the assumption that if
the Japs pounced on us, I would be expendable rather than the CO.
Luckily that never happened. Remarkably it never crossed my mind either
then or later that I would be killed. Others might, but me, never!

'We continued marching further eastwards. Our casualties up to this
stage were not too bad, but were increasing. Two further major problems
were arising. The supply drops were becoming less frequent, but infinitely
worse was how to deal with the wounded. Initially we tried to carry them
on improvised stretchers, but soon realised in the thick jungle it was not
possible. I recall leaving about ten of our lads in a deserted village. We
shook hands with them as we left, with everyone trying to keep a stiff
upper lip. We knew that they hadn't a cat in hell's chance of surviving and
what made it more painful, was that they also knew. Terrible decisions to
make! Most of our lads thought it better to be killed outright than be
badly wounded.

'Still marching eastwards. Would we reach China? If not, where? No
one seemed to have any idea. We reached the Shweli River and waited
five days until rubber dinghies were dropped by the RAF. I crossed in a
party led by the CO. A couple of days later as we were walking down a
chaung I remarked to the Sergeant-Major that we had come down here
the day before. His comments are unprintable. I said to him that about a
mile further on the chaung turned sharp right and there was a large tree
blocking the way which we had to clamber over. Sure enough, twenty

minutes later there was the tree! Even those at the top with the maps and compass were not infallible in that part of Burma!

'On 26 March we received the good news – we were going back to India. "Thank Goodness" was the general reaction. We received a big ration dropping at Baw, but the Japs were waiting for us and several of our lads were killed. An officer who had been instructed to take a Sergeant and several men to attack the Japs from the far side went in the wrong side with the result that the Sergeant and several others were killed. Wingate demoted him to Private on the spot and transferred him to 5 Column. The following day I was with that column and found the column commander, Major Fergusson, had promoted him to Sergeant. When we came out eventually all was forgiven or forgotten and he retained his officer's rank and in due course became our adjutant.'

Arthur Willshaw at Brigade Headquarters continues:

'By 20 February the whole force was across the Chindwin, operating behind the Japanese lines. The first action came when a Burma Rifle patrol ran into a Japanese patrol near Sinlamaung. From information gained, it was learned that there was a big concentration of Japanese troops at Homalin. It was thought that the Japanese were preparing a push through Assam, but within a week all Jap forces in the northern Burmese theatre were re-deployed to contain the infiltrating Chindits. Life seemed good as stories of successful sorties were received – the main railway between Mandalay and Myitkyina was blown in several places - road blocks were successful and the enemy was being engaged wherever it suited us to engage him.

'The only real bad blow to our morale was the dispersal of 2 Column – most of them young Gurkhas – who ran into a bad ambush outside Kyaikthin and were never able to re-form as a column. Day followed day, travelling mainly by night we climbed the mountains into the Hukawng Valley, very aptly called the Happy Valley, down the valley towards Shwebo and down to the banks of the Irrawaddy. Our air supply was working quite well but the Japanese were reinforcing troops in the area and rarely were they more than two hours behind us. The drop would be organised, the area chosen, in would come the planes, there would be a mad rush to collect our supplies and regularly we would leave with the sound of Japanese machine-gun fire in our ears. Each of us carried about six days' rations and we made up with rice and juggary, a kind of local sugar extract from cane, which each column obtained by purchase from the Burmese villages they passed through. A well-tried recipe of these days was "Bamboo Baked Rice". Take a twelve-inch length of bamboo cane about one inch in circumference, fill it to within two inches of the top with rice, add one inch of water and plug the open end with clay or leaves. Put on to a burning fire and let the outer bamboo skin burn away. Take out of the fire, allow to cool and peel off the burnt bamboo. This makes a stick of rice already cooked which you can break off like a stick of rock and eat a half inch at a time. Such a stick of rice will last for weeks before going sour.

'The Irrawaddy was crossed much later than was expected and, with the monsoon due, a quick decision had to be made whether to press on up into the Chin Hills and lie out the monsoon period, or attempt to get back to India with information urgently needed by the General Staffs. By this time the Japanese had reinforced their troops and were strongly emplaced between the Shweli River and the Burma Road. Further Japanese troops had been sent up from Meiktila, Myingyan and Mandalay and were now strongly emplaced between the Irrawaddy and the Chindwin. Dropping areas became harder to find and almost every time we left the jungle on to the tracks linking village with village we ran into Japanese.'

Wingate pondered his next move. He had successfully transported 2,200 men and 1,000 animals across the Irrawaddy in the direction of Mongmit and had no doubts that he was entering the second and more fruitful phase of operations. He hoped that Herring and his Kachins would be ready to receive him in the Kadaung Hill Tracts. Supply dropping had proved an unqualified success and the radios were working adequately. However, he was not to know that between him and the hill tribes lay a dry hot belt of waterless forest, freely intersected by motorable tracks and heavily patrolled by Japanese. In addition, the enemy had not been idle. After Fergusson crossed at Tigyaing a battalion of Japanese troops had been trucked to the area and a further regiment was distributed at posts up and down the river on both banks.

As the columns moved deeper into enemy territory they found themselves in late March and early April in a great bag formed by the Irrawaddy and Shweli Rivers, and across the mouth of the bag ran a motor road. By now the Japanese hornets' nest had been well and truly aroused and substantial reinforcements were being moved into the area. In addition the rivers were being patrolled and eventually the Japanese confiscated all the boats they could find. They were aware that the villages would attract the Chindits in search of food and guides, so they occupied them. Needless to say this caused enormous problems, in particular for the columns whose radios had been lost or destroyed and who were unable to call for resupply by air. Captain Herring waited five days for Lieutenant-Colonel Alexander and his group to make the rendezvous and on 29 March he had to move on himself. The Japanese were searching for him and his men, he had no radio and there was no sign of support. After a long journey he made his way out via China. Alexander and his group finally arrived at the RV on 8 April.

Wingate's columns were now so far east that the RAF could no longer supply them. The transport aircraft had the range, but the fighter escorts did not. Instructions were received from India to return home immediately. It was easier said than done. Mike Calvert's column carried off a masterful ambush on 23 March and destroyed a full company of Japanese troops. However, that day Wingate cancelled his operation against the Gokteik viaduct and ordered Calvert to return to India by any route. Fergusson was ordered to bring 5 Column to rejoin the Brigade Group and participate in a supply dropping at Baw, before attempting to recross the Irrawaddy. Unfortunately his column would go hungry as a fierce fight in a village would split his force and lead to the loss of two-thirds of his men over the coming weeks. The attempt by the Brigade Group to recross the Irrawaddy would fail, leaving Wingate with no option but to disperse his columns. Each would be sent off in different directions, with instructions to split up into smaller parties on the way. It would be easier to forage for food in small parties and easier to hide from their hunters as they tried to evade the Japanese and escape to India. It would be a game of cat and mouse all the way.

On 26 March, Wingate held a conference of column commanders on the Hehtin Chaung. He told them that they were returning to India at all speed and would try to recross the Irrawaddy at Inywa, the same place they crossed on their outward journey. Wingate reasoned that it was the last place the Japanese would expect them to try. In order to reach the river without alerting the enemy to their intention, Wingate proposed a fifty-mile forced march followed by a swift crossing of the river.

On 27 March, the columns set out for Inywa. Wingate later reported:

> 'Owing to the carelessness of a Burma rifleman our tail was attacked by an enemy patrol about 1400 hours. I sent a verbal order to Major Fergusson, the commander of the rear column, to ambush our tracks to prevent the enemy following up, and continued to march north. Fergusson decided to leave the main body and make a false bivouac and generally to engage whatever enemy might be about. This was not my intention. However, he was successful in making the enemy attack his dummy bivouac. But at 0300 hours on the twenty-eighth, he endeavoured to pass the village of Hintha. This village was at the junction of several tracks frequently patrolled by Japanese and probably held a company.'

The sound of 5 Column's fight at Hintha echoed through the night as the rest of the brigade group marched for Inywa. At 1600 hours on the twenty-eighth the exhausted men arrived four miles short of Inywa and laid down for a three-hour rest before moving down to the Irrawaddy. When they reached the river at 0300 hours on 29 March, they expected to meet Colonel Wheeler and his Burma Rifles Headquarters party, who had been covering their tracks when the columns crossed motor roads.

However, they had missed the rear column and gone on to the Operational Rendezvous at Debin.

Wingate was depending on the Burma Rifles to obtain boats and men to paddle them and it took until 0600 hours to gather about twenty country boats of various sizes, with paddles for only half of them. Eventually some native rowers were rounded up, ten RAF dinghies were inflated and the crossing began. A platoon of 7 Column had just begun to land on the west bank when firing began. Apparently a force of Japanese were living in the village one mile upstream and Wingate could see twenty or thirty of them running along the river bank. Soon mortar and automatic fire began to sweep the river. Snipers began to fire aimed shots at the men on the east bank, one of which went through Major Scott's map as he stood on the bank. When the first boat was sunk, the native oarsmen began to scurry for safety. Wingate estimated that the remaining six boats would require two and a half days to transport the brigade group of just under a thousand men, already exhausted after marching fifty miles in forty-eight hours. The mantle of responsibility rested heavily upon Wingate's shoulders that morning. Allen Wilding was one of the men who came under fire during the attempted crossing:

> 'As soon as we arrived at the river, I was told to take my ciphers, my Sergeant and a transmitter across the river and be ready to encipher and send a message to the RAF for help if our crossing was interrupted. As the only canoe immediately available held but three plus the paddlers, we decided to take one of the bomber dinghies which I had acquired at Argatala and tow it. I put the transmitter in the dinghy. To my horror we were fired on from the west bank. I much regretted the dinghy which was bright yellow! It is a very odd feeling when you, personally, are fired at, especially for the first time. Also the noise made by bullets ricocheting off the water is a bit intimidating! The paddlers, who were locals, knew that the Japs would kill them, but were pretty sure that in spite of my lurid threats, I would not, so they turned back and we regained the east bank. Very sadly, Sergeant Crawford of the Royal Signals was killed. It was rotten luck, he was hit by a bullet which had ricocheted off the water and, going sideways, hit him in the throat, killing him instantly. I reported to the Brigadier who, fortunately, had seen it all. We withdrew from the bank and rested. Thinking about it all these years later we should, of course, have forced a crossing. It would have been costly, but not so costly as the alternative. But this is with hindsight.'

Private Charles Aves was one of the men who reached the west bank:

> 'As quietly as possible, we made our way to the small boats at the bank of the river where boatmen had been paid to ferry us across. I think I was in the second or third boat. We proceeded across the river and it seemed ages getting across. I suppose there were eight or ten of us in the boat. Just

as we and a couple of other boats reached the bank, the Japs opened up with mortar and automatic fire from a point some few hundred yards north of our landing. We couldn't see them, for they were well concealed in a copse. We scrambled ashore to find Lieutenant W. and a few men from the first boat standing around. I shall never forget the Lieutenant; he was eating cheese from a tin with a penknife quite unconcerned about the firing which was directed on to the boats trying to get over, also at the troops on the other side.

'Contrary to what has been written before, we were not under fire on the west bank. The Japs did not have control of this area. I firmly believe that it must have been only a patrol of Japs with a mortar unit and automatic fire. Perhaps also with a sniper. I can vouch for the fact that we were not fired at on the bank. For some reason Lieutenant W. decided that I would attack the enemy position. Yes, ME. He told me to make my way across an open paddy field to a point some two hundred yards away and direct some grenades on to the Japs wherever they were. I looked at him in disbelief. I couldn't see the enemy, I had never used a grenade launcher, I only had two grenades and no launcher attachment. I told him this but he found a launcher and told me to just fix it on the end of the rifle. I was completely in the open as I crossed this paddy field; had there been any Japs looking they could have mown me down easily. I made myself as small as possible and safely reached this point.* What was I to attack? I couldn't see anything. There was no firing at this time. Just a small forest of trees. I decided to return and ask for further instructions. When I got back to the main group I found them forming up to move off. Had the Japs been any stronger I am sure they could have attacked us. The total number of men that formed up was sixty-five. One Captain O., one Lieutenant J., one Second Lieutenant W., two or three Sergeants and some Corporals and about fifty other ranks. I asked about Captain Hastings, who had been my platoon officer until he was promoted to column adjutant. I was told that the boat he was in had been hit and he was flung into the river and swept away.

'In retrospect we could say that had we attacked the Jap unit it is possible that the rest of Wingate's force could have crossed reasonably safely, but I don't know what orders our senior officers had. I believe we had no means of signalling across the river and at this time most of the men were ill and short of food. The sixty-five of us who had crossed the river moved quickly away and a few miles later made camp in dense jungle. This was the rendezvous point for those who had crossed the river,

---

* Charles Aves told the author that there was one reason why he may have been singled out for such a foolhardy exploit. Some time previously the men had been told by Lieutenant W. and a Sergeant that there was no chocolate being dropped with their meagre rations. However, one night Charles came across the Sergeant eating chocolate and challenged the officer about his claims that none had been dropped. He did not reply, merely turned his charger around and rode off.

but by the morning no one else had turned up. We waited another day and then our officers led us off towards the Chindwin. Captain O., our senior officer, had maps so we knew where we were going, but we were very short of food. It was decided to make for a village where we hoped to obtain some rice and a little rock salt.

'After a couple of days we came to a village, a friendly one we hoped, without any Jap troops nearby. We each obtained a wedge of cooked rice within a large banana leaf envelope. The rice was delicious. The Burmese have a way of presenting boiled rice like I have never tasted since. We ate half of this and went on our way.

'A number of men were feeling pretty bad by now and a particular friend of mine, Freddy Raffo, said to me, "I'm not going to make it, I can't go on any more." I knew Fred wasn't married, but he had an elderly mother who lived alone in a small house in Salford. I said, "You can't give up, it's all right for you, but what about your mother, all on her own waiting for you, you've got to make it for her sake." We split up all his equipment and took his rifle and carried it all for him. I am glad to say Fred did get out and he thanked me later for saying what I did at the time.

'We made our way slowly for another day and at about one p.m. the officers decided we would have a rest and a brew-up. We flung our weary limbs down in the dried bed of a river. Two men were posted as sentries and we took off our packs, laid down our rifles and made some tea. I was with Corporal Stan Hickman; I did not know him very well, but he was a good chap, who came from South London. We were relaxing and completely off guard when suddenly we heard the sound of footsteps running through the trees. Looking up we saw the two sentries running for their lives past us. They didn't say anything, but at the same moment we heard shots being fired and shouts from some twenty yards away. I went to run, for everyone else had gone, but Corporal Hickman said "No, don't go." I stayed with him and then we saw them, about fifteen yards away, coming at us. We moved like lightning, carrying only our rifles. We ran up the nullah and as we did so we both grabbed a pack each left by someone else. We broke the speed record and managed to climb up behind some rocks; there were a few of our party there and we poured rifle fire on where the Japs were coming from. After a while we ceased fire. We couldn't see the Japs but we could hear them shouting to each other. I think they must have been looting the packs left behind. We withdrew up the hill and then sorted ourselves out. There was Lieutenant J., two sergeants, Corporal Hickman and seven other men. Corporal Hickman and I looked into the two packs we had picked up; mine was Captain O's and contained all the maps on the way to the Chindwin. In the other that belonged to Lieutenant W. was a quantity of silver rupees. We then found that we only had two water bottles between us. We went back to the site of the attack, but the Japs were still there, so we took off west as fast as we could without a stop for two hours.

'As night fell, we took stock. We all had rifles, ammunition and grenades, but no food and little water. The Lieutenant was a good officer who decided to involve us all in decisions if needed. We had another bonus, me, as I was the only one who could speak any Burmese, thanks to Stan Allnutt. Anyone can make themselves understood in their quest for food, but I was able to ask the villagers for the headman and for the position of the nearest Japanese.

'In the morning we decided to make for the nearest village. Most of us really found ourselves during this period. We enjoyed being in the jungle, the thicker the better, and we felt safe. We could find paths among the undergrowth, however indistinct and we knew that they would eventually lead to water or a village. The first village was quite near and I went in first with Lieutenant J., while the others kept a look out. They were very friendly and helpful, all smiles and generosity. In fact our experience showed all the Burmese to be very helpful, with one exception; I can't recall the name of the village, but shall call it Maungde.

'We had travelled quite a few miles, probably about twenty each day, when we reached Maungde. We knew this village was different to all the others, we could tell straight away there was something wrong. The headman was uneasy; we always watched out to see whether anyone disappeared when we entered a village and it seemed to us one or two shifty characters moved out of sight. We didn't hesitate, let's get out now, no messing. We didn't give them a chance to call on any Japs, we shot through like lightning, and disappeared over the horizon with no casualties.

'It transpired that some others of our original group were betrayed when they went through the same village and a number of them were killed by crossfire and mortar fire when they left. On arriving safely at Imphal the survivors of that group reported the behaviour of those villagers and HQ arranged to send a plane over and a couple of days after we left, the village was bombed.

'There was one village where they laid on a real feast for us – meat and vegetables, rice and fruit – and we spent quite a time with them. We augmented our food a couple of times by throwing grenades into lakes and bringing out the concussed fish, stewing and eating them. Eventually we found our way to the Chindwin without too much alarm, although our boots and socks were worn out and our feet were suffering badly. We were almost in sight of the Chindwin when to our great pleasure we ran into a patrol of Seaforth Highlanders. Their role was to be on the look out for us and help us get boats over the Chindwin. A patrol of Japs a few days previously had inflicted some damage on a Seaforth patrol and this group who met us were going out to look for them. After seeing we were fed they led us to the boats and we proceeded up the river for a couple of hours to a point of safety on the west bank where we were greeted by another patrol. We still had quite a bit of trekking to get over the escarpment where there was transport to get us to Imphal. We eventually arrived in Imphal some three months after we had left and were taken to hospital where we had luxury baths, new clothing and good food. Then most of us collapsed with malaria; I was delirious for forty-eight hours but came to in chastened mood. A couple of days later Wingate came to visit us. When I mentioned my feelings about the two officers running away and leaving maps and money behind, he became serious and said, "We won't wash our dirty linen in public, will we?" I never have until now.

'The officer who led us out became quite morose and did not seem to want to acknowledge any of the party that came out with him. It was strange as we had all been so close and we all did our share of helping him as well as him helping us. Some time later we understood that he had received a letter from his wife, who was a stage actress at the London Palladium, to the effect that she had fallen in love with somebody else. Later he blew himself up when demonstrating a new form of plastic grenade.

'The pride of we survivors in our accomplishment at being the first to hit back at the Japs after all our reverses along with our faith and belief in our leader was paramount. General Wingates descendants can be immensely proud of his individuality, bravery, foresight, technical brilliance, unorthodoxy and understanding of his ordinary troops.'

For Lance-Corporal George Bell, the day of reckoning had arrived. The Irrawaddy crossing attempt had failed. Now what?

'After a further supply drop, the decision was made to split up into smaller parties. Some headed for China, while others stayed together and marched due west. Our party under Lieutenant Pearce, about fifty strong, went north-north-west. Before splitting up we shook hands with our pals in other parties, several of them we would never see again. Our party included three officers and two Burmese who were in the Burma Rifles and could speak both English and Burmese. They saved our lives, as they were able to enter villages and obtain information about the whereabouts of the Japs. Apart from the one occasion when they got drunk as newts in one village on rice wine!

'After leaving the other parties we made for a small village on the Irrawaddy, only to find as we arrived there about dusk there were only two Burmese there. The village had been moved to the other bank several years before. It transpired that our maps were dated 1912! We decided, although it was pitch black, to make for another village several miles north. Fortunately as it turned out we got bogged down in the thick jungle and halted and slept for a few hours. When eventually our two Burmese lads went into the village the following day, they found a large party of Japs had been there that night. After that lucky escape I always felt that someone above was looking after me and the lads for the rest of the campaign.

'As soon as it was dark I, together with my section and a villager rowing, crossed the river, in a boat similar to that used in the Oxford and Cambridge boat race. I can still vividly remember the water came up to a few inches from the top. I couldn't swim and was I pleased when we reached the other side, despite not knowing whether the Japs would be there. Fortunately they weren't. Throughout the night the boat crossed and recrossed until everyone was over. By that time we had no means of contacting our air base and had to rely on rice bought from the villages. Boiled rice, no salt, for breakfast, lunch and dinner! Having had no change of clothes for some time we all became lousy. After a couple of days we forgot all about it. We had more important things to worry about. Leeches were another problem. They got everywhere and I mean everywhere. We had been told that if you stubbed them with a lighted cigarette they would drop off. That advice presupposed we had cigarettes. We hadn't. I was lucky being a non-smoker, but to those heavy smokers lack of a cigarette was almost as bad as lack of food. We called into a small village one day where some of the lads bought some tobacco. But how to smoke it? We had no paper. That also brought other minor problems! One of our lads had carried a bible throughout the campaign and had a heart-searching battle with his conscience as to whether to tear a few pages from it. He still had a few matches left and the desire to smoke was greater than his religious convictions and he rolled a couple of cigarettes. A few puffs was all he managed, but it sufficed.

'We marched on about twenty to twenty-five miles per day, with little food, crossing the railway line and two minor rivers. One day, marching along a track in thick jungle, we picked up a Burmese who could speak some English. What he told us didn't ring true, so we decided to take him along with us. The following day our two Burmese lads went into a village and when we followed them the headman stated that our prisoner had been there with Japs a few days before and was probably a Jap spy. It was decided it was too dangerous to let him go and that he should be shot that evening. My section took him away from the others and one of the Burmese shot him through the head. I had never seen anyone killed like that at short range and as he slipped to the ground he gazed at us with such a look of surprise and condemnation. Unfortunately the shot hadn't killed him and the Burmese finished him off with a machete. Much later it struck me that we had been judge, jury and executioner. That night we had difficulty in sleeping, not because of what we had seen, but because of a swarm of small insects buzzing round all night. An omen?

'A few days later, calling into another village, we found a villager with a British rifle, which he could not account for. We decided he should suffer a similar fate, but later the saner councils prevailed and after taking him along for a couple of days we let him go. I don't think he realised how lucky he was.

'The rest of the campaign was a steady slog, with only a couple of incidents of note. We set off early one morning with no food in our packs. I had brewed up with a tea bag which had been used at least twenty times before. Around midday we were walking along a dried-up river bed when we saw some parachutes in the trees to the right. We went carefully towards them in case it might be a Jap ambush, but it was a definite ration dropping, presumably for some other party. We found enough for eight days' rations per man and left some behind in case of any stragglers. Exactly eight days later when we had almost finished our rations, we were in a small village when a British plane came over and, having seen us, the pilot dropped a small canister in which he had scrawled a note asking whether we were some of Wingate's lads and, if so, did we want a ration dropping. We marked out on the ground using strips of parachute how many there were of us and where we wanted the drop. We waited almost a couple of days but nothing happened and knowing the dangers of hanging around too long, we reluctantly moved on with no rations.

'About this time we stopped at a small stream for a brew up. Two of our lads, whose feet were in a shocking condition, were bathing their feet in the water when the order was given to move off. They said they would stay a short while and catch us up. A few hundred yards down the track we ran into a villager who told us that there was a large force of Japs nearby looking for us. We sharply turned down a small track away from the village and a few minutes later realised the two lads were not with us. A section was sent back to the stream, but could find no sign of them. We heard later that two British soldiers had been killed in that village. They were the only two casualties in our small party since we crossed the Irrawaddy.

'We pushed on, eventually reaching the Chindwin, where we walked down the east bank for some time and then found some boats in a village. Some Burmese ferried us across to the other side, just north of Tamanthi which we did not enter as Jap patrols often stayed there. We continued westwards over mountains 8,000 feet high until we reached an Assam Rifles outpost. Here we shaved off our beards, realising how thin we were. Most of us had lost two or three stones. After a few days' rest we set off again on foot, knowing that we were safe. Remarkably that made matters worse. Our incentive to keep going was no longer there. Physiologically and mentally we were in a poorer state. Several of our lads were in an exceptionally poor physical condition and myself and two others were told to stay behind to try to keep them going. Rather hard work! Eventually we hit the road and were transported to the hospital at Kohima. Sadly Lieutenant Pickering and Private Sullivan died there. After all our privations it was heartbreaking.

'Looking back at the age of seventy-seven, I am glad I was in the 1943 expedition. It taught me self-confidence, not to take the ordinary things of life for granted, and the enjoyment of a comradeship which is sadly lacking in our society today.'

Major Scott's 8 Column arrived at the Irrawaddy just before the attempted crossing began; 7 Column and Brigade Headquarters were already there. Nick Neill, a young subaltern from 3/2nd Gurkhas attached to 8 Column as an animal transport officer, recalled the scene as the boats carrying the bridgehead platoon came under enemy fire:

> 'This was the first time I had heard the sound of Jap medium machine-guns. They had a much slower rate of fire than our Vickers MMGs and their distinctive tok-tok-tok-tok noise was imprinted in my memory from that moment on. British troops eventually christened them "Woodpeckers". The area we were in on the eastern bank of the Irrawaddy was a vast stretch of open paddy fields and I had a clear view of the far bank of the river, some two miles away. I could not see any sign of our men, but I could see the bursting Jap mortar bombs from time to time. A group of men were approaching me across the paddy and when they came closer I realised that they were a group from Brigade HQ, led by Wingate himself. He was still wearing his sola topee, but now had a beard like the rest of us. I remember thinking that he looked just like a figure straight out of the Bible. As he passed by he was almost trotting, and his speed was causing his pack to bump up and down on his back. His eyes were wide and very staring; he called out to me and the others of my column standing nearby, "Disperse, disperse, get back to India." I recall thinking to myself, "My God, the man's gone mad. Here we are, a force of some 700 men, we have a platoon already across the Irrawaddy and he's not prepared to carry on with the crossing. This is too improbable to be true. There must be some other explanation to his behaviour."'

As Charles Aves and the sixty-four other men from 7 Column tramped westwards away from the river, Wingate led the remains of his force east, back into the jungle. Perhaps if the bridgehead party had attacked the Japs firing on the boats, while the remainder of the troops forced a crossing, the story would have had a different ending. One can only speculate. As Nick Neill and 8 Column made camp that night, Major Scott told him that all mules and chargers were to be released during the next day's march and driven away from the column as they could become a hindrance when the time came to head for India. Nick was aware of the cruelty that the Japanese often showed to animals and as his own charger, Rate, nuzzled his face with his soft nose, he stared up at the stars and cried. He continues:

> 'The next morning we hid the saddles and other equipment as best we could. Johnny Carroll made the mortars and MMGs as unserviceable as possible and hid them. Only the big radio-carrying mules were to be retained until the following day, when we were due to receive our final air drop, after which they would be released as well. From this day on, each man would carry his own pack, rations and bedding.

'The following day we received our air drop and then, for the first time, I was invited to join Scotty's 'O' (orders) Group. It was indeed true that all columns of the brigade were to be split up into much smaller groups and were to find their own way back to India, or China, the latter country being the nearest to us now. Our one radio in the column would go with Scotty's group after we had dispersed – lucky for some!

'Wingate had now played us his final ace card. He had taken us deep into enemy-held territory and now we were required to return to safety in penny-packets, on our own and without any communications, thus condemning us to receive no further administrative or tactical air support. In my judgement, we should have forced a crossing of the Irrawaddy when we had the chance and when we were in considerable strength. We would of course have taken casualties during the crossing, but these, I believe, would have been far fewer than those ultimately suffered by the brigade as a whole during the retreat we were about to carry out in small groups, without any inter-linking support of any kind. I asked Lieutenant Tag Sprague, who commanded the column's commando/demolition section from 142 Company, if he and his small band of commandos might like to join my Gurkhas and I for the return journey. Much to my pleasure and relief he agreed readily to my suggestion. He was four years older than me and had fought in Norway with 1 Commando. We have remained friends to this day.

'Scotty gave us the map co-ordinates of a number of DZs to the north where the RAF would be dropping supplies and to which we could go if we required further supplies during our withdrawal. He then issued us with maps and compasses, the first time I had been given such navigation aids! Now in the middle of a wilderness, with the same poor knowledge of map reading as before, I was being required to take my small group of ill-trained young Gurkhas over hundreds of miles of inhospitable terrain and through the whole of the Japanese 33rd Division, who were already searching for us with the intention of preventing our escape. It is perhaps not surprising that I should have been so critical of Wingate's training methods and battle tactics.

'So, in the early part of April, Tag and I, with my fifty-two Gurkhas and his dozen or so BORs, split from 8 Column to begin our long march back to the Chindwin. We crammed ten days' bulky rations into our packs, the only supplies we would have unless we could buy some from villages on the way. I was given 400 silver rupees for this purpose and I put them into one of the two basic pouches on my web belt. They weighed a ton, as did my pack, and I nearly fell over as I put it on. The only way I could stand up straight was to place my rifle butt on the ground behind me and poke the muzzle underneath the pack to take the weight. But carry it I did. A man's pack from that day on carried very literally his lifeblood and it was never, ever to be discarded.

'Tag and I decided to march in a northerly direction to try to recross the vast Irrawaddy somewhere along its stretch where it flows east-west between the big villages of Bhamo and Katha. We would have to avoid Shwegu though, as that village contained a Jap garrison. Every escape group had been given a few soldiers from Nigel Whitehead's platoon of 2 Burrif and we were delighted to find that we had Naik Tun Tin and four riflemen attached to us. An outstanding NCO, Tun Tin and his men were Karens and he had been educated at a mission school. He was very intelligent and spoke excellent English and was to prove to be of tremendous assistance to us. Sadly, however, we were soon parted from him. It took four days to reach the Irrawaddy, near the village of Zibyugon. The sal trees were in blossom; they smelt like a wet flannel and whenever I scent such a smell my mind goes back to that day at Zibyugon, and our brief stay there while we searched for boats to take us across the river. Tun Tin and two of his men changed into civilian clothes and went into Zibyugon to try to find boats to carry us across. He was successful and on the night of 11/12 April four or five boats appeared and ferried all of us across the river.

'We made camp four miles from the Irrawaddy. We had crossed the major river obstacle between us and safety. We still had to cross the Chindwin and other smaller rivers, but they should present us with little difficulty, providing we crossed them before the monsoon rains broke in late May or early June. We had over 200 miles to cover before reaching the Chindwin. By the morning of 14 April we had crossed the Kaukkwe Chaung, a north-south flowing river which joined the Irrawaddy and entered the village of Thayetta. Tun Tin was arranging the purchase of rice, chicken and vegetables while I sat down to remove my boots and examine my sore feet. I noticed briefly a villager leaving the village on a bicycle and heading north. I thought nothing of this at the time and did not realise the significance until later in the morning.

'We had not gone far from the village when, totally out of the blue, an ambush exploded abruptly to my immediate left. I can remember roaring out to my men "Dahine tira sut!" (Take cover, right!) before diving for cover myself into the bushes to the right of the track. I remember I wasn't actually frightened – which surprised me – but I was totally and utterly shocked. Never, ever, during any of my previous training had I been taught any of the approved contact drills; certainly the counter-ambush drill was unknown to me. I was utterly appalled to realise that I simply did not know what to do to extract myself and my men from our predicament. A Jap gunner was firing his LMG immediately opposite me from the jungle on the far side of the track and another was firing at the men who were behind me. I could see the smoke rising from his gun muzzle and his bursts of fire were hitting the trees and bushes above my head. When the Jap gunner stopped firing to change magazines I roared above the noise of the continuing rifle fire, "Sabai jana ut! Mero pachhi aija!" (Everybody up! Follow me!). I leapt to my feet, turned away from the track and crashed through the jungle, calling to my men to follow. I looked around and saw some of my Gurkhas and Tag's men running parallel to me. When we halted, there were only twenty of us. Tag and I, eleven Gurkhas, six of Tag's men and one Burma rifleman. I did not believe that many of the others had been killed, but those missing were without maps and compasses. My guilt at not being able to do better for them in the ambush, and being unable to maintain contact with them afterwards, hung very heavy on my conscience and still does to this day.'

It was clear that the villager who had left Thayetta on his bicycle had gone straight to the nearest Japanese outpost to alert them. The survivors of the ambush had to put as much distance between them and the village as possible, before making camp for the night. The next day they set a course westwards for the Chindwin, straight across country. They did not see a track again for three weeks. After a couple of days, Sergeant Sennett and the five other British commandos asked Tag Sprague if they could turn about and head east for China. They planned to make for one of the pre-arranged drop zones, collect some rations and then make for China. Tag told them frankly that they were mad to go to the DZ area, as the enemy would probably be waiting there by this time and by going towards China they would be heading into the unknown. They were adamant, however, and with reluctance Tag gave them a map and compass and allowed them to go. They were never seen again.

As the days passed, the men got weaker. Fortunately the Gurkhas' knowledge of what wild plants and fungi to eat helped eke out their meagre supply of rice. Food was so scarce that Nick never cleaned his mess tin at all. Any residue would harden on the sides of the tin, to soften next time a meal was cooked, before being scraped off with his spoon and eaten. They were now infested with lice which lived in their shirt seams and socks. They did not bother them during the day, but made them itch so much at night that they slept without clothes. Any scratches quickly turned into sores.

Eventually they reached the Mawhun–Mawlu road, which ran parallel to the Myitkyina–Rangoon railway a couple of hundred yards away. They crossed without delay and entered the Mawhun Reserved Forest. They had eighteen miles to go, as the crow flies, to the Meza River. When they got there, the river was only fifty yards wide and with little water in its bed. From there it was another twenty-two miles to the Zibyu Taungdan Escarpment. It would be hard going. Nick recalls:

'During one part of the journey, my tired mind, with its sights set forever on the Chindwin, recalled a time from the past when my mother used to sit me on her knee and, bouncing me up and down, she would sing the old American negro spiritual hymn "One More River", the words from which so aptly fitted both my frame of mind and our ultimate aim:

> One more river, that's the River of Jordan,
> One more river, that's the river to cross,
> One more river, that's the River of Jordan,
> One more river, that's the river for me.

The Jordan of the hymn became the Chindwin of my thoughts and prayers. It helped me push my tired legs ever westwards.

'Sleep at night did not come easily at this time. We were only using game trails, but at night we would move as far away from the trail as possible and, like hunted animals, seek the thickest cover available. My blanket was used during the day as a pad between my pack and my back and by nightfall it would be soaked through by my sweat. It was a pretty chilly thing to wrap around me, particularly if we were on very high ground. Then one night it rained very hard. It was on this night, with the rain water soaking through my already damp blanket and running down the slope either side of where I lay, that I really started to pray to God for deliverance. I suspect that many a soldier, in times of grave danger and misfortune, has prayed to his Maker for help, just as I did in those dark days. Then we met the buffaloes in the Namma Reserve Forest and I began to think that some of my prayers were being heard!

'Each day two of my riflemen, 107871 Bandilal Limbu and 107524 Dhanbahadur Rai, would volunteer to scout ahead of our small party. Tag or I would follow behind them and concentrate on reading our compasses. Suddenly on the morning after the heavy rainfall, Bandilal turned to me and whispered, "Bhainsi, saheb. Hanum, ki?" (Buffalo, Sir. Shall I shoot?) Sure enough, there were four village buffaloes wallowing in the water of a fairly deep-sided chaung just ahead of us. Manna from heaven! Tag and I looked at each other. Should we take the risk, or would the firing of a shot alert a hostile villager? We were nearly starving and had to take the risk. Tag took Bandilal's rifle, aimed carefully at the nearest buffalo and killed the unfortunate beast cleanly with one shot. The other buffaloes scattered in panic at the sound of the shot, which I hoped was muffled by the steepness of the chaung banks. The men dragged the buffalo out of the chaung and proceeded to butcher it on the spot. Soon a large fire was built from the driest wood, to minimise smoke, and the meat was smoked and roasted in the fire in no time at all. We were so hungry that many of us ate quite a number of pieces of meat before they were properly cooked through, with the blood running down our chins. Soon the buffalo had disappeared. Our stomachs were full to bursting and we had some left over to carry with us on our journey.'

It was now the middle of May and they still had another month to go before reaching the Chindwin. They crossed the Zibyu Taungdan, the escarpment, by struggling along a very prominent river called the Chaunggyi, shaped, in its course, like a dog's leg. It cut through the escarpment via a pass, then continued its journey west to flow into the Uyu River, which in turn flowed west to join the Chindwin about two miles south of the big village of Homalin where there was a large Japanese garrison. The ten-mile stretch was to take them three days, through ankle-deep soft sand and knee-deep water.

Another Gurkha rifleman was lost during an encounter with a truck load of Japanese, which curiously was being pulled by an elephant. They were all now very weak and Naik Harkabahadur had gone down with a severe bout of malaria. They took his equipment from him and he staggered along without a word of complaint. They were now just sixteen miles from the Chindwin.

Chapter 5

The Long Way Home

On the evening of 29 March, when Wingate ordered his columns to withdraw to India, 1 Column was the furthest from home, bivouacked six miles west of Mongmit. In the morning Lieutenant-Colonel Alexander ordered all but seven mules to be released and all heavy equipment, including mortars and machine-guns, to be dumped. Three days earlier Wingate had sent a message to Southern Group: 'Remember Lot's wife. Return not whence you came. Seek thy salvation in the mountains. Genesis XIX.' However, there was no salvation to be found in that direction. Herring could wait no longer for them and although the Kachins provided food for the hungry Chindits, the Japanese were everywhere.*

For a while the column continued eastwards, but at 0800 hours on 2 April sentries spied Japanese infantry deploying below the ridge on which they were bivouacked. As the tired men took up firing positions, the Japanese formed up in three lines and charged, yelling as they ran through the scrub. The Gurkhas held their fire until the enemy was nearly upon them, then opened fire at point-blank range. The first line of troops was decimated and those following took cover and began to fire back and throw hand grenades. Lieutenant Ian MacHorton was hit in the leg and left behind after the column disengaged at nightfall. Amazingly he later continued westwards on his own and made it back to India and safety. He later co-wrote *Safer Than a Known Way*, a rather dramatised version of his adventures, well worth hunting for in the second-hand military bookstores.

Their last mules gone and the wireless set destroyed, 1 Column and Southern Group Headquarters continued eastwards. A Gurkha Brahmin came upon them and led them on a detour to the south-east to avoid the enemy searching for them. It had been twelve days since their last supply drop, when at last they reached the village of Kunka. Subedar Siblal Thapa later recalled, 'We had eaten little but leaves and shoots for nearly a week. My stomach was beginning to think that my throat was cut!' For two days they fed and rested, then continued in a circle, eastwards, then north and finally west, back in the direction of India.

*Note: George Dunlop wrote to the author – 'Wingate should have known that he was sending 1 Column and Group HQ into a death trap. It was the area in which the Japs were confronting the Chinese Yunnan Armies.'

By 13 April they were on the banks of the Shweli River and commenced crossing on bamboo rafts. However, the enemy arrived and the crossing was halted, leaving five men marooned on the far bank. Captain Weatherall went to the bank of the river to seek them and was killed by a burst of machine-gun fire. The next twelve days saw the column very short of both food and water and when they finally arrived at Singyat, on the east bank of the Irrawaddy, on 25 April, they learned that no boats were to be found. Japanese troops were garrisoned only five miles away, so Alexander decided to attempt a crossing right away. At 1830 hours Alexander, together with Major Dunlop and forty others, began to swim the 1,500 yards to the far bank.

Meanwhile, Lieutenant Chet Khin of the Burma Rifles had discovered two small boats in a nearby chaung and the remainder of the column began to cross, a few at a time. During the evening Subedar Padanbahadur Rai with fifty-nine men joined the queue on the riverbank. Attached to Wingate's Headquarters as Defence Platoon, they had been left behind when Brigade Headquarters re-crossed the river and continued westwards on their own. The crossing continued throughout the night and as the men reached the west bank they quickly took cover and moved on in their dispersal groups. As dawn broke, the covering platoon under Naik Devsur Ale began to cross. Then the Japanese arrived. Running along the west bank, they opened fire on the boats when the platoon was a mere fifteen yards from the shore. The boats were sunk and only the platoon commander and one rifleman escaped.

The hunt was now on with a hundred miles to go to the Chindwin. Some groups disappeared without trace, decimated in ambushes or fallen by the wayside as starvation and exhaustion overtook them. Lieutenant Wormwell was taken prisoner by the enemy while only fifteen miles from the Chindwin. Major George Dunlop, who was later chosen by Wingate to head an aborted project to teach the ways of the Chindits to Chinese Army officers, described the fighting withdrawal of his column to the author:

'Captain Weatherall was killed when we attempted to cross the Shweli River. Patrols sent out up the river encountered the enemy and a fight developed. We did not get across and so I had to change my plans and try to get back to India. I had hoped to get to India via China as Gilkes, the commander of 7 Column, did, but there were far too many enemy about. According to General Mutagatchi he ordered three divisions to catch us, although they failed at that time. Weatherall's death was a terrible blow. His Gurkhas worshipped him and their morale was hit hard. I told Alexander at the time that our troubles had now really begun and that our one object was to get as many men as possible back to India. We crossed the Irrawaddy and the railway more or less intact, but then disaster befell us.

'The "ambush" at the Mu River was really the final stage of a day of encounters with the enemy and his Burmese helpers. Despite patrolling the banks of the river which we had to wade, the Japs caught the tail end of the column in the water. The rest of us were in thick secondary undergrowth awaiting the completion of the crossing. As the fight developed the enemy mortared the area and there were casualties. Men were there one moment and had disappeared, usually for good, the next. It must have been at this time that Alexander was hit and very soon died. The procedure on these unmanageable occasions was to carry out the dispersal drill taught by Wingate. This happened and when we met at our RV Lieutenant Clarke told me what had happened to Alexander. He fell seriously wounded and was last seen being carried into cover by Lieutenant De la Rue and Flight Lieutenant Edmunds. The latter officer was captured and held prisoner until the fall of Rangoon in April 1945.

'Captain Chet Khin and I parted company after our last proper battle with the Japs near Maingyaung in the Zibyu Taungdan hills. We surprised the Japs while they were preparing a trap for us. Realising what was about to be sprung on us and being near the Chindwin, and with so much evidence of the Japanese on the footpaths, I had given orders about what everyone was to do. They were to the effect that as soon as the enemy opened fire, we were to extend quickly to either flank and attack. No withdrawal. The trap was sprung from three sides, but chiefly in front, and this was done. Fighting occurred in scattered groups for some time. This is when the largest number found themselves under Chet Khin's command. They eventually reached the Chindwin, found some boats and crossed. Chet Khin was later awarded the Military Cross. This final dispersal came near the scene of our first encounter with the enemy nearly three months earlier, on 18 February, when we gave the Nasu battalion a good hammering. We had underestimated the results of that fight, because only a few bodies had been found. Chet Khin was lucky enough to have the fighting, and better, part of the column under his command. I was left with HQ, muleteers without their mules and the British troops.

'We were very hungry. Villages were few and far between and held unhusked rice and little else for immediate use. Food gathering was strictly controlled and was done by the Burma Rifles. John Fowler did the issuing of what little there was. Private foraging was an offence. However, at this time we had virtually nothing to eat for a week and Lieutenant Nealon commanding the British demolition platoon asked permission to try for food in Maingyaung. There, he was attacked by the Japs and the survivors captured. He was about the only one to survive to the end of the war. Extreme hunger tends to blur the judgement and my party was scattered by an enemy attack after we had shot a buffalo near the Chindwin and we were forced to cross as best we could. By that time the Japs, with Burmese help, knew where we were and there were no boats. Thus those who could, swam the river. A company of Mahratta's was at the confluence of the Yu and Chindwin rivers and helped us on our way. It was about the tenth of May.

'When I got back to Tamu in the middle of May, I was ordered to report to IV Corps commander, Lieutenant-General Scoones, as soon as possible. This I did. At the time I knew nothing of the fate of anyone in the "Northern Group". General Scoones told me to give him a written report as soon as possible, and sent me to hospital in Imphal, where I found a lot of survivors from other columns and learned that Wingate was alive. A 77 Brigade HQ had been established in Imphal and I asked the chief clerk to have my report typed for General Scoones. That is the last I saw of it and I don't know if he even got it. A lack of information about our group became apparent when the books started to come out. I later met Wingate out walking before breakfast one day at Imphal. His actual words to me were, "I ought to have you court-martialled!" and he then turned about and stomped off. I don't know if it was to do with my report, or indeed if he was serious. I didn't see him again for many months and no mention was made at any time of the misadventures of number one group. I suspect that he was conscious of the fact that in sending us east when the rest turned for India, he had treated us as expendable. Getting back, with the very good help of Chet Khin and his Karens, rather upset all the glowing reports which had been rushed out for propaganda purposes.'

When Major Mike Calvert received the message to return to India he was only 100 miles from the Burma Road. He initially decided to head for China or Fort Hertz in the north, but to do that he had to cross the Shweli River. Although they discovered that enemy pickets were in every village, they tried to cross over at night on 27 March, using sapper rafts of bamboo encased in waterproof ground sheets. A Japanese patrol arrived on their side of the river just as the crossing began and two men were marooned on the far side when Calvert called off the attempt. Calvert was prepared as usual and Sergeant-Major Blain and his men ambushed the advance section and killed the lot. They made good their escape and moved back into the jungle to rethink their plans. Calvert sent out scouts who discovered that there were large enemy forces in all of the larger villages and a force of seven hundred had just arrived at Myitson. Squadron Leader Robert Thompson radioed the news to India and the village was bombed, causing 200 casualties. Calvert realised that forcing a crossing of the Shweli in the face of enemy opposition would lead to heavy casualties, so he abandoned his idea of heading for China or Fort Hertz. He preferred to try to take the column back to India in one piece, but his officers declared their preference for dispersal in small groups. Calvert decided to go for dispersal and wasted no time in organising one last supply drop. When their packs were full Calvert divided his column into nine groups: Major Calvert, Lieutenant Jeffery Lockett and his commandos; Squadron Leader Robert Thompson and Doctor Rao with the RAF detachment and 15 platoon; Lieutenant Harold James and

Captain Taffy Griffiths, Burma Rifles with 13 platoon; Captain George Silcock (Column 2ic) and Second Lieutenant Denis Gudgeon with 14 Platoon; Lieutenant George Worte and Captain Roy 'Mac' McKenzie, each with a platoon of muleteers; and Subedar Siribhagta with Jemedar Cameron and support group personnel. The last two groups contained headquarters men and Karens, one led by Lieutenant Ken Gourlay and Alec Gibson and the other by Subedar Kumba Sing Gurung and Subedar Donny of the Burma Rifles.

On the afternoon of 30 March Calvert gathered all his officers together and drank a toast of rum. 'Good luck to you. We have been a great team and I thank you for your efforts. I hope that we will all meet again on the other side of the Chindwin.' Wingate later remarked that the groups that used routes south of Indaw–Banmauk had the hardest time, with the exception of 3 Column. It passed by routes south of Wuntho, some days before anyone else, and reached the Chindwin in good spirits and condition. This he attributed to the excellent orders of Calvert and the early adoption of dispersal.

Harold James, Taffy Griffiths and 15 Platoon marched to the Irrawaddy, found a large sampan with a Burmese family on board and paid them to carry their party across. No sooner had the first boatload got across than Bobby Thompson and his men arrived. He sent a runner back to Calvert with the message '*Ventre à terre to the river*'. Once across the river Calvert wanted to join forces and attack the railway on the way back. The others demurred, deciding discretion was the better part of valour. Undeterred, Calvert and his commandos decided to go out with a bang. At the dead of night they laid their charges and Calvert felt in his pocket for his time pencils, which would set the explosives off after they had left the scene. To his horror he realised that he had failed to follow his own rules and nick the pencils with a penknife, so many nicks to each colour, so that they would be easy to pick out at night. There was a Japanese working party nearby, so striking a match would be very risky. 'Lift up that kilt of yours,' said Calvert to Lockett. The young, bearded, toothless Scot watched warily as Calvert struck a match under his improvised black-out curtains and sorted out his pencils. Lockett muttered darkly about suing Calvert for damages. The other groups heard the distant sound of explosions as Calvert's charges cut the railway line in five places again. As the Japanese flocked to the area, Calvert and his party went to ground in a thick clump of bamboo. 'What the hell do we do now?' one officer asked. 'Let's have a cup of tea,' suggested Lockett. And they did.

Bobby Thompson and Taffy Griffiths combined their parties and travelled onwards together, finally meeting a Sikh patrol on the east bank of the Chindwin at 1400 hours on 14 April. They were the first of the brigade dispersal groups to reach home. The following day Calvert and his party crossed over. Subedar Kumba Sing Gurung's group escaped into China, but Alec Gibson, Denis Gudgeon, Ken Gourlay and Subedar Siribhagta were taken prisoner. The other groups made it safely back to India. George Silcock took half of his party across the Irrawaddy on sapper sampans, but when Denis Gudgeon tried to follow with the rest of the men, their rafts began to sink and they had to turn back. Eventually Denis and his party of eleven Gurkhas and one Burma rifleman bribed a boatman to take them across and they struck out on their own for the Chindwin. The exhausted men got within a few miles of safety when suddenly Denis collapsed. He ordered his men to continue without him. They returned for him next day, but could find no sign of him. Recovering a little, Denis had moved on and reached the village of Tanga on the east bank of the river. He recalled, 'I was drinking tea from a bone china tea cup and beginning to feel rather apprehensive, when there was a commotion and I looked up to find myself staring down the muzzles of a dozen Jap rifles.'

Out of the 360 men in 3 Column, 205 eventually recrossed the Chindwin. For his courageous leadership Major Calvert was awarded the Distinguished Service Order.

When Wingate led his Brigade Group back towards Inywa on the Irrawaddy River, 5 Column was given the job of rearguard. However, they were in a worse shape than the other columns, having missed some supply drops and had stopped to slaughter a mule in a dry stream bed. Unfortunately, a Burma rifleman left the bivouac area to answer the call of nature and stumbled into a Japanese patrol. Wingate heard the firing and forged ahead with 7 and 8 Columns, sending a message back to 5 Column to ambush their tracks. However, Fergusson decided to draw the enemy away from the main body instead, by establishing a dummy bivouac and laying booby-traps.

Around 0300 hours, 5 Column reached the village of Hintha. They could not find a way around through the thick jungle, so Fergusson decided to lead his men through the village itself. The Major was in the lead as they approached a fire with four men sitting round it. As they got closer he realised that the men were Japanese and pitched a hand grenade into the middle of the fire. Fergusson later recounted that all four fell over outward on to their backs with perfect symmetry. The explosion heralded the start of a pitched battle in the dark. Sergeant Peter Dorans lay at the side of a track and rolled grenades into the midst of one party of Japanese. Lieutenant Philip Stibbe led his platoon into the village, but was wounded when a Japanese machine-gun opened fire. Fergusson too was hit in the hip by a grenade splinter and soon after ordered the 'Dispersal' to be blown on the bugle. As the column broke up into dispersal groups to head for the RV at Inywa, a wounded Philip

Stibbe realised that he was holding up his party and ordered them to continue without him. A brave Burma rifleman, Maung Tun, volunteered to stay with him. In the morning he ventured forth to seek food and water for Stibbe, but was captured by the Japanese. He was tortured to reveal the officer's whereabouts, but held out and paid for his silence with his life. Eventually Stibbe staggered back to the village in search of water and was captured by the Japanese. He would spend the next three years in Rangoon jail and later recounted his experiences in his book *Return via Rangoon*.

The day after the dispersal at Hintha, Fergusson and some of 5 Column rejoined Wingate at Inywa. Other members of the column joined forces with 7 Column for the trek home via China. Bill Aird, the column doctor, found himself in charge of some sick and sorry from both columns and amazingly saw them all the way back to the Chindwin, where they were captured. Aird and most of the men would die in captivity. The column radio was lost during the battle at Hintha when the mule carrying it was shot and fell into a gully. They were now unable to call for a much needed supply drop. Fergusson decided not to try to cross the Irrawaddy, but to cross the Shweli instead and get into the Kachin Hills where food and friends could be found.

One hundred and twenty men from 5 Column, including Fergusson, reached the Shweli and persuaded two Burmese boatmen to carry them across in their three-man dugouts. They were ferried across during the night, but then discovered that they had been deposited on a large sand bank in the middle of the river, with eighty yards of water still between them and the far bank. Fergusson later recalled:

> 'There is no word for it but "nightmare". The roaring of the waters, the blackness of the night, the occasional sucking of a quicksand were bad enough, but the current was devilish and must have been four to five knots. It sought to scoop the feet from under you and at the same time thrust powerfully at your chest. It was about four feet six or more deep and if you lost your vertical position, you knew as a black certainty that you would disappear down the stream for ever.'

Some who tried to wade across were swept away, their cries echoing through the darkness. Many men lost their nerve and remained on the sand bank. Signaller Byron White was one of those who gritted his teeth, clenched his rifle tightly above his head and walked slowly into the chest-deep water. He told the author:

> 'It was soon up to shoulder height and so fast flowing that it was difficult to keep one's feet on the bottom. Just in front of me was one of our younger lads and we were trying to keep as quiet as possible, but he was shouting "Mother, Mother help me." I got close to him and in no uncertain terms told him to shut up. Afterwards I was sorry for what I

said. I never saw him again. He didn't make the crossing. We moved on slowly against the fast-flowing water, expecting to walk out on the far bank on dry land. Instead, to our dismay the bank rose sheer out of the water, about ten to twelve feet above the water level. Somehow some of the lads had managed to get out on to the top of the bank and were able to reach our outstretched arms and assist us up the slippery bank.'

Many men made it across, including all of the wounded and some of the Gurkhas, the smallest men of all. The rest refused to follow. Fergusson could not remain and jeopardise the safety of the men who had put their faith in providence and made the crossing. It was an hour before dawn and Japanese patrols could be expected at any time. He later explained, 'I made the decision to come away. I have it on my conscience for as long as I live; but I stand by that decision and believe it to have been the correct one.'

Fergusson was now down to nine officers and sixty-five men. Forty-six others had either drowned or remained behind on the sand bank. At daylight the Japanese arrived and took them all prisoner. A couple of days later the depleted column reached the village of Zibyugin and obtained some food. News reached them that the Japanese were on the way and they quickly withdrew to the outskirts of the village. One of their sentries did not return to the bivouac and there was still a need for more food and information on enemy dispositions, so Lieutenant Duncan Menzies volunteered to take a small patrol back to the village. The four men walked into a Japanese patrol and after a brief fight, Menzies and Gilmartin were captured. Fergusson and the rest of the party waited until the next morning, then continued their journey to the north-west. Later that day, the Burma Rifle Headquarters, about 100 strong, reached Zibyugin and attacked it. The small number of Japanese in the village withdrew and the Burrifs discovered Menzies and Gilmartin. They were dressed in Japanese uniforms, their beards had been shaved and they had been tied to trees and used for bayonet practice by the Japanese. Gilmartin was dead and Menzies dying when Colonel Wheeler, the battalion commander, arrived on the scene. Menzies asked for a lethal dose of morphia and gave Wheeler his watch, to be sent to his parents if Wheeler reached India safely. It was not to be. One minute after Wheeler gave Menzies the morphia the Colonel was shot through the head by a sniper and killed. The two friends were buried together.

As the weak began to fall by the wayside, Fergusson decided to split his seventy men into three equal groups. Captain Tommy Roberts, the commando platoon commander, took one and Flight Lieutenant Denny Sharp another. The third was led by Fergusson and included Lieutenant Jim Harman, who was wounded twice at Hintha. Fergusson's party finally crossed the Irrawaddy courtesy of two boys of thirteen or fourteen who thought the whole thing a great lark. Fergusson suspected they had borrowed the boat, unknown to its owner.

Fifteen days later they crossed the Chindwin. Denny Sharp's party reached safety the same day, but Tommy Roberts was not so successful. Five of their party had crossed the Irrawaddy when the Japanese attacked the remainder, forcing them to withdraw. Two weeks later and fifty miles further upstream the nine survivors crossed over and marched for four more days before they bumped a thirty-man Japanese patrol. Although they killed seven of the enemy, they had to surrender after two of their party were killed and five wounded. Roberts was the only member of the expedition to be flown to Singapore for interrogation. He was put to work on the notorious Siam railway, but survived until the war's end. Out of the 318 members of 5 Column who marched into Burma, only ninety-five got out. Twenty-eight more survived Rangoon jail, but many others had died in captivity. Fergusson later described the story of 5 Column's part in the expedition in a book entitled *Beyond the Chindwin*.

7 Column had been split in two when Wingate called off the crossing of the Irrawaddy at Inywa. When the order to disperse was given, the column commander, Major Ken Gilkes, decided to head for China. They had been joined by about 110 members of 5 Column who had failed to rejoin Major Fergusson after the fight at Hintha. Major Gilkes quite correctly separated those he considered physically capable of completing the journey to China, from those who were too weak or sick and ordered them to return to India by various routes. Many would be lost on the way. One of the parties, under Lieutenant Musgrave Wood, reached Fort Hertz in good condition. The larger party, mostly comprising 5 Column men, was not heard from again.

Major Gilkes led his men south over the Mongmit–Myitson Road and then marched north-east to Nayok on the Shweli River, crossed over on 11 April and moved into the Kachin Hills. After a long journey they climbed a broad belt of mountains and linked up with Chinese irregular troops. The inhabitants of the first Chinese village fed all 150 of them and refused any payment. 'You have fought the enemies of China. The least we can do is feed you,' they were told. The Chinese guerrilla officer at Lenma remarked that he was delighted to meet British officers with uncreased trousers who made no demands for beds to sleep on.

Eventually they reached the Salween Valley front where the Japanese had been advancing when Wingate took his brigade into Burma. There they watched a seven-day battle in which the Chinese routed the Japanese, who had transferred a full division to Burma to deal with the Chindits. They then crossed the Salween and later the Mekong Rivers, using guides supplied by the regular Chinese Army. Eventually they reached Kunming, having marched 1,500 miles since leaving Imphal. They were greeted with flags flying and a band playing military marches and the commander-in-chief at Kunming lodged them in the best building in the town. They were given baths, new clothes and haircuts and the Chinese General even advanced Gilkes enough money to pay his men.

The Dane, Erik Pedersen, who had joined up with Mike Calvert at Nankan when separated from his column, was wounded in the head at Baw and could not sit on a horse without help. He was supported in the saddle by relays of men for several hundred miles until he recovered sufficiently to walk and fight with the rest of them. Only sixteen men from 5 Column reached China safely. They had acted as rearguard all the way and had lost eleven killed in four actions. Eventually Major Gilkes and his men were flown back to India from Kunming in planes of the US Tenth Air Force.

One man from 7 Column who did not make it to China was Private Leon Frank:

'I was in a group of thirty men under a Lieutenant from the Sherwood Foresters and we decided to make our way northwards to Fort Hertz which was still in British hands. The idea was that we would take some guides from a village, who could take us on to the next village, and so on. We did this successfully for a while, then we had these two guides who were leading us up a hill towards a cross-shaped junction of tracks. Suddenly one dived left and the other right and disappeared into the jungle. In front of us across the track was a Japanese patrol. Well, we just melted into the jungle either side, but the Japs had spotted us. We hoped that if we were quiet enough they would just go away, but one of our chaps looked up and for no apparent reason shouted 'Japs!' and gave our position away. They started to open fire on us, so we turned and rolled and scrambled down the hill. We did everything we could to put them off our tracks and eventually eluded them. We realised that our party was too large and too obvious a target, so our Lieutenant told us it was every man for himself. Myself and five others, including Lance-Corporal Jordan, decided to go east and try to get into China.

'We became like bandits; we would go into villages and demand rice and food at gunpoint. We eventually came to a hillside with a hut on the side of it and a stream below and settled down to rest. Someone should have been on guard but we were very exhausted. Next thing we knew the door burst open and in came a Jap soldier with a fixed bayonet and stabbed Jordan in the hand. He was about to have another go when an officer called him off. We walked outside to find a half moon circle of Japanese soldiers with a machine-gun in the centre, pointed at us. I remember turning around and saying, "The bastards are going to shoot us in cold blood!" Fortunately we had been captured by the Imperial Guard, who were professional soldiers. They tied our hands and led us to their camp. We were fed and given various jobs to do around the camp. I was made a batman to one of the Japanese officers and had to sleep with five other Japanese batmen. One of the soldiers could speak English. He had been a barber in Tokyo and asked me to go to his hut for supper one night.

He gave me some rice and kidneys to eat and invited me to go to Tokyo after the war and meet his family.

'After about ten days we were put on a truck and sent to Maymyo. On the way we stopped at another jungle camp and our escort left us in the hands of the camp's personnel. We were taken into a hut and made to kneel in the execution position with our hands tied behind our back. A big Japanese officer came in whirling his sword and we thought our time had come. However, it was just a sick joke. When we got to Maymyo we were beaten up by the Korean guards, who were just as bad as, if not worse than, the Japanese. Eventually we were sent to Rangoon by train, crammed into cattle trucks for the three-day trip. I remember when we stopped at Mandalay the door was opened and we saw one of the big six-foot Imperial guardsmen who had captured us. He went away and came back with a bunch of bananas which he gave to us. Our next stop was block number six, Rangoon jail. I was the only one of the six of us to survive.'

Leon Frank was joined in Rangoon jail by another 7 Column member, Fred Morgan. He was among the two platoons of the column that had already crossed the Irrawaddy at Inywa when the Japanese intervened. Apparently he was not with Charles Aves and his party and was soon bagged by the enemy. He told the author:

'As soon as we landed a decision was made to move off in small groups as quickly as possible, since we did not want to attract too much attention to ourselves. After all, we had no idea as to the strength of the Jap patrol. The small group I was with was led by Lieutenant Stock.

'We had paused for a while, resting our heads on our packs, when all of a sudden a number of Japs came tearing up the hillside towards us. Needless to say we beat a hasty retreat up the hill. Somehow the Bren gun was left behind and I handed my rifle to someone and went back for it. I grabbed it, but found the magazine was empty and therefore useless. On the way up I started to strip the gun and began throwing the pieces to the four winds. I finally caught up with Lieutenant Stock and found he was in possession of a revolver, but no ammunition. I think we had words with one another over that omission. We eventually lost contact with each other and I met up with him again in Rangoon jail.

'Now I was all by myself. I was alone, tired and frightened. I found myself climbing a very large hill and when I reached the top I started down the other side and began to cross a paddy field. No sooner had I got to the centre of the field when I heard shouting and what appeared to be animal noises. I stopped and turned around to see three Japanese running towards me. One of them had a sword and the other two had fixed bayonets and they started to prod me in the stomach. The Jap with the sword slapped my face and then knocked me to the ground. My hands were tied behind my back and I was marched back to what must have been an advanced post, complete with a look-out tower, situated just outside Wuntho. I was interrogated by a very tall Japanese officer, who asked me all sorts of military questions about the strengths and whereabouts of the British Army in India. I replied that that sort of information was not available to an ordinary NCO. I was accused of lying and beaten up again!

'Along with a number of other Chindits I was taken to Maymyo, in which there was a Japanese field prison. Here we were made to learn their language, in particular the various words of command. It behove us all to learn as quickly as possible in order to avoid being beaten up. At the end of the working day, which was spent digging air raid shelters and repairing houses, we had to stand around a flag pole with the Japanese 'Rising Sun' flag fluttering in the breeze. We had to bow towards the east in honour of their Emperor. After this charade we had to have a sing-song. Much to the amusement of the guards, a mate of mine, Sergeant Gilbert Josling, and myself used to sing Max Miller's song "I fell in love with Mary from the dairy". Sadly, Sergeant Josling did not make it home from Rangoon jail. Our compound was surrounded by very heavy iron railings and the Japanese guards used to patrol around this perimeter. Every time the guard passed by, we had to stop what we were doing and bow. At this time I was sitting on the ground with Sergeant Josling's head in my lap, because he was very ill with beri-beri, so I did not get up and bow. The Jap saw me and started shouting obscenities at me, so I laid Josling's head down gently and went over to the fence and bowed. The Jap thrust his rifle through the railings butt first and belted me in the stomach and testicles for not bowing to him in the first place. When I returned to Josling he had passed away.'

Major Walter Scott and 8 Column joined up with Headquarters Northern Group and its commander, Lieutenant-Colonel Sam Cooke, for the journey home. Scott wanted to try to take his column home intact, but gave Nick Neill and Tag Sprague permission to leave separately with a group of commandos and Gurkhas. The main body marched northwards towards Fort Hertz and reached the banks of the Shweli River on 1 April. They managed to get a line across the river and began to cross in two dinghies, lashed to the line to prevent them being carried away. Captain Williams and thirty-two men had reached the far bank safely when an NCO in one of the dinghies foolishly cut through a knot in the main rope and the two dinghies and their occupants swirled away down river with the curses of their comrades ringing in their ears. They were never seen again. Captain Williams and his party set off on their own, but were ambushed on the way and only one of their party survived.

On 3 April the RAF dropped more dinghies to the column and they crossed the river and continued north towards Katha and Bhamo on the Irrawaddy. On 19 April they reached the Irrawaddy and lay in wait on the bank of the river for two days, hoping that a boat would pass their way. On the third morning a large native boat approached the bank and Scotty and Private Jim Upton jumped into the river and seized it. It held fifty men and they were soon across. Private Dennis 'Topper' Brown managed to keep a diary of the trek home. He recorded the speech that Colonel Cooke made to the men, the day after they crossed the river:

> 'It was not very encouraging. The gist of it was that he had orders from HQ to make the return journey to India, but that if he had his way, we would fight on to the last man and last bullet! You can imagine how that went down with the rank and file! I did hear that at one time he suggested that the RAF should drop soap, towels and razors, until it was pointed out that you can't eat them! The next day, our last mule, carrying the radio, keeled over and died. We radioed for one last supply drop, smashed the set and continued our journey.'

The rendezvous for the supply drop was a clearing near Bhamo, a large town 150 miles behind Japanese lines. On the way they ran out of rations and were all in a poor state when hope returned to bolster their flagging spirits. As he marched along through the dark jungle, Major Scott noticed that the track ahead of him was growing lighter, as if he were approaching the end of a tunnel. Soon he was standing at the edge of the jungle, looking out on what was probably the largest patch of open ground in northern Burma.

The following day, Sunday 11 April, the Chindits scanned the sky, praying for a supply drop. Captain Johnny Carroll, the support group commander, was one of them: 'Colonel Cooke agreed that we should work out the best area for a supply drop using white maps and socks. I suggested that we mark out PLANE LAND HERE NOW. Colonel Cooke said that we could not issue orders to the RAF and should therefore mark out REQUEST PLANE LAND HERE NOW. As the noise of a supply plane could already be heard, I suggested we start without the word REQUEST and add it later if time permitted.' The planes came over and dropped supplies to the waiting Chindits. One of them circled lower and saw the message. Flying Officer 'Lumme' Lord tried to land, but the area was too short and too rough to put down safely. A message was dropped to the men: 'Mark out 1,200-yard landing ground to hold twelve-ton transport.'

On Tuesday at dawn the Dakota rescue plane took off. Flying Officer Michael Vlasto and his crew were given a pair of Army boots each to walk home in if the plane did not land safely. When he reached the clearing, a white line was marked out on the field, together with a message: LAND ON WHITE LINE. GROUND THERE V.G. The crew braced themselves as Vlasto made his approach. They touched down and the pilot hit the brakes, coming to a halt just at the end of the strip. The plane was soon surrounded by bearded, malnourished men. Who would go out in the plane? There was only one answer: the wounded went out first – Corporal Jimmy Walker, who had dropped out of the column with dysentery and an infected hip, but had dragged himself along behind them; Private Jim Suddery who had been shot in the back, the bullet going right through him; and Private Robert Hulse, shaken every couple of hours by violent fits of vomiting. Lieutenant-Colonel Cooke also went aboard. This was a controversial decision which provoked much discussion among those left behind. A photographer on the plane took a picture of the Colonel smiling and reading *Punch* magazine, in contrast to the looks of suffering, emaciation and profound relief on the faces of the others. Fifty years later one of those who walked out remarked to the author: 'A round of bread and jam would have been more use to them than a read of *Punch* magazine. If you want my opinion it wasn't a case of wangling a seat, but that Scotty was glad and eager to get rid of him! And of course there were more deserving cases who should have gone.' One of those was Topper Brown, who staggered on to the Chindwin while suffering with dysentery, after escaping death when they were ambushed at the Kaukkwe Chaung, and then came down with typhus fever and had to be carried seventy miles on a stretcher by Naga tribesmen to the Imphal road.

Eighteen men were counted into the plane and the cargo door was closed behind them. Corporal Bert Fitton, who played left half in the company football team, helped Lieutenant-Colonel Cooke and the sick and wounded into the plane. He found himself locked in and about to take off and pleaded with the pilot to let him out. Back on the ground he told Major Scott, 'I came in on my feet and I'd like to go out the same way,' and rejoined his comrades. Michael Vlasto gripped the control column as the end of the field rushed towards his plane. The runway was too short and they were overloaded. With knuckles white and his face dripping with sweat, he pulled back on the stick and the plane staggered into the air, brushing the treetops below. 'God bless number eighteen,' he said. Sadly, number eighteen was later killed.

The Chindits hoped that more planes would be sent to take them all home and divided themselves into groups in anticipation. It was not to be. One plane arrived and dropped a message to Major Scott. It read:

> 'After very careful consideration I have reluctantly decided not to allow the pilot to take the risk of attempting to land his plane again. Apart from the actual landing risks there is considerable danger of interference from Japanese land and air forces. This must, I realise, be a very great disappointment to you and all your men. We will do all in our power to help you in and patrols are now operating east of the Chindwin to meet you. I have no doubt at all that you will be able to reach the Chindwin safely by one of the two routes given you by Fergusson. Have just heard Wingate crossed the Chindwin today. Hope to see you soon. G. Scoones, Major-General, Corps HQ. 29 April 1943.'

Before the plane departed it parachuted more supplies to the men, including a large bundle of boots. The message was clear. A map of the route taken by Major Fergusson was also dropped to Major Scott and the disappointed men shouldered their packs and continued their journey. Company Quartermaster-Sergeant Duncan Bett continues the story:

'We were all scared of being left behind. When we dropped down exhausted at night it was so dark under the jungle canopy that you could not see your hand at the end of your nose. It was like the tomb. I remember waking up suddenly once and I couldn't see a thing or hear a sound. No mules, no sentries, nothing. I thought I had been left behind when the column moved on before dawn. I scrabbled around in a panic, feeling for another body and the relief was indescribable when I felt someone else there on the ground. It seems hard to believe, but several men were left behind in the dark. Presumably they were so exhausted they didn't wake up and were not missed in the confusion when the column moved off.

'We broke up into parties of forty or so, to make our way back to India. A day or so later we were bivouacked on the bend of a chaung when we were attacked by Japs who had crept up under the cover of a thunderstorm. As we retired to the river bank I passed another Colour Sergeant who had been shot in the leg and was unable to walk. He asked me to shoot him as he knew the Japs would not bother to take him prisoner if he could not walk. I could not do it and had to abandon him to his fate. He was never heard of again.

'On reaching the river bank, which was very high and steep, I sank over my knees in the mud with the weight of my pack, which weighed about seventy pounds. I was forced to slip it off and it rolled down the bank and disappeared in the muddy water with all my newly acquired food and gear. I was left with what I stood up in, a rifle and a bandolier of .303 ammunition.

'As we neared the railway we picked up a Burmese who offered to lead us across the railway between Japanese posts. Although we were very suspicious he led us safely across at night and, just as dawn was breaking, to the entrance to a village. The Lieutenant in charge of our party placed a Sergeant and the men in some cover a short distance away while he, a warrant officer and myself leant against an earth bank outside the entrance to await the return of the Burmese. Meanwhile a large covered bullock cart trundled past within touching distance, on its way to the paddy fields. After some time firing broke out where we had placed the rest of the men. The bullock cart had obviously been full of Japs and if we had tried to see what was in the cart we would not be here now. We ran into the village, which was deserted, and in the centre of an open area was a dugout with a sloping ramp and the Burmese was hiding inside. I tried to put a round up the spout of my rifle to shoot him, but it jammed. I did not have a bayonet or a grenade and as I was being fired on from the other side of the village I reluctantly had to leave him and run for cover. I then got stuck in the tangled undergrowth, still being fired at, before breaking free and getting away from the village. From then on there were only the three of us. We had a map which was of little use, but we knew if we kept going west we would eventually reach India, which we did in about two months, picking up food in villages on the way. Just after dark we once went into a hut and obtained a chicken which had its neck wrung by the villager, who folded it over and bound it with some fine bamboo. It was deposited in a bamboo basket which I slung on my back before we went on our way in the brilliant moonlight. After a while we heard sounds of revelry in the distance and hastily dodged off the track and lay down behind a small bank in the dry paddy fields. It was a number of villagers who had obviously been celebrating in the next village. Just as they drew level there was a tremendous fluttering from my pack. The chicken was not dead and it was making frantic efforts to escape. I got the pack off and tried to wring its neck, but instead pulled its head off and it ran around headless in circles making what seemed to us to be a tremendous noise until I managed to fall on it and quieten it. We could not believe we hadn't been noticed and they must have been very drunk on the local rice beer.

'We successfully avoided any Jap patrols and crossed the Chindwin in a dugout canoe we found hidden at the river bank. After spending the night in a woodcutter's hut on the Indian side of the Chindwin we set off up a track towards Somra in the Naga Hills. After a time a voice shouted "Tairo" ("Halt" in Urdu) and we ran into a machine-gun post manned by the Assam Rifles. We were escorted to their headquarters several miles back and, after being fed and sleeping for about twenty-four hours, carried on towards Kohima. We were put in the Somra District Officers bungalow the following night, when suddenly shots rang out and we thought "Japs!" but it was the DO firing at rats with his revolver. We did not appreciate his efforts, but put it down to his being "round the bend" being stuck in such a place for years.'

Wingate divided his own brigade headquarters column into five dispersal parties: the Brigadier's party, mostly commandos, some RAF and Lt Spurlock; a party of Gurkhas, mostly muleteers, under Major Conron; a party of Burma Rifles from the propaganda section and some Gurkha muleteers under Lt Molesworth; a party of British other ranks under Major Ramsay and Captain Moxham; and a party of British other ranks under Captain Hosegood and Lt Wilding. Wilding's party was about thirty strong. He recalls:

'We were instructed to go north, cross the Shweli, swing west and go home, a distance of some 200 miles. First of all we received an enormous drop by the RAF. This included some rum and some chocolate bars, a gift from the RAF station, bless them. We were very grateful, because when I opened my rations I found that every bar of chocolate and every cigarette had been stolen, presumably by the packers. How mean can you get?

'We withdrew from the drop area for a few miles and just at nightfall we had the grisly job of killing our remaining mule. To maintain silence we had to cut his throat, a difficult and literally bloody job. I suppose we should have eaten him, but he had been with us for many miles and we were fond of him. It was 30 March 1943.

'We reached the Shweli on 1 April. It was only about 200 yards wide and not very swift flowing. I was sure that any competent swimmer could manage it. However, only about eight men could swim and that included the officers. This was a blow. We made rough rafts from dead bamboo, but when we launched the first after moonset we were greeted with heavy fire from the north bank. We withdrew. I wonder if this rather supine behaviour was the product of slinking about behind enemy lines for six weeks and, perhaps, very inadequate rations. We had become furtive and had lost our aggression. Had it been possible to arrange a reasonably bloodless (on our part) battle early on, it might have helped. We had two choices. The swimmers could cross that night and the rest could make their own arrangements, or we could stick together. It is arguable that the proper course was to get the swimmers over and back to India, but I suggest this might win battles, but will not win wars. The men had a right to leadership and we decided to stick together. I think it was the correct decision, but only three (including myself) who could have swum survived.'

Wilding's party spent the next couple of weeks resting and preparing for another attempt to cross the Irrawaddy. One of the Burmese Jemadars was wounded and captured during a recce to Inywa and a British Private got lost while out searching for water and was presumed captured. The party made some more rafts and set out for the Irrawaddy. However they found themselves in a mangrove swamp and could not get through. They then decided to try to go east, cross the Shweli where it was but a stream, swing north and go into the Kachin hills and there sweat out the monsoon. It was only eighty miles, but they had hardly any supplies left, so they decided to find a village and obtain some food. There was not much food to be found, but the headman offered to put them over the river for a consideration, a very considerable consideration. Wilding continues:

'That evening, 21 April, he and his "brother" took us at racing speed to the river. It was night and we were not exactly sure where we were. We embarked, paddled round one island and disembarked, handed over nearly all of our money and set out for the hills to the west. Alas we found a wide stretch of water between us and the hills; it was the main river. We had literally been sold up the river.

'The next six days are very confused in my mind. We searched the island, it was about a mile long and half a mile wide. We found a village and persuaded the villagers to sell us a meal, but this only occurred once. I had two black-outs which were alarming. When travelling in a hot country beware when the sweat getting into your eyes stops stinging – this denotes that you need salt.

'On 29 April we found a boat that floated. We decided that Second Lieutenant Pat Gordon, Lance-Corporal Purdie and Signalman Belcher, with Burma riflemen Orlando and Tunnion as paddlers, should make the first trip. They reached the other side, then we heard Pat rallying his men and a good deal of firing and then silence. Orlando and Tunnion survived but the others were all killed. I was very sad. I thought that the first boat load would have the best chance, but I was wrong.

'We split up into small groups and hid in the elephant grass, but on 2 May the Japs, or possibly the Burmese police, set fire to it. The flames came very close, but I was not burnt. We then rendezvoused and discovered that only one rifle was serviceable, the one belonging to Lance-Corporal Willis. Since leaving Imphal eleven or twelve weeks before, nobody had thought of having more rifle oil dropped and now you could hardly move the bolts. Lance-Corporal Willis had used mosquito repellent cream, and it worked. I would ask the reader if he would order his men to attack a well-armed enemy with rifles that would not work. We didn't even have bayonets. And so, alone and very frightened, I went into the village – and that was that. The Japs were away searching for us and the Burmese tied my wrists rather cruelly tight with a sort of bark string, the scars are still just visible. In spite of this discomfort, when the men arrived I curled up and slept for hours. It is a frightful thing to be a PoW. You have failed. You have lost your liberty and you have a nagging feeling that you should have done better. When the Japs returned to the village they were really quite decent. They released me from the very tight bonds on my wrists and let me sleep for twenty-four hours.

'We proceeded to Tygiang where we lived in what must have been the school house and were given three meals of curried chicken and rice each day. Shortly afterwards we set out for Wuntho, then Maymyo, where the missing Private Simons rejoined us. Our time in Maymyo was pretty ghastly. I think we were there for about a fortnight, it seemed like years. Then another quite horrible railway journey to Rangoon. Our party when the brigade broke up was thirty strong. Twenty-four of us arrived in Rangoon. Seven of us survived. Captain Hosegood was a great personal friend, a very gentle and very good man. I never heard him say anything unkind about anyone, even a Jap. He died in Rangoon in April 1945, of a heart attack I think. Two hundred and ten Chindits, including our party, arrived in Rangoon. By the time we were liberated two years later, 168 of the 210 had died or were deliberately killed, a survival rate of about one in five. Even taking into consideration the fact that we had rather a rough time before capture, eighty per cent casualties among prisoners of war shames the Japanese Imperial Army.'

RAF radioman Arthur Willshaw was still with Brigade Headquarters and would remain with Wingate all the way home to the west bank of the Chindwin. His story continues:

'The Brigadier made the decision to split us up into smaller groups, each group being told to find their own way back to friendly territory. Our wireless sets were now almost useless – there wasn't time to keep the batteries charged. Air supply became almost impossible with the Japs so close to us and with poor wireless communication. Most of the mules in the Head-quarters Column were by now battle casualties and the few that were left were slaughtered to provide sustenance for the journey back to India. I was part of the group under the direct command of Brigadier Wingate which was preparing to go straight back through the Japanese lines, planning to use almost the same route that we had come into Burma by. And so the worst period of the campaign began. We were attacked while crossing the Irrawaddy and it was here that we lost Squadron Leader Longmore, himself a strong swimmer, who was in a canoe that overturned with many non-swimmers in it. From 7 to 11 April some seventy miles were covered and fresh Japanese troops hounded us most of the way. Then into mountainous country, where we clambered up and down rocky cliffs, almost from boulder to boulder with a slip meaning a drop of some 100 feet into boulder-strewn gorges. The important thing was to keep moving, to try to keep ahead of Japanese information.'

After Wingate divided his headquarters column into dispersal groups and sent them on their way, he took his party of forty-three deep into the jungle, where they remained for a week. The remaining mules were killed by having their throats cut rather than risking the sound of rifle shots. This was done to prevent them giving their position away and to fill the bellies of the men before they began the long trek home. For six days they ate mule for breakfast, mule for lunch and mule for dinner. On the seventh day they ate the horses.

On 7 April Wingate made a second try at crossing the Irrawaddy, twenty-five miles south of Inywa. Captain Aung Thin of the Burma Rifles could only find one boat and it would take but seven people at a time. Signaller Eric Hutchins was in the last party, together with Squadron Leader Longmore, Flight Lieutenant Tooth, Flight Sergeant Fiddler, Lieutenant Rose of the Gurkhas, Private Dermody and Private Weston of the King's. He told the author:

'The first six boat parties made their way safely to the opposite bank. Eventually the boat returned for us, but when we reached the opposite bank we could find no trace of the others. Wingate's excuse, when we met him later, was he "thought" we had been captured by the Japanese, whereas he had abandoned us without maps or any means of finding our way back to our own lines. Such is my regard for a commander who later became world famous.

'So we set out west only to find we were on an island in the middle of the river. Our problems now really began, because we could not find a suitable boat. Eventually we found a boat that had seen better days and decided to take a chance crossing at night, using our rifles as oars. Of course the inevitable happened and the boat capsized. I and others swam to the west shore, where we had to rescue two of our party who were clutching a floating plant because they could not swim. At light of day we found that Squadron Leader Longmore was missing. Later at the end of the war I found out that he had remained clutching the boat and floated down river and was eventually captured. I understand he survived the Japanese prison camp.

'We found we were on another island and right opposite a very large village and most of the inhabitants walked across the shallow water to the island, presumably out of curiosity. We had lost everything when the boat capsized and had no arms to defend ourselves, except that I still had a hand grenade. We went with the villagers and enjoyed a meal of rice and obtained two sacks of rice, cooking pans, a flint stone to make a fire, salt and juggery, the latter unrefined sugar. Suddenly there was a commotion in the village and the locals started to disperse, which was a signal to us that the Japs had arrived. We made a quick retreat and proceeded to climb the hills behind the village and make our way westwards.

'Our progress after that was mainly at night, avoiding paths and villages. I remember the beautiful clear moonlit nights with the stars to guide us. I often look for a constellation set at dead 270 degrees which we used as our direction arrow as we kept walking westwards. Daytime was spent trying to sleep in the intense heat with no water, setting out at dusk to find water and cook a meal. I was suffering severely from dysentery, but somehow raised the strength to carry on.

'As we neared the Chindwin we found a small chaung in which were some pools of water containing fish. We caught one by swimming under water, but then became greedy and thought if we threw my grenade into the water we could have a real feast. This was not to be because the grenade failed to explode as I had forgotten to prime it. On seeing the river valley of the Chindwin we now became over-confident and started to abandon our policy of avoiding footpaths. On rounding a bend we ran into a Japanese sentry guarding the path. We immediately plunged into the jungle to our left, but Weston was captured because he was too weak to react quickly. We were forced to stand in a marsh for thirty-six hours while the Japs set fire to it to try to draw us out. Meanwhile we could hear the screams of Weston as they slowly tortured him to death with their bayonets.

'On the second night we came out of the marsh only to walk straight through the Jap-occupied village. We walked on down the path leading to the Chindwin and then, practising the usual dispersal drill on leaving a path, hid in the jungle nearby. Within fifteen minutes a party of Japs came down the track, following our footprints by torch light. Fortunately for us they hesitated where our footprints finished and then carried on. This was our cue and we retreated deeper into the jungle. Within half an hour they were back searching the spot we had left. We were now under real pressure and headed for the Chindwin, but could not find a boat to cross. We were walking along the path on the river bank and came to a small clearing with Lieutenant Rose leading. He suddenly turned round and yelled 'Japs' and in the sudden rush to retreat I fell over. I scrambled to my feet, leaving behind the rice sack I was carrying. The others had a good fifty yards' start on me and machine-gun bullets were whizzing all around. I think I broke the world record for 200 yards and reached the jungle on the opposite side of the clearing before the others. Here we lost Lieutenant Rose and I heard after the war he was later captured and also survived the prison camp.

'We decided to regain the hills and walk northwards hoping there would be fewer Japs to encounter in that direction. We came upon a hut in the middle of a paddy field and found a native sitting inside. He immediately beckoned us to lie down in the paddy and pointed to a road about fifty yards away where Jap lorries were moving. He indicated to follow him crawling on our bellies to a small copse, where the miracle occurred! He brought us food twice a day for three days while we got our strength back. He could not get us a boat but when we drew bamboo poles he understood and on each night visit he brought two bamboo poles. Finally we had enough to make a raft and took them down to the river at the dead of night and our saviour tied them together. We had no money and could not reward him, but gave him a note saying how he had helped us and that he should be rewarded by the British if he produced the document. This man, a complete stranger, possibly a Buddhist, displayed all the ethics of a Good Samaritan and has remained in my deepest thoughts all my life, and I am now seventy-four years old. That day in 1943 on the banks of the Chindwin I learned to believe in miracles.

'I was the only strong swimmer and pushed the raft from the rear. Some of the other survivors were too weak to swim and had to be hauled back on the raft. Eventually we reached the other side and rested for the night. In the morning we walked into the nearest village which was occupied by Gurkhas.

'Wingate was my hero before the campaign, but after his deliberate abandonment on the east bank of the Irrawaddy I know he only considered his own safety and not others. He would deliberately abandon anyone whom he considered to be a handicap. This was proved later when our signals officer, Ken Spurlock, who was in Wingate's boat party, was abandoned in a village not far from the Chindwin because he was weak with dysentery. I was weak with dysentery but my companions never abandoned me.'

Another survivor commented to the author that 'Wingate HAD to survive or else all the lessons we learnt so painfully would have been lost – who would have listened to surviving column commanders?' There are two sides to every story and only those who were there have the right to pass opinion.

After crossing the Irrawaddy, Wingate's party, now down to thirty-six souls, faced the obstacle of the railway. It was heavily patrolled and every bridge and station was guarded. The jungle petered out ten yards from the line, but Japanese soldiers were on guard duty 400 yards away to their right and left. They closed up together and all crossed in one rush, disappearing into the jungle on the far side. They put five more miles between themselves and the line before stopping for a rest. For the next several days they marched through the Mangin Mountains between the railway and the escarpment. Their boots began to fall apart and diarrhoea, dysentery and jungle sores began to take a heavy toll. Men began to fall by the side of the track and there was nothing that could be done for them. No one had the strength to carry the sick. The survivors stumbled onwards. Wingate drove his men on, urging them not to fall out of the column even for diarrhoea. 'Don't worry about your trousers, just keep on marching,' he told them. They kept going only by sheer will-power and faith in Wingate.

The next dangerous stretch was a twenty-mile strip in the Mu River Valley between Pinlebu and Pinbon, Japanese garrison villages that had been attacked by 4 and 7 Columns on the way in. They crossed the valley by night and reached the foot of the Zibyu Taungdan Escarpment. They were faced with a sheer wall of rock 1,500 feet high. Few tracks crossed the escarpment and it was likely that the Japanese would be patrolling them. Before they attempted the climb, the desperately hungry men ventured into a village to buy food. As they were leaving a small Burmese ran after them and offered to guide them across the escarpment using a little known track. Fifty years later, Arthur Willshaw recalled:

'Crossing the Mu River we faced the last sixty miles over almost impossible country to the Chindwin. It was here that we met an old Burmese Buddhist hermit, who appeared one evening just out of nowhere. He explained, via the interpreters, that he had been sent to lead to safety a party of white strangers who were coming into his area. He was asked who had sent him and his only answer was that his God had warned him. It was a risk we had to take, especially as we knew from information of friendly villagers that the Japs, now wise to our escape plan, were watching every road and track from the Mu to the Chindwin. Day after day he led us along animal trails and elephant tracks, sometimes wading for a day at a time through waist-high mountain streams. At one point on a very high peak we saw, way in the distance, a thin blue ribbon – the Chindwin. What added spirit this gave our flagging bodies and spent energies! All our supplies were gone and we were really living on what we could find. A kind of lethargy was taking its toll, we just couldn't care less one way or the other – it made no difference to us. The old hermit took us to within a few miles of the Chindwin and disappeared as strangely as he had appeared.'

At noon on 23 April Wingate's party reached the other side of the escarpment and gazed upon the Chindwin Valley. Arthur Willshaw continues his story:

'A villager we stopped on the tracks told us that the Japanese were every-where, that it would be impossible to get boats to cross the river as they had it so well guarded. Wingate selected five swimmers who would, with himself, attempt to get to the Chindwin, swim it and send back boats to an agreed rendezvous with the others. These swimmers were Brigadier Wingate, Captain Aung Thin of the Burma Rifles, Captain Jefferies, Sergeant Carey of the Commandos, Private Boardman of the 13th King's, and myself.

'At four a.m. on the morning of 29 April 1943 the six of us set out for the river. Soon we struck a terrible stretch of elephant grass, seven or eight feet high and with an edge like a razor. We reconnoitered along it but could see no end to it, and no track through it, so the decision was made – 'into it'. Each man in turn dived headlong into it while the others pushed him flat; after a few minutes another took his place at the front. In four hours we had covered about 300 yards and were making such a noise that we feared the Japanese would be waiting when we broke out of it. We pushed our way into a small clearing and collapsed – I couldn't have gone another foot and I know that we all had the same sickening thought. After all we had been through, how could we find the strength to go on? Then Wingate crawled to a gap in the grass and disappeared, only to reappear within minutes beckoning us to join him. We pushed our way another few feet and there it was – the Chindwin – right under our noses. Arms and legs streaming with blood, we decided to chance the Japs and swim for it right away.

'Among the many things I asked for on my stocking-up visit to Drigh Road at Karachi was a number of 'Mae West' lifejackets. I had carried mine throughout the whole of the expedition; I wore it as a waistcoat, used it as a pillow, used it to ford rivers and streams – and I still have it! It was to save my life and that of Aung Thin that day. Blowing it up, I explained that I would swim last and that if anybody got into difficulties they could hang on to me, and we would drift downstream if necessary.

How I feared that crossing – even though the Mae West was filthy and muddy it would soon wash clean in the water, – and what a bright orange coloured target it would make for the waiting Japs! And so into the water – ten yards, twenty yards, fifty, one hundred, now almost just drifting, thoroughly exhausted. Aung Thin with a last despairing effort made it to my side and together we struggled the remaining fifty yards to the other bank. We dragged ourselves up the bank and into cover – I still relive those fifteen minutes waiting for the burst of machine-gun fire that didn't come.'

Major John Jefferies almost did not make it. After swimming about forty yards he had to let go of his boots and rifle and at about 100 yards from the bank the tattered shreds of his shirt sleeves wound themselves tightly around his arms completely imprisoning them. He kicked out desperately with his legs and forged towards the bank. He began to swallow mouthfuls of water and his kicks grew feebler. He felt an enormous weariness and began to lose consciousness. Then his feet touched bottom and he dragged himself through the shallows and collapsed on the beach. Wingate was waiting for them. He had strapped his Wolseley helmet to his chest, where the thick canvas made an airtight and waterproof float and did much to support him during his swim. The hat would remain with him until his death.

The exhausted men struggled on for five more miles to the nearest British outpost, where a group of British officers were sitting on ration tins drinking tea. They were given hot sweet tea with condensed milk, bully-beef stew, rum and cigarettes. A day or so later Major Gim Anderson and the rest of Wingate's party were carried across the Chindwin, narrowly escaping capture by a platoon of Japanese from the 114th Infantry Regiment who had been tracking them. Arthur Willshaw was back in the Promised Land:

'And so on to Tamu, Imphal, Dimapur and into hospital. We were looked after by Matron Agnes McGeary, a charitable lady who had won a medal for gallantry at Dunkirk. I went into Burma nine stones in weight and came out a mere five and a half stones. After a month in hospital the adventure was over for me. Later by air to Delhi and Bombay and then the first boat home via the Cape. Air Marshal D'Albiac certainly kept his promise!'

Nick Neill, Tag and their eleven riflemen took ten days to cover the sixteen miles to the village of Sahpa on the east bank of the Chindwin. They had passed through the area in February after crossing the river with 8 Column and they hoped to find a friendly villager to help them across the river. Upon reaching the village they discovered that the Japanese had recently collected every single boat from all of the villages on the east bank of the river and taken them north, to be guarded by the garrison at Homalin. Neill recalls:

'Suddenly we saw again the Chindwin, the River of Jordan of my hymn. At this point it was some 250 yards across and fast flowing. Tag and I could probably have swum it without arms and equipment, but none of my men could swim and we would not leave them. I went to stand on a little open rise on the bank of the river and gazed longingly across to the safety of the other side. Suddenly I heard a shout from the far side, "Ko ho?" I could not believe it, I was being hailed in Nepalese. I shouted back at once, "Hami Thard Sikin Gorkha haun. Tyahan dunga chha, ki? Yatapatti rahenachha" (We are the Third Second Gurkhas. Is there a boat over there? We find there is none on this side). Immediately the reply came: "Euta chha, ma pathaidinchhu. Parkhanu hos, hai!" (There is one, I will send it. Please wait!)

'I stood the men to, and we took up defensive positions with our backs to the river. Most of our rifles were rusty due to the lack of oil, although my tommy gun was still in working order. I prayed to God that the Japs would not jump us at this eleventh hour. Eventually a small dug-out type boat appeared, being paddled upstream against the strong current by a single boatman. It could only take four men at a time, so I sent Havildar Budhiman, the sick Harkabahadur and two riflemen in the first boat. It took twenty minutes for the return journey and three more trips before Tag and I clambered down the steep track to the river's edge, placed our packs in the centre of the dug-out and carefully climbed aboard. We rounded the bend in the river and saw a tiny encampment on the west bank. It was the V-Force post at Hwemate and we could see the smiling faces of the others waiting to greet us, together with the British officer commanding the post. We had made it! We would live to fight another day!'

They did not realise just how lucky they had been when they reached safety on the west bank of the Chindwin at 1400 hours on 6 June 1943. A V-Force reconnaissance patrol crossed the river the next day and went to the village at Sahpa. There they learnt that a Japanese fighting patrol of platoon strength had been tracking Tag and Neill's party for a week. They had been very close on their heels and had arrived at their crossing point on the bank of the Chindwin a mere half hour after they had crossed.

Rifleman Brian Soppitt *(centre standing)* of 26 Column, 1st Cameronians was wounded at Blackpool and evacuated before the block was overrun. Jim Higgins on his left and Jim London *(right)* served with 90 Column.

Major Ron Degg took over command of the 1st South Staffords following the evacuation of Lt-Col Richards after being wounded at White City. Richards killed seven Japs before he was wounded, but sadly died later in India.

Rifleman Tulbahadur Pun of 3rd Battalion, 6th Gurkha Rifles won the Victoria Cross at Mogaung on 23 June 1944.

Major Jimmy Blaker of 3rd Battalion, 9th Gurkha Rifles won a posthumous Victoria Cross on 9 July 1944, whilst charging a machine-gun nest at Point 2171.

Officers of the 1st Battalion, South Staffordshire Regiment, killed in action in Burma 1944.

Bert Gilroy of the 1st Battalion, Lancashire Fusiliers wearing Corporal's stripes and Chindit badge on his right sleeve.

LEFT: Piper Bill Lark of the 2nd Battalion, Black Watch. His bagpipes were dropped to him by parachute and he played them to herald his battalion's last attack on Labu on 7 August 1944.

Chapter 6

Prisoners of War

The research for this book began in 1995, the year that Britain celebrated the fiftieth anniversary of the ending of the war with Japan. The lessons of history are often lost with the passing of time and many are unaware of the barbaric cruelty and suffering that was the lot of anyone unlucky enough to find themselves prisoners of the Japanese. Two Chindit survivors have kindly given permission for their stories to be told, lest we forget.

Second Lieutenant Alec Gibson was one of three young officers from the 8th Gurkha Rifles sent to join 3/2nd Gurkhas just days before Wingate's expedition set off for Burma. Alec and Harold James joined Mike Calvert's 3 Column and Ian MacHorton joined George Dunlop's 1 Column. Harold and Ian finally made it back to India, but Alec Gibson found himself a guest of the Emperor:

'MISSING FROM 4TH APRIL – LAST SEEN SWIMMING THE IRRAWADDY. That was the message sent to my parents in July 1943. They were to hear nothing more from me until I was reported recovered from the enemy on 30 April 1945.

'Following Wingate's dispersal order we were trapped on the east side of the Irrawaddy and my party was unable to find boats, so swimming was the only alternative. After two abortive attempts I found myself alone with one Gurkha when we were jumped by eight Burmese Independent Army soldiers who tied us up and dragged us to the nearest Jap outpost some five miles away. At Maymyo we had to learn Japanese drill; commands were shouted at us in Japanese and we were expected to understand them. If we got it wrong we were knocked down with rifle butts, pick handles or bamboo canes. We managed to learn in about two days! As a deliberate policy of humiliation we were lined up at least once a day and subjected to considerable face slapping by the Jap guards. Every now and then one of the prisoners would be called out for interrogation and you knew that you would have to undergo considerable punishment before you got back again.

'At this camp I met one of our Gurkha Subedars wearing an armband with the Jap Rising Sun, the sign of the Indian National Army. I asked him how he could do this and he replied, "Do not worry Sahib – I have plans to get out of here." I heard later that after training with the Japs he and the rest of the Gurkhas were given arms and sent to the front where they promptly killed the Japs with them and then went straight across to the Allied troops.

'From Maymyo we were taken to the Central Jail at Rangoon and on arrival we were put into solitary confinement. The cells were about nine feet square with one small window, dark and gloomy, with only the stone floor to sleep on. We were given one blanket each. We could not speak to one another and were only taken out for interrogation. I was only there for a couple of weeks, but some prisoners spent months there. I was then transferred to one of the open blocks of the jail. The officers were in two rooms on the upper floor, about twenty-six of us to each room. There was no glass in the windows so in the monsoon period the rain poured in. We slept on the floor with our one blanket and used anything else we had as a pillow. As the Japs took everything we had from us when we were captured, we had little other than the clothes we had been wearing since leaving India in February 1943. Most of the time we only wore a fandoshi or loincloth made of a rectangle of cloth and a piece of string. As our boots fell apart we walked barefoot and soon our feet got pretty tough.

'Everyone including the officers had to work. We worked on the railway, dug up unexploded bombs, repaired roads and bridges, unloaded stores at the docks and cleared up damage after air raids. If anything went wrong the man concerned and the officer in charge would be beaten up. Some men were permanently on cooking duties and did their best with the rations we were given, chiefly rice and vegetables with occasional pieces of meat we scrounged from outside, or a pigeon caught inside. Sometimes we had a sort of porridge made from ground-up husks of rice. It tasted horrible but contained Vitamin B1 and was a great help against beri-beri. We also had tea, or rather hot water with a few leaves thrown in, no milk and no sugar.

'The one thing which really worried us was being injured or becoming ill as medical treatment was almost non-existent. We had several medical officers with us as prisoners, but they had virtually nothing in the way of medicines or equipment. Jungle sores or ulcers were treated with copper sulphate crystals, dysentery with charcoal and creosote tablets, beri-beri with grain husks. Incredibly, two successful amputations were carried out with the crudest of instruments and no anaesthetics. Most of us suffered from ulcers, dysentery, beri-beri, dengue fever etc. at some time, but if it developed into a serious condition it was usually terminal. Two-thirds of the complement of the camp died.'

When Lieutenant Allen Wilding arrived at Rangoon jail, there were plenty of familiar faces to greet him. Ken Spurlock was there from Wingate's party, so was Johnny Nealon, last seen by George Dunlop when he went into a village to look for food during 1 Column's trek home. From 5 Column were John Kerr, left behind wounded at Kyaikin, and David Whitehead who had been led into an ambush by a Burmese which left him with seven bullet holes in his body and five in his clothes. For those poor souls who were sick or wounded, there was little succour to be found in the jail. Allen Wilding recalls:

'The "hospital" was an old bug-ridden building situated in the compound of Block 6. There was a sort of 'greenhouse' staging made of wood all round, on which the sick lay and alas often died. To give some idea of the infestation of bed bugs, we took the staging on one side down and the floor seemed literally to move with the bugs crawling to the other side. For those fortunate to have never encountered a bed bug, they are brown but otherwise resemble a ladybird and they smell awful when crushed. There were no beds or sick room equipment of any kind, not even bed-pans. There was an empty lime drum which dysentery patients could use if they had the strength and resolve; otherwise – well, to wash a dysentery patient's blanket when you have no tub, no soap or hot water, just cold water and a bit of concrete to bash it on, is rather unpleasant! I know, I have done it.

'At first the "hospital" came under the care of Lieutenant Brian Horncastle (King's Regiment). He was a wonderfully kind chap and worked really hard to make the "hospital" work. After his death American Second Lieutenant Waldo Cotten (USAAF) took over and he did his best too, but neither had any medical knowledge, just common sense and compassion. Then our brigade senior medical officer, Major Raymond Ramsay (RAMC), was released from solitary. It was a disgrace that he was kept there so long while our poor chaps died at the rate of at least one a day. Words cannot convey enough praise for his work, his devotion, his gentleness and his ability. After the war they gave him an MBE just as if he had been a Beatle, or me. Never was a man's work so grossly undervalued and rewarded in such a niggardly way by "The Brass"! He was NEVER undervalued by us!

'Through all these changes, one man soldiered on: Sergeant Scrutton of the King's. He was a jewel. He knew nothing of medicine, he was a bricklayer's labourer in civilian life, but he had a fund of common sense. Sadly he died, worn out with the work and, I suspect, frustrated because he could do so little for his charges. A surprising number of people were prepared to take a turn at dressing tropical ulcers. In particular I remember Sergeant Jock Masterson and a huge Colour Sergeant named Beatie who had been a "loom turner" from Hawick. I have vivid memories of Jock dressing, very gently, an enormous sore high up on the thigh of a youngster of nineteen. So deep was it that you could see the femoral artery pulsing, so Jock had to be extra careful. Despite Jock's devoted care the poor boy died. One of the Chindit officers had a jungle sore which became gangrenous. The smell was so bad that, at his own request, he was moved out of "hospital" for the sake of the other sick. I liked him very much but found that a half hour visit was all I could manage. A friend of his, a Canadian Flight Lieutenant named Wheatley, used to sit with him for hours, although on at least one occasion he was physically sick when he left. When the patient (and never was the word so appropriate) died, Ken was there to hold his hand. What more can you do for a friend?

'The Japs did provide an equally comfortless hut for the cholera patients. In spite of Major Ramsay's heroic work, it proved impossible to save any of them or Corporal Brown of the KOYLI, a brave chap who volunteered to nurse them. So did the "cultured" Japanese care for those unfortunates who were ill when under their care. Even allowing for their belief that to become a prisoner was a lasting shame, their behaviour was disgraceful. To the average Westerner, the Japanese are a polite race, good at miniaturisation, making television sets and motor cars and motor cycles which are expensive to repair, and who are much addicted to making money, buying golf courses, folding paper, arranging flowers and torturing trees into unnatural shapes. To the average serviceman who has experience of them, they are admirably brave and well disciplined, very noisy and shockingly bad shots. To a Far Eastern prisoner of war, they are cruel, callous, brutal, unhygienic and really rather incompetent administrators.

'It is difficult to describe really serious inhumanities without risk of hurting widows, children and friends of those who died in Japanese hands and this is a risk I will not take. They had one nasty habit of making a prisoner stand for hours in the sun without headgear, sometimes holding a heavy stone over his head. One poor chap was made to stand on his head. This might have done him real harm so I shouted to him to collapse and with a couple of chaps rushed out and made a great to-do about taking him into the "hospital". He survived. They kept people in solitary for too long. The record once stood at 100 days, but this was greatly exceeded. The cells were small and often shared by two or three people. There was no exercise period and the only facility was an old ammunition box, usually leaking, for use as a latrine. After the bombing of Tokyo all flying personnel captured were kept in solitary confinement. I am aware of at least three men who were deliberately killed.'

Calculating the number of survivors from the expedition is no easy feat and depends on which source one consults. Official figures suggest that 77 Brigade entered Burma just over 3,000 strong, comprising seven columns, Brigade Headquarters, two group headquarters and the Burma Rifles headquarters. Just over 2,000 had apparently re-entered India by the first week of June; 2,180 was the final figure. Of the remainder, some

450 were battle casualties. A further 120 Burma riflemen were given permission to remain in their home areas. Of the remaining 430, the majority must have fallen into enemy hands, or died on the tracks on the way home. Apparently only 210 Chindits reached Rangoon jail and only one in five survived to the end of the war. The official history of the 3/2nd Gurkhas states that when they reassembled in Assam under Major Emmett, losses amounted to 446 of all ranks. Of this number approximately 150 returned afterwards. In all seventy-four were reported as prisoners of war; forty-five escaped after capture. One historian has recorded that the 13th King's went into Burma 721 strong and only 384 returned to India. He suggests that seventy-one of those captured survived imprisonment, although that figure seems too high when considering the conditions in Rangoon jail.

So what did Wingate's first expedition achieve? Arthur Willshaw MBE, BEM, who swam the Chindwin with Wingate, considered:

'We had operated successfully behind the Japanese lines and had proved that the RAF could support a large long-range penetration group. In fact, one of the most important results of the expedition was that the supply dropping had been a brilliant success and even exceeded Wingate's own expectations. Thus supply dropping by air was proved possible and came into its own. We also proved that the Japanese were not invincible in the jungle – the enemy had suffered many times the number of our own casualties and, more damaging, lost a lot of face.'

In his after-action report Wingate pointed out that the strategic value of the campaign was negative. However, he went on to say:

'It prevented a number of developments and upset the enemy's plans, but there was no attempt to use it offensively. It is possible that the enemy has not grasped the possibilities of long-range penetration, by a foe who controls the air, as a vital part of a general offensive. Thus the great value of the campaign is that it has demonstrated the power of columns to penetrate as far as they please into enemy-occupied Burma. In this case the columns were not of high fighting calibre and were not supported. They were none the less able to traverse the immense tract of Burma. The enemy did his utmost to arrest the penetration. He did not succeed at any time. It ceased because enough had been done and the force had only sufficient strength left to get out. To sum up, when long-range penetration is used again, it must be on the greatest scale possible and must play an essential role in the re-conquest of Burma. It is the one method in which we are superior to the Japanese. The possibilities have been demonstrated. Do not let us throw away the harvest by Lilliputian thinking or piecemeal squandering of resources. The number of columns is limited only by the number of aircraft available to feed them. From the tactical and strategical points of view, the more the better.'

Wingate went on to suggest that, of the 2,200 survivors of the brigade, at least 1,600 were of the 'wrong type' and should probably not be sent in again. The remainder constituted a core of personnel qualified beyond all others for command, training and general use in connection with the expansion required. Among the officers who reached India were two capable of commanding brigades and nineteen possible column commanders. Wingate proposed that a command should be set up at once to control long-range penetration in all its phases: doctrine, training, planning and, later, control in the field. Measures should be taken at once to raise no fewer than six long-range penetration groups out of the proper materials. The strength of each group should be in the neighbourhood of 8,000 all ranks.

By the time the report was written, General Wavell had been replaced by Auchinleck and although Wavell had shown his faith in Wingate by arranging for 111 Brigade to be formed while Wingate was still in Burma, there was little enthusiasm for Wingate at GHQ India and his ideas for a larger LRP force were ignored. It was at this stage that fate intervened. The newspapers back in England were filled with the exploits of Wingate and his men. Indeed that was his intention when he briefed the journalists before the expedition set off. After eighteen months of one defeat after another, it was seen as a long-awaited victory over the Japanese and Wingate became a national hero. What the staff officers at GHQ Delhi could not have foreseen was that the newspapers would fall on the desk of one man of immense influence: Winston Spencer Churchill, the Prime Minister.

Churchill sent for Wingate and on the night of 4 August 1943 he arrived at 10 Downing Street. Churchill was about to dine alone and asked Wingate to join him. Churchill later wrote, 'We had not talked for half an hour before I felt myself in the presence of a man of the highest quality.. . I decided at once to take him with me on the voyage.' The voyage on which Churchill invited Wingate to accompany him was to Canada the next day on the *Queen Mary*, to the Quadrant Conference in Quebec where Churchill would meet President Roosevelt. When Churchill heard that Wingate's wife Lorna was travelling down from Scotland by train, he gave orders that it be stopped and within hours the bewildered lady found herself in a car en route to the Clyde. She was going to Canada with her husband too. The aim of the conference was to decide future Allied global strategy, of which Burma was but a minor part. However, in the eyes of the United States, Burma was of far greater importance. President Roosevelt aimed to build up China to the status of a great power within the American sphere of influence. As Britain stood to lose from such a development, Churchill was against it. In addition, Roosevelt hoped to use China as a base from which to conduct air and ground operations against the Japanese.

Relations between Great Britain and China had worsened in 1940 when they closed the Burma Road, the land supply route to China, to placate the Japanese. In return General Chiang Kai-shek had enraged the British by his open support of Gandhi's National Congress Party, whose aim was to throw the British out of India while the war was still in progress. From a practical point of view, Britain did not consider itself in a position to open a major offensive in the Far East until Germany had been defeated. In fact Churchill favoured an amphibious landing on Sumatra, followed by the recapture of Singapore, but the Americans had other ideas. Their priority was the re-opening of the overland route from India to China via northern Burma. The Burma Road from Mandalay was under Japanese control and although the new Ledo Road was being built by US Army engineers, the main supply route was now by air over 'the Hump' – the Himalayan Mountains.

Wingate put forward a plan for the recapture of northern Burma by using LRP brigades together with a southwards advance of Chinese troops under US General 'Vinegar Joe' Stilwell and an eastwards advance by British troops in India. It was just what the Americans wanted to hear. President Roosevelt and the combined chiefs of staff were impressed and offered to aid Wingate with a private air force, solely for the use of his Chindits. Unfortunately, the Commander-in-Chief India, General Sir Claude Auchinleck, did not agree with Wingate's proposals. The British supply lines could not support an invasion of Burma at that time and there were not enough aircraft available to do the job by air. He lacked faith in any co-operation from the Chinese and he objected to the proposed breaking up of the 70th Division to form three LRP groups. These objections were overruled and on 26 August the British chiefs of staff signalled Auchinleck with instructions as follows; provide a Force HQ and two Wing HQs; complete expansion of 77 and 14 Brigades to eight columns each; form three British LRP groups, each of six columns, from 70th Division; form one LRP group from a brigade of the 81st West African Division.

To Auchinleck's credit, he put the wheels in motion as directed. The staff officers in GHQ India were not so co-operative. Their resentment was compounded when another decision was taken at Quadrant. A South East Asia Command (SEAC) was to be set up, with Lord Louis Mountbatten as supreme commander. The new command would take direction of the war in Burma out of the hands of GHQ India and so, it was hoped, provide new energy and new operational efficiency. The ground forces of SEAC would be organised into 11th Army Group, under which would come the troops of General Slim's 14th Army. General Stilwell would be Mountbatten's deputy, among his many other responsibilities, chief of which was persuading the Chinese to move their forces into northern Burma. As far as GHQ India was concerned, Auchinleck would take on the responsibility of training and equipping the Indian Army and developing India as a base for operations. Although GHQ India would try to thwart Wingate's plans, despite their approval by Churchill, Wingate would fight them tooth and nail, even resorting to a privileged direct line to Churchill via Mountbatten, to the chagrin of his superiors in India. Wingate now had a cause, indeed a crusade, from which only death could divert him. His disciples rallied to his call to arms – Calvert, Fergusson, Scott, Lockett, Jefferies, Musgrave-Wood and others from the first expedition stepped forward. This time, though, they would be helped by other brave men, from the United States of America.

One of the weaknesses of the first Chindit expedition that Wingate was determined to improve was the treatment of the wounded. Could the Americans provide light planes to fly them out of the jungle? They could do more than that. In August 1943 Lord Mountbatten met with US General Henry 'Hap' Arnold to discuss plans for American support of the LRP brigades. A new unit was to be formed, comprising a squadron of Douglas C-47 Dakota transport aircraft, a squadron of North American B-25 Mitchell bombers, one of P-51 Mustang fighters and a light plane force of L-1 and L-5s, specifically for the evacuation of the wounded from short airstrips hacked out of the jungle. The new force was to be known as the 1st Air Commando Group, the term 'air commando' allegedly coined to honour Lord Mountbatten, who earlier commanded British commandos as head of Combined Operations. The 'Can Do' attitude of the Americans was exemplified by the appointment of two veteran fighter pilots to command the new force. The commander would be Lieutenant-Colonel Philip G. Cochran, a confident, aggressive and imaginative officer with a distinguished war record in North Africa. His deputy was Lieutenant-Colonel John R. Alison, a tactful, well-educated 'ace' pilot who had flown in General Chennault's 'Flying Tigers' volunteer group. When the two pilots discussed Wingate's ideas with him, they added one other type of aircraft to the inventory of the new group, one hundred Waco gliders, capable of carrying fifteen troops each. The next time the Chindits went into Burma, did they really have to walk, or could they fly in?

Top: Memorial to the men who died during the glider landings at Broadway.

Two Africans escort a Japanese pilot who was shot down over Aberdeen.

Below: A light plane with Yank pilot and three Lancashire Fusiliers on Naman strip in late March 1944. He had arrived to fly Lt Hugh Patterson to White City to see Mike Calvert.

The small one-span railway bridge at Kadu, cut by a seven-man patrol of fusiliers late March 1944.

The Royal Air Force wireless detachment with the Lancashire Fusiliers, commanded by Flt Lt George Allen, a New Zealander. Taken April 1944 in the dry country south-west of White City.

The Commando Platoon of 50 Column, Lancashire Fusiliers lined up beside the railway for an attack, near Sepein in April 1944. Three of the men are from the South Staffords who somehow got in on the act. Note fixed bayonets and Bren gunner on the left.

Part Two

The Chindit Invasion of Burma, 1944

John Lucas began the 1944 campaign with 3rd Battalion, 6th Gurkhas as a Lieutenant and finished it at Mogaung as Acting Major with the Military Cross.

Major Ken Robertson, OC 54th Field Company Royal Engineers, 14th Infantry Brigade. He was responsible for the building of the Chindit Navy at Indawgyi Lake in June 1944.

Group photograph of 45th Reconnaissance Regiment officers prior to march in to Burma. Lt Roger Brewer *(third row, third from left)*, Lt Cyril Baldock *(second row, fourth from right)*, Captain Jimmy White *(second row, third from left)*, Lt Peter Taylor *(second row, second from left)*, Major Bill Varcoe *(front row, fourth from left)*.

ABOVE: Chindits practise loading mules into gliders of the 1st Air Commando Group at Lalaghat, India prior to the launch of Operation 'Thursday' in March 1944. Note the hinged nose and cockpit of the glider.

BELOW: An example of an improvised tug, built by the Royal Engineers who accompanied the Chindits. A truck is lashed between two boats, with its rear wheels removed and replaced by improvised paddle wheels.

Chindits training in watermanship on the Ken River, United Provinces, India in the autumn of 1943. After the problems encountered during his first expedition, Wingate was determined that his men would learn how to cross rivers, both with and without boats.

An elephant is used to transport 3-inch mortar ammunition, for the 1st Battalion, Bedfordshire and Hertfordshire Regiment, north-west of Indawgyi Lake in July 1944.

Men of the 1st Battalion, Bedfordshire and Hertfordshire Regiment at their midday halt in the Lakren Hills, west of the railway corridor in May 1944. Privates Harris and Gardner in the foreground.

Officers of the 16th Foot; the 1st Battalion, Bedfordshire and Hertfordshire Regiment. *(Left to right)* Lieutenant J. C. Salazar, Captain D. C. Franklin, Lieutenant 'Red' Carter.

Captain George Grossmith, Royal Engineers, after 16 Brigade flew out of Burma in May 1944. He was at Indaw with Jack Wilkinson's 2nd Leicesters.

The reconnaissance platoon of 16 Column, Bedfordshire and Hertfordshire Regiment, at rest in a friendly village.

Chapter 7

The Gathering of the Clans

Newly promoted to Major-General, Wingate assumed command of Special Force, officially known as the 3rd Indian Infantry Division, comprising six brigades. Two would be led by two of his 1943 expedition column commanders: 'Mad Mike' Calvert was promoted to Brigadier and given command of the 77th Indian Infantry Brigade; Bernard Fergusson was also promoted to Brigadier and given command of the 16th British Infantry Brigade. They were joined by the 111th Indian Infantry Brigade commanded by Brigadier Joe Lentaigne, which had been raised as the second LRP brigade while Wingate was still inside Burma on his first expedition. Brigadier Tom Brodie's 14th British Infantry Brigade became part of Special Force, as did the 3rd West African Brigade under Brigadier Andy Gillmore, the latter a part of the West African Frontier Force. The sixth brigade was the 23rd, under Brigadier Lance E. C. M. Perowne, an old friend of Wingate's from his time at the Royal Military Academy, Woolwich in 1921. However, the 23rd would be taken away from Wingate before he had time to commit them to action, leaving him with five brigades under his direct command. The 14th, 16th and 23rd Brigades would be formed by breaking up the well-seasoned 70th Infantry Division commanded by Major-General Symes. It was a controversial decision.

Order of Battle

3RD INDIAN INFANTRY DIVISION (SPECIAL FORCE)

Commander:	Major-General Orde C. Wingate DSO, later Major-General W. D. A. Lentaigne.
Deputy Commander:	Major-General G. W. Symes
Brigadier General Staff:	Brigadier D. Tulloch
Headquarters:	Rear HQ at Gwalior, central India; main HQ at Imphal and later Sylhet, Assam; forward HQ at Shadazup, Burma

Each brigade comprised a number of columns of troops. The column numbers of the British units referred to either their old infantry line numbers or from the line numbers of the column commander's former regiment, i.e. 16 Column = 16th Foot.

3RD WEST AFRICAN BRIGADE

Commander: Brigadier A. H. Gillmore,
                              later Brigadier A. H. G. Ricketts DSO
6th Bn Nigeria Regiment; 66 and 39 columns
7th Bn Nigeria Regiment, 29 and 35 columns
12th Bn Nigeria Regiment, 12 and 43 columns

14TH BRITISH INFANTRY BRIGADE

Commander: Brigadier T. Brodie
2nd Bn The Black Watch; 42 and 73 columns
1st Bn Bedfordshire and Hertfordshire Regiment; 16 and 61 columns
2nd Bn York and Lancaster Regiment; 65 and 84 columns
7th Bn Royal Leicester Regiment; 47 and 74 columns

16TH BRITISH INFANTRY BRIGADE

Commander: Brigadier B. E. Fergusson DSO
2nd Bn Queen's Royal Regiment; 21 and 22 columns
2nd Bn Royal Leicester Regiment; 17 and 71 columns
51/69 Field Regiments, Royal Artillery; 51 and 69 columns, fighting as
   infantry
45th Reconnaissance Regiment, Royal Armoured Corps; 45 and 54
   column, fighting as infantry
54th Field Company, Royal Engineers, support

23RD BRITISH INFANTRY BRIGADE

Commander: Brigadier Lance E. C. M. Perowne CBE [1]
Headquarters column; 32
1st Bn Essex Regiment; 44 and 56 columns
2nd Bn Duke of Wellington's Regiment; 33 and 76 columns
4th Bn Border Regiment; 34 and 55 columns
60th Field Regiment, Royal Artillery; 60 and 68 columns, fighting as
   infantry

77TH INDIAN INFANTRY BRIGADE

Commander: Brigadier J. M. Calvert DSO
Headquarters column; 25
3rd Bn 6th Gurkha Rifles; 36 and 63 columns
1st Bn The King's (Liverpool) Regiment; 81 and 82 columns. To 111 Bde
   in May.
1st Bn The Lancashire Fusiliers; 20 and 50 columns
1st Bn South Staffordshire Regiment; 38 and 80 columns
3rd Bn 9th Gurkha Rifles; 57 and 93 columns. To 111 Bde in May
Hong Kong Volunteer Company, support.[2]

111TH INDIAN INFANTRY BRIGADE

Commander: Brigadier W. D. A. Lentaigne, later
                              Brigadier J. R. Morris CBE DSO, [3]
1st Bn The Cameronians; 26 and 90 columns
2nd Bn The King's Own Royal Regiment; 41 and 46 columns
3rd Bn 4th Gurkha Rifles; 30 column
Plus units under command of Lieutenant-Colonel J. R. Morris

102

MORRIS FORCE

Commander: Lieutenant-Colonel, then later Brigadier J.R. Morris

4th Bn 9th Gurkha Rifles; 49 and 94 columns [4]
3rd Bn 4th Gurkha Rifles; 40 column [5]

DAH FORCE

Commander: Lieutenant-Colonel D. C. Herring

Kachin Levies

BLADET FORCE

Commander: Major Blain

Gliderborne demolition engineers

5307TH COMPOSITE UNIT (PROVISIONAL), US ARMY

Commander: Brigadier-General F. D. Merrill, later Colonel C. N. Hunter, known as 'Merrill's Marauders'.

Comprised three battalions organised in columns and originally trained by the Chindits. Under direct command of General J. Stilwell and operating with Chinese forces in the north of Burma.

MAJOR SUPPORT UNITS

1ST AIR COMMANDO GROUP, US ARMY AIR FORCE

Commanded by Colonels J. R. Alison and P. Cochran, USAAF. Provided casualty evacuation and close air support to Special Force. Also limited transportation to supplement that of Eastern Air Command. Disbanded 1 May 1944.

ROYAL ARTILLERY

'R', 'S' and 'U' troops, 160th Field Regiment
'W', 'X', 'Y' and 'Z' troops, 69th Light Anti-Aircraft Regiment [6]

Notes:

1. Diverted to support 4 Corps and removed from Special Force order of battle.
2. After the fall of Hong Kong in December 1941, some members of the Hong Kong Volunteer Defence Corps escaped to mainland China. In early 1943 they were flown over the Himalayas in RAF and USAAF planes to Assam. They formed the Hong Kong Volunteer Company and were languishing in Deolali when Mike Calvert arrived to inspect them. They all volunteered to join 77 Brigade.
3. When Brigadier Joe Lentaigne was moved from command of 111 Brigade to command Special Force as a Major-General, Lieutenant-Colonel 'Jumbo' Morris was promoted to Brigadier in command of 111 Brigade. However, as he was tied up with command of Morris Force, operational command was passed to Lentaigne's Brigade Major, Jack Masters. Amazingly and rather unfairly, he was not promoted in his new role, but was expected to give orders to higher ranking officers in the various columns.
4. Originally the garrison battalion at Broadway, they left to join 77 Brigade but were diverted to reinforce 111 Brigade at Blackpool.
5. The battalion was divided by Brigadier Lentaigne after delays in crossing the Irrawaddy. One column was sent to join Morris Force and the other remained with 111 Brigade.
6. Equipped with twenty-five-pounder field guns and 40 mm Bofors and used to defend strongholds and blocks such as Broadway, Aberdeen, Blackpool and White City.

The arrival of orders to join Special Force came as more of a shock to some units than others. The 45th Reconnaissance Regiment was a light armoured unit, formed to spearhead the attack of an armoured division. To be told that they would be losing their armoured cars and receiving mules in their place was a surprise indeed. Shock would adequately describe the impact on the men of the 51st Field Regiment, Royal Artillery and their fellow gunners, the 69th Anti-Tank Regiment, Royal Artillery, when they were told that their sacred guns were to be taken away from them. After the exodus of skilled men such as armourers, they were only able to form one column each and had to be filled out with drafts of infantry.

While the organisation and movement of units was underway, Wingate made one of his rare mistakes which almost cost him his life. On the way out to India from England in September 1943 he landed at Castel Benito in North Africa, together with his small staff. Lieutenant-Colonel Derek Tulloch, later Wingate's Brigadier General Staff, recalled: 'It was hot and dry and we were all thirsty. The airfield canteen bar was not open yet and there was no one there to look after us. Wingate impatiently threw some flowers out of a vase in the canteen and drank the water. This resulted in his having a very severe attack of typhoid a few weeks after his arrival in India which put him on the Dangerously Ill list for several weeks.'

When Wingate arrived in Delhi his reception was cold and hostile. Mountbatten would not arrive for three more weeks and Auchinleck was having to raise a force against which he had strongly objected and over which he would have no operational control. It soon became clear that GHQ India had no faith whatsoever in Wingate's plans, despite the decisions taken at the Quadrant Conference in Quebec. No one believed that an invasion of Burma could take place until Germany had been defeated, and certainly not in 1944. Lord Louis Mountbatten arrived in Delhi on 7 October and Wingate met him at the airfield. The following day he was taken into hospital, seriously ill with typhoid. Mountbatten immediately clarified the situation; Special Force was to be raised in the exact form that Wingate had been promised at Quadrant and unqualified support must be given to him. In hospital Wingate was a difficult patient and Matron McGeary, who had nursed the Chindits after their return from the first expedition, was summoned from Imphal to tend him. On 1 December he assumed command of Special Force at Gwalior.

Colonel Claude Fairweather of the Royal Signals had had an interesting start to his war. On the last day of evacuation, he had been picked up by a destroyer from the Mole at Dunkirk. He had not had the chance to remove his boots for the preceding twenty-eight days! The end of 1943 saw him in Madras as chief signal officer for an Indian Corps:

'I received a message from the Signal Officer-in-chief India, General Vivian, to report to him in GHQ Delhi immediately. When I did so his first remarks were, "Ha Fairy, have I got a job for you." We went along the corridors of GHQ and came to a room. The General knocked at the door and went into the room and I followed. I saw a man with a beard sitting at a large table, surrounded by maps and papers; there was no other furniture. We went up to the table and the General said, "Wingate, this is Fairweather." I was standing facing him and felt like the little boy in that famous painting "When did you last see your father?" Wingate never got up, just looked up and said, "You are to be my chief signal officer. You will be receiving a lot of American WT equipment etc., there will be a number of brigades with their own signal sections. I have just returned from America with the Prime Minister and with the brigades and some American signals you will have six months to organise your signals before our next very large campaign. You will go to Gwalior, my headquarters and report to a Brigadier Tulloch, my chief of staff, who will put you in the picture. That's all." The General and I then went out and we stood looking at each other and he said, "Well!" I looked at him and said, "What a rude b————! I will have some trouble with him." In the end I liked him and we got on well together because I was not afraid to talk to him and argue.

'One day Wingate, Tulloch and I went to a meeting with General Slim and while we were waiting we were having a drink of whisky and we talked about after the war and what we might do. Derek Tulloch hoped to continue in the Army which he did and became a Major-General. I hoped to return to my tugboats on the River Tees and Wingate, without any hesitation, said; "I am going to be commander of the Israeli Army," which was his ambition.'

Allied strategy had been changing while Wingate was recovering from his brush with death. At the end of November Winston Churchill and Roosevelt met Stalin at Tehran. Amid the confusion of the Sextant Conference, which took place in Cairo and Tehran between 23 November and 10 December, two things became clear. The first was that on the one hand Churchill wanted to avoid involvement in Burma in 1944; indeed he told Mountbatten that despite the agreement made in Quebec with the Americans, he meant to have 'a landing on Sumatra or nothing'. On the other hand, the Americans fully intended to implement the decisions made at Quadrant, namely the recapture of northern Burma and the reopening of the overland route to China. It later became obvious to Tulloch that 'Special Force had to be kept in being in case the Americans forced the British to honour the pledges made at Quadrant'.

The detailed politics of the situation soon became clear to Wingate, who was nobody's fool. As far as he was concerned, he had but one mission and that was to get his men into Burma and fight the Japanese. To that end he was given his orders by 14th Army commander General Slim and Major-General Stratemeyer, USAAF, who would provide most of the aircraft required. His mission was to block the flow of supplies and reinforcements northwards to the Japanese 18th Division facing Stilwell; to create a situation favourable for a Chinese advance across the Salween; and to inflict the maximum damage and confusion on the Japanese in northern Burma. Wingate in turn gave his orders to his brigades. 16 Brigade was to walk in from Ledo to Indaw and capture its two airfields. If all went well, Wingate could present Churchill with an all-weather airfield in the heart of Japanese territory into which a British division could be flown. 111 Brigade was to fly in by glider and Dakota. They were to operate south of Indaw, assisting 16 Brigade by blowing up railway bridges and ambushing the roads. A small gliderborne force known as 'Bladet' would also demolish some railway bridges. Mike Calvert would fly his brigade into two clearings deep in Burma, code-named 'Broadway' and 'Piccadilly', and then establish a fortress block astride the road and railway running northwards to supply the Japanese troops facing Stilwell. 'Morris Force', comprising a battalion of Gurkhas, was to land at 'Chowringhee' east of the Irrawaddy River, make its way to the mountains adjacent to the road from Bhamo to Myitkyina and carry out raids in that area. Lieutenant-Colonel Herring's 'Dah Force' would assist Morris by raising bands of Kachin tribesmen to fight the Japanese. They would land by glider at a clearing east of the Irrawaddy codenamed 'Templecombe'. Three of Wingate's six brigades would be committed, with three remaining in reserve. These could either be used to relieve the others after the 90-day limit after which time Wingate considered the men to be exhausted, or used for any other plan that came to mind. And Wingate's mind was full of plans. The fact that he only allocated one battalion to blocking the Bhamo road indicated that he was not convinced that the Chinese in Yunnan wanted to advance into Burma in the first place. Mike Calvert's men could certainly block the road and railway supplying the Japanese opposing Stilwell, but that would only be of benefit if there was heavy fighting going on, where the lack of supplies or reinforcements could mean defeat for the 18th Division. Indaw, however, was uppermost in his mind and two of his brigades were to effect its capture.

The new operation was to be named 'Thursday' and would begin on a moonlit night in early March, a full month after 16 Brigade began its walk in. The Air Commandos and Eastern Air Command, together with units of the RAF, would fly the Chindits into clearings in Burma from which they would steal through the jungle to their objectives. Although 25,000 Chindits would be available to fight, as opposed to the 3,000 the previous year, they would still have to face the might of the Japanese divisions inside Burma, unless of course something happened to occupy them and that something, Wingate knew, could be a Japanese invasion of India and there were signs that a Japanese offensive was in the making. Wingate, indeed, was counting on it.

To give the reader a greater awareness of the composition of Special Force and the men who were to walk into history through the mud, blood and suffering of the second Wingate expedition, we will hear from some of the men who now found themselves 'Chindits' and would carry the fight to the Japanese in 1944.

10603606 Trooper Arthur Withey, 45th Reconnaissance Regiment, 16 Brigade:

> 'The regiment arrived at Bombay in June 1943 and we were posted to Doolatty. After a while we were sent to Bangalore by rail and we were there for about three months. After the usual training schedules, parades etc., we were posted to Jhansi where we underwent jungle training. This consisted of sixteen-hour forced marches through scrub land with a forty-pound pack on our backs, plus a twenty-eight-pound Bren gun and ammo. We did this for about ten weeks and it toughened us up for the long walk. In late November we were on the move again, this time to the Assam border where we again made camp for a month, checking our kit, dyeing our vests and pants in tea and checking our weaponry. Our next move was by truck, driven by West Africans up the hilly roads and over the mountains in Assam towards the Ledo Road. That ride was really hair-raising; a steep drop on one side for hundreds of feet with the Africans driving with one foot on the pedals and one foot hanging out of the cab. It was to be our last ride for a long time. Of all the brigades in Special Force, ours was the only one scheduled to walk into Burma and it would be a long trek indeed.'

Captain Arthur Shadbolt, Royal Engineers, attached 2nd Battalion, The Black Watch, 14 Brigade: After taking part in the break-out from Tobruk, Shadbolt spent time clearing mines and his unit suffered fifty per cent casualties. Later they were sent to Rangoon, but it fell to the Japanese before they arrived, so instead they were sent to Bombay:

> 'We disembarked to be met by a very formal ceremonial party complete with band. I reported to a Colonel on a very large horse and in the best military tradition requested oil, fuel and rations. The reply was unexpected: "Put your indents in three months in advance." That very night we replenished our stocks illicitly and proceeded to our rendezvous 200 miles away. We spent a considerable time training and undertaking engineering tasks, such as bridge and dam building. Each driller was accompanied by a man with a stick to kill snakes, and there were plenty of

them. One day I was talking to Archie Wavell (the son of General Wavell), who commanded a company of Black Watch, in his office tent. The Company Sergeant-Major came in and said, "Orders, Sir?" I promptly excused myself but was told to stay. A Jock was marched in, dealt with and the order given: "March him out, Sergeant-Major." On the way out the man muttered something and the order was given: "March him back in, Sergeant-Major." Archie said, "What did you say, my man?" "Nothin' Sir," replied the Jock. "I distinctly heard you say something, now, what did you say?" "I said fuck you, Sir." Archie replied, "And fuck you too. March him out, Sergeant-Major." At Ranchi Officers' Club I ran into a drinking contest between medics and sisters from the nearby hospital, versus sappers and gunners. Some had disappeared under the table by the time I decided to go outside for a leak. I stepped over a low hedge and fell down a thirty-foot well into three feet of water. After three or four hours the drunks came looking and when they located me they sat on the top of the well and ordered more booze. Then there was a great argument among the sappers as to what sort of knot to tie in the rope they had found. I spent forty-eight hours under observation in hospital, visited by all sorts of curious people wanting to see the silly b——— who had fallen down the well.'

Captain Geoffrey Straight, 1st Battalion, The Cameronians, 111 Brigade:

'General Wingate came to visit us at Dukhwan Dam, where we had been learning a little about river crossing, just before we were due to start our journey across India to Assam and Burma. He spent quite a while with the CO, Lt-Col Gillespie, and the 2 i/c, Bill Henning. The men of the battalion were paraded for him to address. No officers were permitted to be present, but whatever he said, the men subsequently appeared to be both inspired and impressed. Later came dinner in the Mess. Wingate sat opposite Gillespie and Henning and I was lucky enough to be sitting next door but one to the great man. There was no doubting the power of his personality and I was fascinated by the jagged scar in his neck, which I presume was caused by his earlier attempt at suicide. Conversation across the table with our senior officers was formal and limited. I could readily detect an extremely tense atmosphere between the three of them. The next morning he was gone and twenty-four hours later so was Gillespie, who left to become GSO 1 (Training) in Central Command. I felt very sorry for Gillespie whose treasured ambition it had been to lead his own battalion into action. That was not to be, however. He said goodbye to us with great dignity and self-control, but his eyes were glistening with emotion. He was a good man and I liked him a lot.

'Within the next few days we were on our way. From Saugor, where we entrained, we moved slowly across India, stopping frequently, making tea from the hot water in the engine; across the Brahmaputra at Mymensingh in boats; finally in another train to Silchar. As we detrained a Sergeant asked me if I would look after 2,000 rupees for him; he had been lucky at cards on the way. Then we tackled the Silchar–Bishenpur track. Up one side of a mountain and down the other was roughly a day's march. Getting mules across rickety bridges over rushing streams was not exactly a picnic, but in about five days we were at Bishenpur, just south of the Imphal Plain. Naga warriors watching us along the track must have wondered what the hell was going on. We bivouacked at Bishenpur for a few days. Someone managed to set fire to a small ammunition dump and a few bullets were sent whistling through the air. The main entertainment under a glorious March full moon was watching the gliders carrying men of the King's, being towed eastwards towards Broadway on 5 March. Some planes towed only one, but others pulled two. A stimulating sight that raised the tension and excitement a degree or two. We were taken to Tullihal airstrip and shown a plane, a Dakota of course. The next day we would be on our way. The Chindit invasion of Burma had begun.'

Chapter 8

Operation 'Thursday'

It was the evening of 5 March and Wingate was furious. Despite giving specific instructions to Colonel Phil Cochran, USAAF, to keep all aircraft away from the two landing zones, he had sent a photo reconnaissance plane to fly over the clearings and check the area for Japanese troops. It was fortunate that he did. The film was hastily developed and rushed to the command group on the airfield. It showed that 'Piccadilly' was covered with logs.

Had someone spilled the beans? Did the Japanese know that an airborne invasion was about to begin? Photographs of the landing zone had appeared in an American magazine, taken by a photographer that was in Michael Vlasto's C-47 when he landed to take out some of Scott's sick and wounded from the same clearing in 1943. Did the Japanese block the airstrip afterwards? Wingate took Mike Calvert to one side. As commander of the troops about to embark Wingate was right to seek his opinion. Calvert was adamant, the operation should go ahead and he would take all of his men into the other landing zone 'Broadway' and accept a slower build-up. General Slim, as usual, was a picture of calm and nodded his agreement to the new arrangements. As Cochran rushed to brief his pilots on the new plan, Lieutenant-Colonel Walter Scott rearranged his men and equipment and the gliders were hitched up to the tow-planes. Scott was now commanding the 1st Battalion, King's (Liverpool) Regiment and they filled most of the gliders, along with a company of the 1st Battalion, Lancashire Fusiliers under the command of Major Shuttleworth. American engineers and their equipment were also coming along to construct a Dakota airstrip, into which the rest of 77 Brigade would be flown. There was a shortage of C-47s so each aircraft would tow two gliders, one on a short line, one on a long line. It was a risky business and a glider had been lost with all occupants during training when the glider on the long tow had moved forward and struck the glider in front of it. In order to restore morale, the air commandos had been told not to blame themselves for the accident; the Chindits would go with them 'Any Time, Any Place, Any Where' and this became the motto of the air commandos.

One by one the aircraft took off, circled the airfield and headed eastwards. Inside one of the leading gliders Mike Calvert looked out into the darkness at the Chindwin river thousands of feet below. 'It gleamed

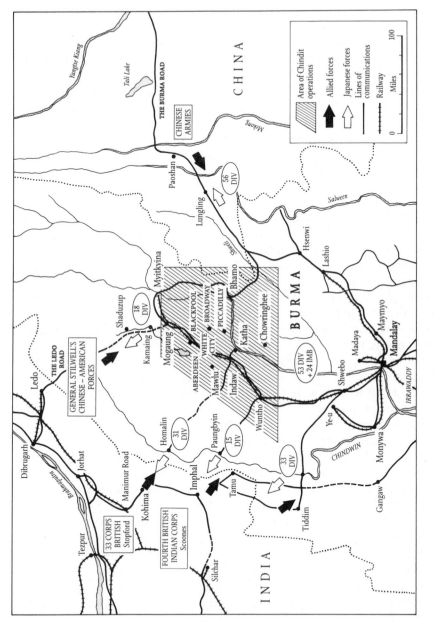

Special Force area of operations March–August 1944.

below us in the moonlight and although I was not swimming across it this time I almost wished that I was still the leader of a small band of odds-and-sods, wandering more or less as I wished, instead of the commander of thousands of men in a carefully planned operation, with all the responsibilities attached.' Calvert's men stirred themselves as Broadway came in sight and the tow was cast off. Silence enveloped the glider, broken only by Calvert's Anglo-Chinese batman, Lance-Corporal Willy Young, cracking jokes in his usual cheerful way. The glider pilot, Lieutenant Leese, peered into the darkness then banked steeply, his jaws moving rhythmically as he chewed gum. The ground came up with a rush, then a hefty bump as they touched down. Ahead of them was the wreckage of a glider. Leese pulled back on the stick and the glider took off again, cleared the wreck and came down again on the other side. Calvert noticed that Leese was chewing his gum a little faster now as they crashed down again, a stanchion of the glider hitting him in the back as the glider broke up on impact. 'All out,' Calvert shouted and leapt out at the head of his men. Then the reason for the bumpy landing became obvious: there were a number of deep furrows across the field, where the Burmese had used elephants to pull timber to the river during the monsoon. The undercarriages of the leading gliders had been destroyed by the furrows and they could not be pulled out of the way as planned. Overhead in the darkness more gliders descended and soon the area was strewn with wrecked and damaged gliders. In the distance, Calvert could hear the occasional crash as a luckless pilot came down in the trees.

Before leaving the airfield at Lalaghat, Calvert had agreed with Wingate that he would signal 'Pork Sausage', the favourite dish in the cookhouse, if all went well or 'Soya Link', the loathed sausage meat substitute, if all went badly. At four a.m. on 6 March he reluctantly ordered his radio operator to send 'Soya Link'. When Calvert surveyed the field, he discovered that casualties had been heavy. Sixty-two gliders had taken off, but only thirty-seven arrived at Broadway. Eight had been recalled, but seventeen had suffered broken tow ropes on the way and had landed God-knows-where. Eight of them came down on the British side of the Chindwin River, but nine others landed on the Japanese side, causing confusion among the Japanese preparing for an invasion of their own. Sixty-six of their occupants were never seen again. Calvert's casualties were three dozen killed and thirty injured. Only seven of the American engineers, plus one of their officers, had survived the landings and they possessed only one small bulldozer and a jeep and towable scraper for equipment. They set to work immediately to build an airstrip. As dawn broke Calvert realised that he now had over 500 men in place, with 30,000 pounds of supplies and there was not a Japanese soldier in sight. He ordered the signal 'Pork Sausage' to be sent to Lalaghat. Wingate's mood changed from despair to elation.

During the day a dozen light plane pilots bravely flew over 400 miles of enemy territory to take out the casualties. That night sixty Dakotas landed, bringing in 900 more men. A second operation began the same night to fly the advance guard of 111 Brigade into 'Chowringhee', a landing zone some fifty miles south-west of Broadway between the Shweli and Irrawaddy Rivers. It was an inconvenient change of plan for the brigade, destined originally to fly into Piccadilly. Now they would have to cross the Irrawaddy to help 16 Brigade at Indaw.

As the build-up continued, Broadway was fortified with anti-aircraft guns and the 3rd Battalion, 9th Gurkhas arrived to garrison the stronghold. The two columns of the King's would remain as well, as floater columns circling the stronghold. By 11 March, nine thousand men had been flown in, together with 1,200 mules and 175 ponies. As Wingate issued an order of the day, which included the famous phrase 'All our columns are in the enemy's guts', Calvert assembled his men and marched westwards, towards the railway.

One of the King's men who did not make it to Broadway was Arthur House, a twenty-one-year old Private who was one of the occupants of glider number 19B, one of two gliders being towed by a C-47:

'Our glider carried nineteen men and a load of ammunition. The pilot was Flight Lieutenant Martin J. McTigue from Pennsylvania; our battalion padre Captain Patterson sat in the co-pilot's seat. We had been in the air for two hours when the pilot suddenly called "We've been cut loose!" We were at 7,500 feet, in darkness and over thick jungle. We were all in the hands of our pilot. He circled, it seemed endlessly, looking for a clearing. Eventually he made his decision. Seeing two high trees above the jungle "almost like goal posts", he said later, he steered in between them; the impact tore off the wings and the glider, at high speed, careered through the jungle, coming lower and lower until it stopped with a shuddering crash.

'Although we had been thrown around like rag dolls there was no panic at all. I kicked the glider door open and we stumbled out into the jungle. We were all badly shaken and nursing cuts and bruises. Two men were injured: a Corporal thought he had suffered a rupture and a Private had a broken jaw. We went back into the glider to help the pilot only to discover that Captain Patterson the padre had been killed in the crash. He was the only one in the party who could speak Burmese, so his death was a double blow. Arms and equipment were sorted out, look-outs posted and Sergeant McGee, who had assumed control of the patrol, assessed our position. The pilot had no idea how far we might be from Broadway and as we had no maps McGee decided our best chance of survival would be to head due west and try to march back towards the Chindwin River. This meant at least 150 miles through Japanese territory, but if we could make it we would be able to fly in again to join the King's. We had the sad task of burying Captain Patterson. He had been a popular figure in the battalion, small, wiry with a dry sense of humour; he had been a Methodist minister in Burma before the war.

'We moved off into the jungle and before daybreak we stopped, made a brew of tea and decided to rest up for the remainder of the day. It was decided to march only in darkness and for three nights we did this until we walked into some swamps. We only just managed to rescue the injured Corporal before he drowned and after that we overruled Sergeant McGee and decided to march in daylight. For the remainder of the week we marched due west, seeing plenty of evidence of the enemy: remains of camp fires, papers and packets in Japanese printing. By now our rations had gone and we knew that before long we would have to go into some villages for food.

'At the start of the second week we reached a large village. After watching it for some time we assumed that there were no Japs there and went in to be greeted by the head man. They treated us to a meal of fish, rice and fruit and gave us some eggs and rice to take with us. They told us the Chindwin River was a week's march away. For the next few days we marched, twice seeing Japanese, but not coming into contact. We had to risk going into villages to buy food – with the Burmese money that we all carried – and in one village we had the feeling that we were being watched.

'We marched on, getting even nearer to the river and when we least expected it we walked into an ambush. A sudden burst of fire, a confusing exchange and we were forced to scatter. I found myself on my own and could hear the Japs raking the undergrowth with their bayonets. How they missed me I'll never know, they were so close. The noise of the search died down and I made off and before long met up with the rest of the patrol. We had lost five men, including the American pilot, and although we waited and moved around we saw no sign of them and could only think that they had been captured.*

'We moved on westwards and a few days later reached the Chindwin. It was very wide and fast flowing at that point and on the opposite bank was a Jap officer, complete with sword, pacing up and down and looking at our side of the river. By nightfall we had cut bundles of bamboo to float across the river with. Suddenly a force of Japanese arrived and, making a tremendous racket, began to cross the river. Sergeant McGee and his runner slipped into the water and began to swim across, saying it was as good a time as any to go. We found the current too strong for the non-swimmers and decided to wait until morning when, moving up river we

---

* All five men were captured by the Japanese. The pilot, Flight Lieutenant Martin J. McTigue, was executed soon after capture by a Japanese officer. Of the four soldiers, only one survived incarceration in Rangoon jail. Sergeant King, Private Sam Booth and Private Blundell all died because of lack of medical attention.

came to a village with four sampans moored on the bank. We "borrowed" these and paddled across.

'Once on the other side of the Chindwin we felt we were almost home, but it took another three days, still without food, before we arrived at Tamu in the middle of a battle between the Japs and the Border Regiment. The Japs were repulsed with heavy losses and we watched them withdrawing with their wounded. They passed within a few feet of us as we stood in the darkness, under cover of the jungle. The Borders were expecting them back when they had regrouped and when news of the arrival of eleven Chindits at Tamu was sent to Imphal they were asked to send us on to Imphal as soon as possible. Before we left we had our first meal in nine days, porridge and sweet tea.

'We left in a truck the next day, a ninety-mile drive through mountains hoping that the enemy hadn't cut the road anywhere. At Imphal we were given a medical. We were all in a poor state, mainly because of the lack of food. Private Bill Griffiths had a flesh wound in his back, John Potter's jaw was broken and Corporal Bill Durkin had a suspected hernia. Intelligence officers questioned us at length about the Japanese we had encountered, especially about the large force we had watched cross the Chindwin near Thaungdut. Suffering from "debility" we were packed off to a hill station, Shillong, for two weeks of regular food and PT. At the end of this we went back to Imphal and asked to be flown back into Burma to join the King's. We were told that this wasn't possible as 81 and 82 Columns had left Broadway and were marching to Blackpool. In the meantime we were detailed to go on supply dropping flights and on one of these our Platoon Sergeant, Hugh McGee, was killed when his Dakota was shot down in flames.

'Towards the end of June we were told that we would soon be able to rejoin the King's as the 1st Battalion was re-forming in northern India. By this time I was the only survivor of our glider crew at Imphal and I made my way to the railhead at Dimapur and after a ten-day train journey rejoined the King's in northern India. The battalion was re-forming at a jungle camp near Malthone. Not many of the men who flew in from Lalaghat were left. Casualties, sickness and men in the unit who had now served their four years abroad and were on their way home had depleted the battalion strength and this was made up by drafts from England. We were visited by General Sir Oliver Leese, Commander-in-Chief India Command, and he thanked us for our efforts in Burma. "The Chindits are finished!" he said. "Now you must get back to some proper soldiering!"

The crass comments of General Sir Oliver Leese notwithstanding, Arthur House had been comparatively lucky in crash-landing so far into Burma. It took so long to return home that he could not be sent in again to join the King's.

Captain Fred Freeman was Arthur's company commander in 'C'

Company, 82 Column and his glider came down south-west of Broadway. He later survived a bad ambush which decimated his column and fought with Mike Calvert's 77 Brigade in the traumatic battle for Mogaung. He told the author:

'The Dakota towing our two gliders went into an air pocket and our glider, on the rear tow, found the tow rope of the glider ahead had wrapped round the wing and started to cut it off. Our pilot had no option but to rapidly cast off. We landed safely on a long sandbank in the Irrawaddy River. The sandbank was nearest to the east bank of the river, whereas we wanted to reach the west bank. About eight of our party of twenty-two were indifferent swimmers and we had 500 yards of water to cross. We used our groundsheets to make a waterproof pack which floated and some troops used their denim trousers as waterwings. If dampened and inflated with the legs tied tightly, these gave considerable buoyancy.

'We laid low in the jungle until the next night when we came out to find a boat to carry us across the river. We found two boats and paddlers and crammed aboard, with only two or three inches of boat above the waterline. We had been warned that the Burmese in the area could be treacherous and we had been told of occasions when they had loaded a boat with troops carrying heavy equipment and they had then sunk the boats in the river with many of the troops being drowned. I kept our Burmese under gunpoint all of the way. The boats kept together as we crossed the river in the moonlight. When we got within wading distance of the bank the boatmen insisted we disembarked. We agreed, paid them with silver rupees and they quietly disappeared.

'We found that we had been landed near a Japanese barracks. We tried going through the adjoining jungle, but the brittle teak leaves gave off a sound like small arms fire. We remembered Wingate's favourite motto – "The boldest measures are the safest" – and moved on to the main track, which took us straight past the barracks. I remember the Japs singing away like anything in the barrack room while we walked on the main path past them. The track led in due course to Katha aerodrome and we walked along this until we came near the far end. A soldier put his head out of a door and saw us marching past. He did not make any sound at the time, but presumably he gave the alarm. We made for the hills and laid up in the jungle. That night we heard the Japs following us and the search continued all day. However, we had the pleasure of seeing a number of bombers attacking Katha and the aerodrome. We continued on our way and crossed the road and railway, eventually reaching the rendezvous at the Kaukkwe Chaung where we were reunited with Colonel Scott and 81 Column. We stayed with them until they returned to Broadway, then we joined Major Gaitley's 82 Column.'

Wingate's decision not to reconnoitre the landing zones at Broadway and Piccadilly was clearly a mistake. The SOE and OSS were both capable of dropping men into the jungle at night to check out and indeed prepare landing strips. They could also have pinpointed the nearest Japanese positions and found all important water supplies. However, it was not to be. As a result, with Piccadilly out of the running, everyone had to be flown into Broadway, thus delaying the operation.

Wingate's master plan included the insertion of Morris Force, the 4th Battalion, 9th Gurkha Rifles, into a landing zone named Chowringhee on 9 March. The LZ was in the same area between the Irrawaddy and Shweli Rivers where Wingate's brigade had been cornered in 1943. However, the loss of Piccadilly caused a change of plan. A hundred miles from the take-off airfield, the men of Morris Force were going about their routine business; a pay parade was taking place and men were cleaning their weapons and kit. One of the RAF liaison officers, Squadron Leader Pat O'Brien, was down at the airstrip hearing an account of the chaos at Broadway from an American pilot when a breathless Gurkha summoned him to an urgent conference with the battalion commander, Lieutenant-Colonel Morris. O'Brien and the other officers present were told that because of the loss of Piccadilly, the advance glider party would be sent into Chowringhee that very night. O'Brien was in charge of the RAF element with the advance party and he left the tent at a dead run. Nine gliders would take the commander of 49 Column, Major Ted Russell, plus six officers and eighty men into Chowringhee. Two of the gliders would carry a grader and tow tractor, essential to level an airstrip into which the rest of the force would be flown. The plan took on an even greater sense of urgency when the news arrived that the bulk of 111 Brigade would follow Morris Force into the same airstrip.

In the officers' tents, chaos reigned. O'Brien recalled feverishly packing his kit: 'Puttees stuffed into trouser pocket, no time to put them on . . . revolver ammunition . . . water bottle to be filled . . . compass . . . diary and exercise book for notes . . . fill fountain pen . . . kukri sheath to be affixed to webbing . . . blanket and groundsheet wrapped around the sharp-cornered K ration packs . . . spare socks . . . double sewn Gurkha hat . . . jungle green hand towel.' Down at the airstrip they were each given a hundred one-rupee notes 'in case your glider crashes', and bundled into Dakotas for the short flight to Lalaghat, where the gliders awaited them.

By nightfall, the advance party was in the air. It was a brilliantly clear night and the Chindwin River was easily pinpointed by the pilots and their map readers. After the previous night when so many gliders had been lost, it was more than prudent to know where one was at any time. The final checkpoint was reached, the junction of the Shweli and

Irrawaddy Rivers, and within the curve of the junction, amid the darkness of the surrounding jungle, was the pear-shaped clearing known as Chowringhee. The gliders cast off their tow lines and began to descend. The ground reached up for O'Brien's glider as it hurtled earthwards at 120 miles an hour. The grass was ten feet high and studded with dried-up buffalo wallows and the glider forced a path through it with a deafening roar. The ten men in the back of the glider were thrown around as it finally slewed sideways into a depression and came to a halt with a crash that detached the starboard wing and forced O'Brien's feet through the instrument panel. One of the gliders was not so lucky. The pilot had made his approach too high and stalled, crashing into the trees with the loss of the three American engineers on board and the destruction of the precious caterpillar tractor. Colonel John Alison radioed Air Commando headquarters and requested that another tractor be sent in by glider the following night. However, Cheetham, the sapper officer, and the twelve Garwhalis of his platoon were not to be put off. They had a dozen kukris and four spades between them and by daylight they had cleared four hundred yards of airstrip. A second tractor arrived by glider that night and an eight-hundred-yard airstrip had been cleared by the morning. Seventy aircraft were scheduled to land that night and the first one in was piloted by General Old, the commander of Air Transport Command, USAAF. For his own mysterious reasons he decided the airstrip was not long enough and barred further landings. The aircraft en route were ordered back to Assam, although six other Dakotas landed without difficulty.

As the circling lights disappeared, the men on the ground cursed and set about extending the strip to twelve hundred yards, hoping fervently that any Japanese in the neighbourhood would not notice the noise of the tractor or the clouds of dust being raised. They were all short of water and no one had any idea where the nearest supply was to be found. A patrol eventually found a stream five miles away. In the meantime Colonel Morris himself had joined the men on the ground and one of his first actions was to ban the lighting of any fires. The Chindits were not amused. The Americans, who were not under the command of Morris, had a huge fire blazing at one end of the strip and the Chindits ambled over to cadge cups of coffee from the unconcerned air commandos.

On the third night everything fell into place and a steady stream of aircraft began to arrive at Chowringhee. One of the first arrivals was Wingate accompanied by Brigadier Joe Lentaigne, the commander of 111 Brigade, together with his Brigade Headquarters and the remainder of Morris's two columns of Gurkhas. Lentaigne and Jack Masters, his Brigade Major, were not very happy. They were on the wrong side of the Irrawaddy and they would have to march west to cross over and rejoin the two other battalions of their brigade which had landed at Broadway:

the 1st Battalion, The Cameronians and the 2nd Battalion, King's Own Royal Regiment. Morris Force was to head off in the opposite direction. Their task was to march eastwards, cross the Shweli River and continue on to the border with China. There they would operate against the section of the Burma Road which runs between Bhamo and Myitkyina in the north and also assist Lieutenant-Colonel 'Fish' Herring of the Burma Rifles and his Dah Force who were to organise resistance among the Kachin tribes. Major Peter Cane, the enthusiastic commander of 94 Column, was sent off first with two platoons and all of the river-crossing equipment towards the Shweli River. The rest of his column, plus its sister column, number 49 led by Major Ted Russell, and Morris himself were to follow on in due course. As soon as the rest of 111 Brigade were in, Wingate ordered the landing zone to be abandoned and the columns moved out to their allotted tasks. It was not a moment too soon. As Morris Force moved through the jungle not far from the airstrip, Japanese fighters arrived to strafe the four damaged gliders still left there. The trials and tribulations of Morris Force would continue until the end of the campaign, and as for 111 Brigade, they still had to cross the Irrawaddy where more problems awaited them.

Bladet was the codename for Blaine Detachment. It consisted of six junior officers and sixty men who had volunteered from reconnaissance patrols of individual columns of Special Force. The unit was trained as a sort of personal arm of Wingate's, to be used for duties such as sabotage, reconnaissance, diversion etc., wherever desirable during the main operation. Engineers trained in the use of explosives were attached; a couple of signallers and three mules to carry wireless and charging machine were also on strength, as was a Burmese interpreter. The unit was commanded and trained by Major Blaine who had been a Sergeant-Major in Mike Calvert's column in the first Wingate expedition. He had been highly thought of and was promoted in the field to officer rank and awarded the DCM.

The detachment's first and only action began during the third week of March when it was landed west of the Irrawaddy in five gliders, by night, on a paddy field landing strip prepared by some of 111 Brigade's Gurkhas. Lieutenant Stewart Binnie recalled the operation:

> 'The landing was a successful shambles. The gliders were piloted by Americans of Cochran's commandos. The first glider with Blaine and myself in it overshot the strip and tore into the jungle, shedding its wings and splitting open through the length of the fuselage. The troops within were able to step out of the wreckage, alarmed but relatively unharmed. The remaining gliders performed with equal acrobatic flair and the one carrying the mules actually looped the loop very near the ground,

pancake-landed and the mules walked daintily out over the wreckage and calmly started to graze.

'The unit bivouacked for the night in nearby jungle, the bivouac including the American pilots who were to be flown out by light plane at first light. They were very unused to jungle and I don't think they slept much, seeing lions, tigers and Japs everywhere. During the night, Blaine realised that he had been injured in the glider crash and was incapable of undertaking a long march in enemy territory. He was therefore to go back with the American pilots and I, by chance the senior Lieutenant, took over command. This was, initially, quite a shock, as apart from CSM Chivers and a couple of engineers, the remainder of the detachment were new to action and it had been anticipated that Blaine's experience would be essential to the success of the operation. I was fortunate in having CSM Chivers to lean on throughout the patrol, as he had been with Blaine in the first expedition and was an excellent Wingate-type soldier.

'Anyway, the troops were of good quality and my fellow officers were keen and enthusiastic. We set about our objective to reach a bridge over the railway near Kawlin on the Mandalay–Myitkyina line, blow it up, make a mess of the railway line and throughout the patrol give the impression to native Burmese – knowing that the information would be passed to the Japs – that there was a biggish Chindit force this far south.

'The operation took about six weeks and was a success. We blew the bridge and a nearby pumping station and cut the railway line in several places. During the patrol the mule carrying the wireless set went over a cliff, falling about 200 feet, and we were incommunicado for most of the patrol. Eventually the wireless was resuscitated enough to permit contact with India and we arranged one supply drop without which we would probably have perished. We were congratulated by Wingate just before his untimely death and told to move on to Aberdeen. This was quite a hike and we became very exhausted and hungry. A period of marching through a dry belt very nearly caused madness due to thirst and one got to the stage of planning the murder of one's best friend for the sake of the small residue he might have in his water bottle.

'At one stage we got lost and hunger and thirst were so affecting us that it was proposed by CSM Chivers that we should take a free vote as to whether we should go on looking for Aberdeen or allow small groups to go it alone and head back over the Chindwin for India. I think that Chivers felt that having done it himself before, he could do it again. Fortunately the problem was solved by the sudden appearance of two Gurkha soldiers at the fringe of the jungle. Our saviours were in bivouac about a quarter of a mile away – Tim Brennan's Cameronians, the King's Own and a couple of columns of Gurkhas. We were made very welcome, fed with bully beef and peaches and cream until we were sick, and allowed to sleep the sleep of the just. Tim Brennan got a message that we were to move on, when ready, to Aberdeen and be flown out as we were too exhausted to participate in any further action. A day's rest and we were on our way. We were ambushed by some excitable Japs a short distance away from the bivouac, but they were as anxious as we were and we escaped with one engineer shot through the kneecap and John Urquhart, my second-in-command, with a bullet burn right across his left breast, lucky fellow, shaken but intact. Two days of tough marching saw us in Aberdeen, happy but very, very exhausted.

'We eventually arrived in Shillong, in Assam, where we were to recuperate. Within twenty-four hours every single member of the unit was in hospital, after an enormous celebratory binge, suffering from malaria or dysentery. I was unconscious for three days with malignant tertian malaria. I thought the initial symptoms were merely those of a gigantic hangover. This extraordinary medical situation was of great interest to me after the war when I trained to become a general practitioner, and it wasn't understood until the discovery of cortisone how, in desperate states, our adrenal glands produce masses of it in an endeavour to keep infection at bay and maintain necessary bodily functions.

'Bladet was disbanded at this stage and individuals returned to their parent units when their health was restored. I then had the dubious pleasure of being trained to command a small detachment of twelve man-pack flame throwers and soon took them into Mogaung to be used by Brigadier Calvert. We were used, I believe rather unskilfully, in a night attack on a village near Mogaung. However, although the tactics were discredited, their use was such a shock to the Japs that the village fell into Calvert's hands with minimal casualties to our attacking force. In this action I lost the sight of my right eye to shrapnel from a Jap grenade, one soldier was killed and the remaining ten soldiers were all wounded to some degree.'

Brigadier Bernard Fergusson DSO was clean out of luck. All the other brigades of Special Force were going to fly into Burma except his. The 4,000 men and 700 animals of 16 Brigade would be marching, or more accurately walking, in a single-file snake sixty-five miles long from head to tail. They would be heading for the Indaw area and travelling through some of the most difficult, jungle-covered, mountainous country in the world.

The start point for the trek was Tagap Ga on the Ledo Road. The luckless muleteers and their charges would have to walk there from the brigade's concentration point at Ledo in northern Assam, the remainder would be carried in lorries. The conditions were appalling. It rained continuously and the muddy road, still being constructed by US Army engineers, followed hairpin bends and rose and fell over 5,000 feet foothills. The bedraggled brigade concentrated at Tagap Ga at the end of January and early February. From there they would take to the hills and all future supplies would arrive by air drop. A track was believed to run southwards over the Patkai Hills to the Chinese outpost at Hkalak Ga and the engineers were sent ahead to widen the track for the mules.

On 5 February the brigade began its long trek, with 21 and 22 Columns of the Queen's leading. Their first obstacle was a 2,000-foot-high hill, with a gradient in many places of one in one. The torrential rain made the track impassable for the mules and their heavy loads, so they were unloaded and the men carried the radios, ammunition, heavy weapons and equipment uphill by hand. By the end of the first day, the rearguard platoon of 22 Column was still on the Ledo Road. Brigadier Fergusson's official post-campaign report read:

> 'The march was the heaviest imaginable. The rain was torrential and almost continuous. No single stretch of level going existed between Tagap and Hkalak, and few thereafter. The cold was intense, particularly at bivouacs over 5,000 feet. The seventy pounds which men were carrying were greatly increased in weight due to saturation with water. A dry bivouac was practically unknown. Leeches were innumerable, but less unpleasant than the Polaung fly whose vicious bites hardened to a septic lump. Wireless communication was difficult and supply dropping on the whole atrocious; up to forty or fifty per cent of the supplies falling hundreds or thousands of feet down the cliffs and becoming a dead loss. Columns averaged nine days to cover the thirty-five miles from road head to Hkalak.'

Each column followed roughly the same daily routine. They would get up at around 0530 hours in the dark and load up the mules. Then they would move off in single file with 'slashers' ahead, armed with dahs (native knives) or kukris to cut their way through the thicker jungle. After two hours' march they would stop for a K ration breakfast, then four hours' more marching before the midday break, which was the best time of day to send radio signals. Thereafter they marched until darkness fell and it was time to set up the night bivouac. Generally the column would halt on the track, turn either left or right and march into the jungle in the same direction for up to five minutes. Upon halting, they would face the same direction in which they were previously heading and would find themselves back in the same column snake, but well away from the track and discovery. The column commander would set up his HQ and a perimeter defence would be organised before fires could be lit and a last meal cooked before everyone settled down in the darkness to try to sleep. Everyone cooked and slept in pairs and if you wanted to wander off to attend to your ablutions, your partner came as well. The idea of pairing up was not only to maintain morale in the jungle, but to lessen the chances of getting lost or surprised by the Japs. If proper precautions were not taken to cover one's tracks, or if a column bivouacked too near to the track, it would inevitably pay the price. The reader may recall the fate of 2 Column in the first expedition, which bivouacked too close to the railway line it had been marching along.

Anyone who fell out of the columns through exhaustion or illness had two choices, to follow on in the wake of the brigade, or to make his way back to the Ledo Road. One man from the Queen's stumbled towards the rear. Someone had put a piece of bamboo on the fire, sealed by its joints at either end. The heat of the fire made the air expand until the bamboo exploded, a piece hitting him in the eye, seriously damaging it. The penalty for putting unsplit bamboo on a fire, thereby causing a loud bang that might reach enemy ears or injury to those nearby, was to carry a Bren gun for three days. Normally the bren was handed on after every quarter of an hour of marching. There were also fatalities. An engineer officer of 69 Column was killed whilst examining a grenade found in a bivouac area. Another man was killed when a 'free' drop of mule fodder hit him. It was wise during a supply drop to find shelter under a tree, but often, particularly for those tending the signal fires, this was impossible. Punishment in the field was a dilemma for the column commanders. Two men were found asleep on sentry duty. They were both flogged by the Sergeant-Major. This was less drastic than it sounds, with the lashes being applied to the man's buttocks. On the same day a man was caught stealing rations at a supply drop. If he had more than his share, someone else went short. During the long halt at midday in the broiling sun he was tied to a tree. Most of the men understood and accepted such summary justice, although after the war one of the two flogged men complained to his MP and his column commander appeared before a court martial. The second man, however, refused to give evidence to support the other and eventually the officer was cleared on the grounds of 'condonation'; That is, the punishment was known and approved of by higher authority, Wingate in fact. Fergusson had ordered one of his 5 Column men flogged on the first expedition for sleeping on sentry duty and afterwards Wingate stated his approval. The man concerned later apologised for his lapse and was killed while fighting bravely in battle.

The Leicesters passed through the Queen's at Hkalak on 17 February and continued as pathfinder battalion. On 29 February they reached the banks of the Chindwin River, having covered 110 miles since the start of the trek. A signal from Wingate arrived: 'Well done, Leicesters, Hannibal eclipsed.'

At that point the river was 300 yards wide, swift flowing with broad, sandy banks bordered by thick jungle. The leading troops of the Leicesters began to cross in inflatable boats. The nearest Japanese outpost was five miles away and to ensure they did not interfere with the crossing Fergusson had arranged for a glider with men of the Black Watch to land on a sandbank near the outpost and cause a diversion, while Captains Jim Harman and Peter Bennett, both survivors of the 1943 expedition, booby-trapped the only track from the outpost to the crossing point. Fergusson had learnt from bitter experience the problems associated with river crossings and he was determined to cross this one in style. At one hour before dusk two air commando Dakotas appeared, with two gliders in tow. They circled once, then the gliders cut loose and made a perfect landing on a sandbank in the river. The noses of the gliders were pulled up and from their bowels were dragged assault boats, complete with outboard motors. All night long the boats sped to and fro, carrying the men and their equipment across the river.

The next day, 1 March, General Wingate landed on the sandbank in an air commando C-64 Norseman plane, with four war correspondents in tow. Fergusson was not pleased. Wingate had left his second-in-command, Colonel Katie Cave, and his rear base signals officer behind to accommodate the journalists. Fergusson took Wingate for a swim in the busy river. 'Last time I swam in the Chindwin,' he said, 'was on the way out, last year, when John Jefferies nearly drowned.' Wingate was worried about the brigade being behind schedule. Mike Calvert and his brigade were due to fly in within the week, followed by Joe Lentaigne's brigade. Fergusson would probably reach the Banmauk–Indaw area around 20 March, instead of the fifth as Wingate originally planned. It was not Fergusson's fault; Wingate had underestimated the terrain over which 16 Brigade had to march and they still had 200 miles to go.

When Wingate took his leave of Fergusson he gave him an operations order which began with a quotation from Zachariah: 'Turn ye to the stronghold, ye prisoners of hope!' Wingate had thought up another original idea. The concept of jungle strongholds was masterful and involved the establishment in the heart of enemy-held territory of an impregnable fortress, from which to dominate the countryside in the manner of a Norman baron. The selected spot should be self-contained in water and must be dug, wired, mined and strongly defended. It must also feature nearby an airstrip 1,200 yards long, which would be defended by anti-aircraft weapons and garrisoned by West African troops. The site must be inaccessible to the enemy, so he could not bring up troops by truck, and should only have a couple of approach routes, which could be patrolled and ambushed. Fergusson was ordered to establish such a stronghold near Indaw and Wingate named it 'Aberdeen'.

On 12 March, eleven days after leaving the Chindwin, Fergusson received a signal from Wingate concerning the approach to their objective, the town of Indaw and its two airfields. Originally 16 Brigade was to pass Indaw, and then swing back and storm it from the south-east. The new signal directed the brigade to make for Indaw direct and establish Aberdeen en route. Wingate rightly appreciated that Indaw was the key to Upper Burma. It was the northernmost centre of communications possessed by the Japanese. Roads led to it from the four corners of the compass and the Myitkyina railway ran through it from south to north. There were a number of important supply dumps in Indaw and the surrounding area, supporting the Japanese divisions opposing General Stilwell in the north and the divisions preparing to cross the Chindwin. The two airfields were also believed capable of operating through the monsoon season and their capture would present the possibility of flying a British division straight into Burma to spearhead its recapture.

At the time Fergusson received the message from Wingate he was moving along the Uyu Valley with 3,000 men and 400 animals in his train. His two columns of artillerymen had already been despatched to seize the town of Lonkin, some forty miles to the north-east, as a favour to Stilwell in return for his co-operation in moving the brigade up to their start line. Suddenly, the leading column of the Leicesters bumped a Japanese patrol, killed one and captured a prisoner. The unfortunate man with a bullet in his leg turned out to be a Gurkha, captured the previous year and pressed into service with the Japanese. He lay on the ground, smiling and shouting '77 Brigade! 77 Brigade!' A week or so later, Fergusson found a suitable site for Aberdeen. It was enclosed on three sides by high hills, the Meza River ran through it and just north of the village of Manhton was space for an airstrip. The columns arrived one after the other and took up residence. It would be home to the brigade for the next six weeks and the 12th Battalion, Nigeria Regiment would eventually arrive to garrison the stronghold.

The two artillery columns, number 51 under Major Dickie of the Burma Rifles and number 69 under Lieutenant-Colonel Sutcliffe, left 16 Brigade at Haungpa on 11 March and headed northwards towards Lonkin, an important communications centre on the Uyu River and in peacetime the centre of Burma's jade mining industry. The artillerymen were tired. Before they began their journey Wingate had visited them and said that they would be carrying sixty-pound packs on their backs. If they (India Command) had listened to him, they would only have been carrying thirty-five. Two of the men later weighed their packs at a railway station on the way to Assam and they were eighty-three and eighty-five pounds each. In addition their rifles weighed eight pounds. Intelligence reports dropped to the columns indicated that there were 1,100 Japanese in Lonkin. The next report stated 400. The few Japanese manning the outpost at Haungpa had fled towards Lonkin as the brigade approached, but one of them had stopped on the track to set up a booby-trap. He had fluffed the job and blown himself up and the leading scouts came across his body the next day.

Four days after leaving the brigade, the two columns approached Lonkin. The last few miles led them along a tortuous chaung and it was well after dark when they collapsed into their bivouac. That night the heavens opened and all were soaked to the skin. At 0430 hours they rose from the soaking ground and prepared to attack. 51 Column was to attack Lonkin from the west and 69 from the east. Major Dickie led 51 Column across the Uyu River and along the river bank towards the western end of Lonkin. They had fixed bayonets and bedecked their hats with foliage for camouflage as they crept forward. Lieutenant Eden and his platoon were the first to find the enemy. Advancing parallel to the riverside track, they disturbed a dog that the Japanese had tied to a tree to give warning of their approach. As his barking echoed through the jungle, the enemy opened fire. Lieutenant Comrie's platoon at the head of the column also came under fire and two men were hit. One died instantly, the other, seriously wounded, died later despite the efforts of Doc Lees and the padre. The column commander walked about surveying the situation, showing an unhealthy contempt for the Japanese snipers, who had begun to shoot from treetops across the river. Eventually Lieutenant Lodge brought up his flame thrower detachment and, led by Bombadier Summers with a Bren gun, advanced on the Japanese foxholes. The enemy opened fire and were met with a hail of bullets from the Bren gun, then the jungle around them burst into flames as the new weapon spewed out its fiery destruction. It was the first use of the weapon in that theatre of war and at once the Japanese retreated. Bombadier Summers received an immediate award of the Military Medal.

The eastern end of Lonkin was cleared against little resistance, although Major Mertz, the infantry company commander, had a lucky escape. They bumped a Japanese patrol and a grenade landed at his feet. He wanted to run, but all power of movement had been frozen. The grenade stared malevolently up at him, but amazingly did not explode. Such are the fortunes of war. The artillerymen had got off lightly, with two dead and two wounded. Only a couple of dozen Japanese had been left to garrison the town, the remainder having left the day before in sixteen three-tonner trucks. Apparently they had received the news that a British brigade was heading their way and decided that discretion was the better part of valour. If they had stayed, it would have been a very bloody battle indeed.

An airstrip was prepared and light planes took out both wounded men, a morale booster for the others who had heard the tales about the wounded being abandoned in the first expedition. Thereafter both columns shouldered their packs and turned towards the south, eventually reaching Aberdeen on 10 April.

Taken on 1 May 1944 whilst crossing the Mawe Chaung, 200 miles behind Japanese lines, this photograph shows most of the Royal Signals Wireless Operating Group attached to 21 Column, 2nd Battalion, Queen's Royal Regiment, 16th Infantry Brigade. *(Left to right)* Corporal Howard, Private Myers, Signalman Beaton, Private Holmes, Signalman Hill.

Major Denis Arnold with his wife Evelyne, taken just before the VJ parade in London in August 1995. The medal on the left of the row is the Military Cross, won during an attack on the Kyunslai Pass by his platoon from the 7th Battalion, Nigeria Regiment.

The final resting-place for two Chindits. Many have no known graves.

Wingate briefing pilots of the 1st Air Commando Group and Chindit officers at Hailakandi, India, on the invasion plans to land at two places behind enemy lines in Burma. Colonel Philip J. Cochran, USAAF, commander of the Air Commandos stands to the right of the map.

Captain Michael Allmand of the 3rd Battalion, 6th Gurkha Rifles, won a posthumous Victoria Cross at Mogaung on 22 June 1944.

Norman Campbell who fought at Blackpool with the 1st Cameronians, photographed just after he joined the regiment.

Old warriors, 50 years on. Brigadier Mike Calvert DSO *(left)* and Brigadier Jack Wilkinson DSO, former CO of 2nd Leicesters, at the 50th Anniversary of the last campaign in Burma on 17 June 1994. Two of the toughest soldiers ever to serve this country.

Trooper Arthur Withey of the 45th Reconnaissance Regiment, who had a lucky escape when his party was surrounded by Japs outside White City. Photographed after returning home in 1946.

Sergeant Roy Vine from the 45th Reconnaissance Regiment was suffering from malaria and pneumonia during the battle of Thetkegyin. When he fell out of the column his friend Trooper Gardner stayed with him and they were later found by the 2nd Leicesters and flown out.

LEFT: Lance-Corporal Charles Tinsley *(left)* and Private Gregson of the 4th Battalion, The Border Regiment, 23 Brigade. The battalion operated in the land of the Naga headhunters, to the rear of the Japanese attacking Imphal, ambushing and destroying their supply dumps.

BELOW: A Gurkha officer from 3rd Battalion, 4th Gurkhas, standing fourth from right (without hat) and his men on training before entering Burma with 111 Brigade. Half of the battalion stayed with the brigade, the rest, 40 Column, joined Morris Force.

Havildar Gapan Pun from 3rd Battalion, 4th Gurkhas, with his platoon. He was promoted to Jemadar later in Burma and killed leading his men in an attack opposite Myitkyina.

Chapter 9

First Blood

L ong before 16 Brigade established their stronghold at Aberdeen, Broadway was fortified as the stronghold for 77 Brigade Rear HQ under Colonel Claude Rome. It was dug and wired and would become a light plane base until the monsoon, garrisoned by a battalion of Gurkhas. It was now time for Calvert to go to work.

Half of 20 Column of the Lancashire Fusiliers under Major David Monteith was sent south to the Irrawaddy to halt all traffic on the river. Boats would only be allowed to pass if they flew the Union Jack. The other half of the column, led by Major Shuttleworth, was to head for the railway line and carry out demolitions between Mawlu and Pinwe. Lieutenant-Colonel Hugh Christie was to take the senior column of the Lancashire Fusiliers, number 50, and cut the road and rail tracks between Kadu and Mawhun. In the meantime Calvert would take the South Staffords and the 3rd Battalion, 6th Gurkhas and establish a block on the road and rail track at Mawlu. The demolitions being carried out either side of Mawlu by the Lancashire Fusiliers would give the brigade a breathing space to establish the block before Japanese reinforcements arrived. As Private Bill Merchant of the Lancashire Fusiliers tramped westwards, shoulders bent under the weight of his pack, he thought back to their march into Assam to prepare for the operation:

'We marched in easy stages through tea plantations and the paradise of Assam where tropical fruits grew in abundance and gorgeous flowering shrubs and trees were everywhere. I can truly say that Assam was the nearest thing to paradise that I had ever seen in my life and the thought went through my mind that perhaps God gave us a glimpse of this paradise before we died in battle in a land we hardly knew anything about, with names we couldn't spell or pronounce! It was here that I first heard the repetitive call of the brain-fever bird which went up and down the scale until one started to count the notes, and just when you thought it had finished it added a few more – hence the name.

'We left Broadway on or about 9 March, heading for the block that our brigade was to establish at Henu. It was the third or fourth day out that we first bumped the Japs after crossing the Kaukkwe Chaung. We were lying down trying to fix bayonets as one of the platoons was passing through us, when a bullet went through my mate Jacko's pack, just missing my head.

127

(We were all paired together to avoid being surprised by the Japs.) Jacko was in considerable pain and I remember telling him to be quiet or we should both get bumped off. We heard a lot of shouting and firing and then the platoon that had passed through us came running back saying that the place was alive with Japs, so we hurriedly retraced our steps back across the chaung. Some of us helped Jacko and we went a couple of miles before we bivouacked for the night in some disarray. We had about eight or nine men missing and a patrol discovered their badly mutilated bodies the next day. A couple of days later a light plane came in and flew Jacko out.

'After this incident we made our way towards the Mawlu area through some very thick jungle and having to take it in turns to hack our way through so that the mules could get through with their wide loads. The heat was beginning to have an adverse effect on our stamina and it was about this time, just after we had climbed over the formidable Gangaw Range and got down into the Railway Corridor proper, that it rained a little and that night we had our first taste of being bitten by leeches. They were everywhere, all colours and sizes, grey ones, black ones, they were on every bush and beside the track where they reached blindly as you passed; small ones, big elephant leeches and some like threads of coloured string, but they all sucked one's blood and then the itching started. We burned them off with cigarette ends. One never got used to them, they would crawl through the smallest aperture and get inside your clothes. But of course, although most unpleasant, they were not as deadly as the ticks which carried typhus.

'As we came down over the Gangaw Range we could hear the pop-pop of rifle fire as the South Staffords and the 3/6th Gurkhas strove to establish the block at Henu.'

The firing that Bill Merchant and his fellow fusiliers could hear was what later became known as the Battle for Pagoda Hill. Calvert had chosen the site for his block during an aerial reconnaissance in an Air Commando bomber. It was near a small hamlet named Henu, just north of the village of Mawlu with its garrison of some 500 rear echelon troops. The road and railway ran next to each other at Henu and a block could be put across both of them at the same time.

The Kaukkwe Valley through which Calvert's men had to march was real textbook jungle – dark, dank, primeval growth with enormous creepers. The two columns of the South Staffords, led by Lieutenant-Colonel Richards and Major Ron Degg, reached the railway first and asked for a supply drop of barbed wire, picks, shovels, ammunition and food. Much of it went astray, so they began to dig in with what they had. One column of the 3rd Battalion, 6th Gurkhas under its commander, Lieutenant-Colonel Hugh Skone, arrived soon after, while the other column under Major Freddie Shaw put in a diversionary attack on the 300 Japanese at Nansiaung, just north of Henu.

The next morning Calvert led his Brigade Headquarters into the valley to meet Shaw's column of Gurkhas. Calvert also had with him his own crack Gurkha Brigade HQ Defence Company under Ian Macpherson. As they neared the block the sound of firing reached their ears. The six platoons of Gurkhas doubled forward towards the sound of battle. A number of Japanese had infiltrated between Degg's and Skone's columns and established themselves around a small pagoda on top of a small hill overlooking the paddy. The South Staffords were not dug in properly and were in full view of the enemy; casualties began to mount. Calvert left Shaw and his Gurkhas with instructions to give him covering fire while he crossed the paddy and thereafter to conform with whatever he did. Together with Squadron Leader Bobbie Thompson, his groom Paddy Dermody and his batman Lance-Corporal Willie Young, Calvert ran across to the South Staffords. Lieutenant Norman Durant later wrote:

> 'By now a third of us were casualties and were extremely glad to hear over the wireless that the Brigadier was on his way and would counter-attack any feature held by the Japs. He came striding up to our hill, rifle and bayonet in hand, took a quick look round and then said to Major Jefferies, "How many men can you spare to attack Pagoda Hill?" "About twenty" "Right, we'll go straight up".

Calvert relived the moment for the author fifty years later:

> 'Standing up, I shouted out "Charge" in the approved Victorian manner, and ran down the hill with Bobbie and the two orderlies. Half of the South Staffords joined in. Then looking back I found a lot had not. So I told them to bloody well "Charge! What the hell do you think you're doing?" So they all charged, the machine-gunners, mortar teams, the officers – all who were on the hill. As we climbed Pagoda Hill, the Japs, entering into the spirit of the thing, got up and charged us. There, at the top of the hill, about fifty yards square, an extraordinary mêlée took place, everyone shooting, bayoneting, kicking at everyone else, rather like an officers' guest night.'

Norman Durant sprinted up the hill and found a path a dozen feet below the pagoda which led to some huts on stilts. He shouted to his Sergeant to follow and doubled along the path, round a corner and into view of the huts. Coming straight towards him was a section of Japanese soldiers, the nearest two just twenty yards away, bayonets fixed. He had a grenade with a four-second fuse in his hand and he threw it over the heads of the two leading Japanese and dived down the side of the hill, wincing as a bullet hit him in the knee. Fortunately his sergeant and a couple of men arrived on the scene and shot the two leading Japs and set about grenading everything in sight until the area was clear. As Durant made his way back to the path he saw a hand-to-hand struggle going on further up the hill:

'George Cairns, the mortar officer, and a Jap officer were struggling and choking on the ground, and as I picked up a Jap rifle and climbed up towards them I saw George break free and, picking up a rifle, bayonet the Jap again and again like a madman. It was only when I got near that I saw he himself had already been bayoneted twice through the side and that his left arm was hanging on by a few strips of muscle. How he found the strength to carry on was a miracle.'

Cairns continued to fight, armed with the Japanese officer's sword, until he succumbed to his wounds. Mike Calvert was there at the end. He recalled Cairns asking, 'Have we won, Sir? Was it all right? Did we do our stuff? Don't worry about me.' After the war the King awarded Cairns a posthumous Victoria Cross, the first of the four that the Chindits would earn over the next couple of months.

Another officer, platoon commander Noel Day, was shot dead by a Japanese soldier feigning death, but on trying to repeat the ruse he was spotted by Day's Platoon Sergeant who promptly despatched him. They found out then that it did not pay to leave wounded Japanese breathing. Fourteen officers took part in the charge, including Major Jefferies, Captain Stagg, Lieutenants Scholey, Day, Cairns, Durant and Williams. All were killed during the campaign except Durant and Williams. Scholey was awarded an immediate Military Cross for his part in the charge, Sergeant Perry an immediate Distinguished Conduct Medal. The day's losses for the South Staffords were three officers killed and four wounded and twenty other ranks killed and sixty wounded. Chindit officer casualties would be high throughout the campaign. Many were volunteers who led by example and many would die leading their men into battle. Cairns himself was a volunteer from the Somerset Light Infantry. Ken Battey later recalled Cairns: 'We were busy training so I did not have much time to get to know him properly, but we did get the feeling that he would be a good man manager as he was not afraid to do his share of the chores. Some officers were rather snooty on this sort of thing, but not George. I feel that we lost a good man.'

From the Brigadier's point of view, the battle had been a success. His men had scored their first victory over the Japanese and it set a standard for the brigade. Fortunately the two enemy companies were from a railway engineer battalion, rather than front-line infantry, but they were still brave men and over half of them were killed by the South Staffords and the Gurkhas who joined in the fighting towards the end.

2100 hours, 15 March, the Mawhun railway bridge, north of Henu. Lieutenant Hugh Patterson and his commando platoon had finished their work. All of the charges had been laid and as the Lieutenant surveyed the scene his thoughts drifted back to the dummy run on a similar bridge back in Assam:

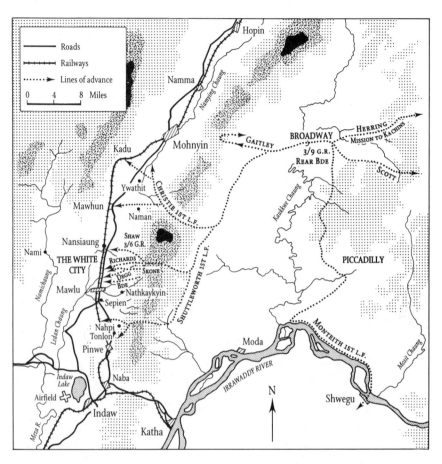

The landing at Broadway and the installation of White City.

'The dress rehearsal was enlivened by the arrival of a crowded train. This, rather surprisingly, detonated the 200 feet of primacord which was connected to the dummy charges and in turn set fire to the railway sleepers on the bridge. The result was quite impressive, resulting in pandemonium and the immediate departure into the surrounding jungle of several hundred passengers and the crew of the train. The crew were eventually persuaded to drive on, but of the rest no more was seen.'

This time the real thing was to be set off by two separate three-foot lengths of safety fuse, fired by igniters. Having lit the thirty-second fuses, Patterson and Sergeant Kemp walked away down the line with the traditional mixture of dignity and haste. 'This is something I've wanted to do all my life, Sir,' remarked Kemp. The charges had been increased by fifty per cent in case they had to be blown in the face of opposition. The

131

mixture could not have been quite correct as the pair were promptly thrown flat on their faces as the bridge went up. Lumps of metal and brick hummed through the air and thudded down all around them, but no one was hit. For the technically minded, 300 pounds of Nobel 808 plastic high explosive, with primer, was used. Each of the three spans was cut with two thirty-pound cutting charges and a fifty-pound cratering charge was dug three feet into the north abutment and fired, leaving a crater ten feet deep. Two piers, eight feet thick and fifteen feet high, supported the spans. One was sunk into the bed of the river and fell victim to a fifty-pound underwater charge, the other was perforated by eight four-pound beehive charges, each of which blew six-inch diameter holes three feet into the pier, which disintegrated when the borehole charges were subsequently fired.

Ten miles to the south of Mawhun, Mike Calvert sent a signal to Patterson: 'Both saw and heard your bang – keep it up!' They did their best to comply, wrecking Mawhun station the next night, before rejoining 50 Column and Colonel Christie. For the next few days the column would be occupied ambushing the road leading to Calvert's stronghold.

The commando platoon of 20 Column also had a demolition task to carry out the other side of Mawlu. Led by Captain Butler and Lieutenant De Quidt they left the column to make their way southwards to blow the bridge at Tonlon Gorge, three miles south of Pinwe. John Mattinson told the author:

> 'While the charges were being laid a Jap truck came down the road at a hell of a speed. We all took cover and I was holding on to a mule that had broken free when the truck reached the level crossing over the railway and stalled. The back of the truck was full of wounded Japanese and was a sitting target, but we had been told not to open fire under any circumstances. After some time the driver got the truck started and went on his way. Lieutenant De Quidt asked me to pull the safety fuse pin out of the time pencil and the bridge blew up.'

Bill Merchant takes up the story:

> 'The bridge went up with a hell of a bang and shortly afterwards two truck loads of Japs came along and started searching the jungle. We had only gone about 400 yards when our mule carrying the radio and ammunition fell down a ravine and landed upside down. We scrambled down but could not move the mule. We could not carry the equipment without the mule and were worried that it might die of fright, so we stayed there all night, with the muleteer stroking the mule to keep him calm. When dawn came the mule got up of his own accord and we made our way back towards Pinwe, where we were to mine and ambush the road. We were waiting to ambush part of a Japanese battalion that was retreating from the Mawlu area. As a qualified sniper it would have been my job to shoot the officer who was leading the Japs. We eventually withdrew the ambush and learned later that the Japs marched down the road only half an hour after we had left. Lucky for them

and no doubt lucky for us too. Sadly a Burmese riding a bullock cart ran over the mines and was blown to bits.'

Mike Calvert's stronghold was about 800 yards wide and 1,000 yards long, ideally situated around a series of wooded hills about thirty to fifty feet high, with numerous valleys in between. There was water nearby and a light plane strip was constructed for evacuation of the wounded. The village of Henu was brought into the defended area and also a slightly higher hill, named OP Hill, which had a good view of the surrounding countryside. The mules and chargers were protected by walls of parachute containers filled with mud and a Brigade Head-quarters and main dressing station were set up. Every day supply planes came over and soon the high trees around the block were festooned with white parachutes. The stronghold was aptly named White City.

The South Staffords manned the defences to the north and east of the perimeter. To the north there was a small open valley about twenty yards across, ending in a wooden knoll. Beyond the valley was a hill which overlooked the block. To the east were several densely wooded hills where visibility was down to ten yards. At the south-east corner was OP Hill from which the Gurkhas had made their charge on to Pagoda Hill. This isolated position was manned by the Brigade Defence Company commanded by Ian MacPherson. The 3/6th Gurkhas manned the south and west sectors of the defences. The south side overlooked a stream and open paddy beyond. The western defences were dug into the highest hills and overlooked the railway and the open paddy beyond. The main dressing station was near the north end in a concealed re-entrant and opposite this on the perimeter was 'Bare Hill' where all of the trees had been cut down and lay as logs all over it. The whole area was soon turned into a fortress. Every platoon and company post was wired in, bunkers were dug and reinforced with wooden sleepers and metal rails from the railway, telephone lines were laid and buried, water and ammunition was stored and mortar and machine-gun fire plans prepared. Eight three-inch mortars and eleven Vickers machine-guns, later increased, were sited to fire across the perimeter wire. The barbed wire was initally six to eight feet deep and supplemented by booby-traps and mines. All that was missing was the Japanese.

The perimeter was probed by the Japanese on four consecutive days with few casualties to either side, but on the fifth day, 21 March, they came in earnest. Just before seven p.m. a fusillade of grenades heralded an attack on the South Staffords in the northern sector. The enemy gained a foothold in two platoon positions and heavy fighting continued throughout the night. At the main dressing station Captain Chesshire listened to the gunfire as he tended the wounded:

'The 38 Column headquarters was being overrun on the other side of the hill. Between them and us was an open area of about 100 yards of short grass, which had been used by a light plane to take out some wounded two days earlier (before a longer strip was constructed near the railway). It was a very dark night, but we could hear the Japs coming as they kept on testing their rifle bolts as they advanced. The mortar crews nearby picked up their rifles and my farrier and groom jumped into their trenches and waited. When the Japs were a few yards away they opened fire and seven Japs fell dead in front of them, one of them almost joining my farrier in his trench. The remaining Japs retreated.'

At dawn Colonel Richards led a counter-attack which threw the enemy out again. He was shot in the chest, but gleefully informed Calvert that he had accounted for seven Japs before they got him. By this time Chesshire and his two orderlies, Hollis and Bate, had about forty casualties in their aid post. Richards was later evacuated but sadly died from complications two weeks later. Major Ron Degg assumed command of the battalion. As the enemy retreated from the block they were attacked by a 'floater' column led by Major Jefferies. The Japs put up a stiff fight and Jefferies was shot dead by a sniper in a tree. Calvert called the column back and thereafter the 'floater' idea was abandoned.

During the same night another Japanese attack had been launched in the area of Bare Hill and 100 mortar shells were fired at the attackers. The following morning Calvert went on to the hill, which was supposedly clear of the enemy, together with his groom Paddy Dermody and batman Lance-Corporal Young. Suddenly Paddy shouted 'Get down!' and pushed Calvert out of the way, before falling, wounded in the groin. There was a wounded Japanese soldier the other side of the tree trunk and Calvert went down on his knees, crawling along the length of the tree and pausing every couple of feet to fire his revolver over the top at the hidden sniper. His shots found their mark and he emptied his revolver into the soldier. As they carried Paddy down to the dressing station Calvert sent the Gurkhas to clear the hill. They killed eleven Japanese still hiding there. The attackers had comprised three companies from the 18th Division and two Railway Engineer Companies. They left most of their men dead in and around the White City perimeter and their adjutant, Lieutenant Satrai, was captured, together with their battalion flag. On the whole, Japanese prisoners lived up to their code of death rather than dishonour and few were ever taken alive. Satrai asked that he be interrogated then shot, but he was flown out by light plane. Later, at a hospital in Assam, he summoned the chief doctor, thanked him for his help and informed him that it was dishonourable to live, so he must now die. He turned his face to the wall and, despite force feeding, willed himself to die, achieving his aim five days later. A post-mortem could discover no cause of death.

The next week was spent strengthening the defences of White City and Wingate himself flew in on 24 March. An attack on nearby Mawlu by the Lancashire Fusiliers and the Gurkhas was carried off successfully and several hundredweight of Japanese Army records were discovered and shipped back to India. From 27 March to 6 April constant patrolling was the name of the game and several more bridges were blown in the neighbourhood. It was however, the calm before the storm.

Wingate's visit on 24 March was the last he made to White City. One of those who met him was Joe Bate, one of Captain Chesshire's medical orderlies: 'My pal, Ron Clifford, and I were returning to our position laden with chaguals of water for the medical section when we met the great man himself, Wingate, walking alone. He stopped us, shook hands and asked us how we were coping there in the block.' It was typical of the Chindit leader, a Major-General then, to stop and talk to his men. When he flew out again, he left Calvert with the words, 'Be of good heart, I will see that you lack nothing.'

Although the fighting had died down around White City for the time being, men were still dying. Joe Bate again:

'One day the Royal Engineers Sergeant, Nick Carter, came running to me shouting, "Come quick Joe, Jock's had it!" I grabbed a stretcher and rushed after him and Captain Chesshire, having heard Nick's shout, followed me. The barbed wire was opened to let us out and Nick led us across the open ground at the north end of the block and into the "jungle" opposite. It was in fact more like an English wood with lots of undergrowth and Nick had to stop every few yards to disconnect the wires attached to booby-traps laid previously by Nick and his Corporal, Jock. We could soon hear Jock screaming out "Where's that ————MO?" and fifty or so yards further on we found him lying in a small hollow in the ground. Just after we got to him, and with him still shouting, we heard Japanese voices approaching and their feet crashing through the undergrowth. At that point we realised that, in our haste, the MO and I had not brought weapons with us and the only weapon we had was the revolver Nick carried. On reflection I think Jock's shouting, which none of us could bring ourselves to subdue, may have saved us, because the Japs probably thought it was a trick, the sort of trick they so often employed themselves. Anyway, after coming close, we heard them going away and we were able to get Jock on the stretcher. The poor chap had terrible injuries, caused by the explosion of the hand grenade he was preparing as a booby-trap. He had lost both eyes, parts of both arms and legs, and had severe abdominal injuries too. We got him out of the wood and Nick and I were carrying the stretcher across the open ground towards the block with Captain Chesshire walking beside us. Suddenly there was a flash and a bang and poor Chesshire leapt two feet in the air. He had stepped on an explosive charge set in the ground to act as a warning of a Jap approach. Sad as the occasion was, the sight of the MO's shocked reaction did cause us to chuckle. Sadly Jock died half an hour after we got him back in the block. He had won the Military Medal at Tobruk when dealing with land mines between the lines and I felt this accidental death was such a shocking waste of a brave young Scotsman.'

Another myth perpetuated by various historians concerns the scattering of the 6th Battalion, Nigeria Regiment after being 'ambushed' while on its way from Broadway to Aberdeen. The battalion was commanded by Lieutenant-Colonel P.G. Day, who was marching with 66 Column and Major Lahosky, a Polish officer who commanded 39 Column. Who better to set the record straight than Captain Robert St John Walsh, the officer who was at the head of the leading Column, number 66, as it first met the enemy:

'We flew into Broadway on 9 March and set off for Aberdeen on the twelfth, over one mountain range, across the eight-mile-wide plain (at night) through which ran the main Japanese lines of communication from Mandalay to Myitkyina and Mogaung and the north, over another range and thence to Aberdeen. It was while crossing that plain that our column had its first encounter with the Japs, and I was the first officer to come under fire, in fact the first man.

'In crossing the plain we had first to cross the main north-south railway and then the main road, before reaching the cover of the wooded foothills on the other side of the plain, which was nothing but open paddy fields. You can imagine, therefore, that we had to be pretty careful to get across eight miles of open country, two miles from a town, with a Jap garrison and patrols out, without being detected. I was intelligence officer at the time and consequently I was leading the battalion across in single file, with the leading platoon commander and a Burmese guide out in front. There was no moon and all was going well until after a couple of miles the railway loomed up in the blackness fifty yards in front of me. I halted the column behind me and said to another officer that we'd better make sure it was safe to cross the railway before moving on. Almost as I whispered this, I suddenly spotted a dozen shadowy shapes moving across our front only thirty yards away – a Jap patrol moving alongside the railway, between us and the railway! The Japs must have seen us at the same time and they opened fire. A furious battle at point-blank range ensued, but it was over pretty quickly and the enemy took to his heels and fled. Unfortunately my pal had been shot in the thigh and severely wounded, along with an officer and a European NCO. The alarm had been raised and before long the Jap garrison from the nearby town would be out looking for us. It was up to us to melt away into the jungle across the plain, six miles away. We had to get there before the moon rose, otherwise we could be seen and followed. There was nowhere we could take our wounded, 150 miles behind the enemy lines, in the heart of their territory; we'd not yet had time to build an airstrip from which to evacuate our casualties, so there was unfortunately no alternative but to leave those three poor devils behind, at the mercy of the Japs. What a dreadful, ghastly business war is. However, there was nothing else we could do, and there was no time to waste.

'We were to destroy an ammunition dump at Bilumyo, a few miles north of Mohnyin, before continuing our march to Aberdeen. However, total confusion reigned, the rear platoons and 39 Column behind us, not knowing what sort or strength of opposition lay ahead. There was a complete dispersal of the battalion, with 39 Column retreating to the foothills they had just left and moving south to cross the valley at a narrower point. Our objective was not of course achieved, the separate groups of 66 Column now making their way to our pre-arranged ten-day rendezvous, which was Aberdeen. My group of sixteen men, including the CO, fortuitously met the complete 39 Column as they were crossing the mountain ridge. The battalion, except two platoons which finished up at White City, was again a complete unit at Aberdeen by the end of March and we remained there as garrison until that "fortress" was abandoned and we were ordered to move north and act as floater columns outside Blackpool. The platoons at White City did not join up with us for three months.'

Kenneth Kerin was the mortar officer for 66 Column and his support group was located two-thirds of the way from the head of the column:

'It was very peaceful, but I remember reflecting at the time that we were rather exposed, and that I should have felt more comfortable had we been following the line of the "hedges" which seemed to approximate to the direction in which we were headed. In course of time my apprehensions were realised as there was a sudden eruption of small arms fire, and the sound of explosions which could have been grenades or mortar bombs. Most of the action seemed to be coming from the front of us, and I noticed the sound of little "thuds" in the grass, or paddy, which I imagined were bullets striking the ground. The column halted and then out of the darkness men started streaming past us, whereupon I signalled the men in my immediate vicinity to get down on the ground facing the hedgerows. As far as I could see in the dark, to the front and rear of me, men were lying in the prone position with their rifles ready for use if a target appeared. We remained on the ground while the firing lasted, and then when it was quiet I got up to collect my men, when I was surprised to find that beyond the distance I could see while prone there was nobody, and I had in all about ten men. I set about looking for 39 Column which I knew was travelling in our rear and bumped into them half an hour later. The column commander altered course, circling back into the bush, eventually crossing the railway at a different point, where it could be crossed under cover. We also laid mines on the line and after we had harboured a mile or so away had the satisfaction of hearing them go off.'

Colonel Day's men had in fact taken a number of precautions according to the 'Wingate Bible'. All rattling equipment had been secured and the mules' hoofs had been muffled with pieces of cloth. Talking was forbidden and march discipline was being maintained. Suspicion later fell on the Shan guides that were at the front of the column; after the column dispersed they were seen leading a party of Japanese trying to pick up their trail.*

---

* The battalion commander was later sent back to India and replaced by Major Gordon Upjohn, the Brigade Major.

Sergeant Jim Paines from the 45th Reconnaissance Regiment upon his return to Comilla in May 1944. He marched into Burma with 16 Brigade and fought at Thetkegyin and White City.

Captain Jimmy White of the 45th Reconnaissance Regiment who won the Military Cross at Thetkegyin, whilst commanding the rifle company of 54 Column. He led five bayonet charges against the Japs and later fought with Mike Calvert's task force outside White City.

Men from the 45th Reconnaissance Regiment persuading their mules to cross the Chindwin River during the march-in of 16 Brigade in February 1944.

The airfield at Broadway under attack by Jap bombers. Note the two RAF Spitfires on the ground in the centre of the picture. Eventually all six were destroyed or withdrawn to India.

Lieutenant-Colonel 'Fish' Herring of the Burma Rifles briefing men of Dah Force on their operation to raise the friendly Kachin tribesmen along the border with China.

1st Battalion, South Staffords hockey team in June 1943, Lieutenant David Wilcox *(sitting centre)*, was wounded four times during the 1944 campaign and was awarded the DSO and American Silver Star. Lieutenant Norman Durant *(standing extreme left)*, was wounded at Pagoda Hill and awarded the Military Cross.

Stan Hutson of the 60th Field Regiment, Royal Artillery, 23 Brigade. After dropping out from his column with malaria and dysentery he struggled through thick jungle and across rivers for two days to find them again. The only words that greeted him from his officer were: 'Ah, you've caught us up then. Good show.'

Bill Merchant of the Commando Platoon, 20 Column, 1st Battalion Lancashire Fusiliers on leave in Karachi after the campaign. He was with Captain Butler's men when they blew the bridge at Tonlon Gorge and later fought at White City.

Two West African Chindits from 43 Column of the 12th Battalion, Nigeria Regiment, together with their mules.

Officers of 22 Column, 2nd Battalion, Queen's Royal Regiment in April 1944. *(Left to right, standing)* Lieutenants Johnston, Wilkinson, Aprey (RE), Page (RA), Lt-Col Close, Lt Fox (missing), Capt Blackburn, Maj Jones, Capt Flint, Capt Rev Pritt. *(Sitting)* Capt Sykes (RE) killed, Lt Damery, Capt Miller, Capt Paul, Lt Hughes, Capt Baker, Capt Chet Khin (Burma Rifles), Flt Lt John Knowles, Royal Canadian Air Force.

LEFT: Chindits from Mike Calvert's 77 Brigade advance towards Mogaung.

Smoke fills the air as another railway bridge is demolished in the White City area by the Lancashire Fusilier commando platoons.

Chapter 10

Indaw and the Battle at Thetkegyin

There would be little rest for 16 Brigade at Aberdeen. Japanese reinforcements were moving into the Indaw area and Wingate wanted the assault to go in while it still had a chance of succeeding. Within days of the launch of Operation 'Thursday', the Japanese had crossed the Chindwin at several points, attacked the 17th Indian Division under General Cowan at Tiddim, and were marching in strength for Imphal and Kohima. The reason for the Japanese offensive was directly related to Wingate's expedition the previous year. Up to that time, the Japanese Army Command had thought the countryside just east of the Chindwin to be impassable for any substantial force of troops and had adopted a policy of defence. Wingate had proved them wrong and caused a rethink of Japanese plans. If one brigade could invade Burma in 1943, perhaps the whole British Army would come in 1944? Perhaps it would be better to invade India first?

Operation 'U-Go' was the result. It would begin with an advance against Stilwell's Chinese in the north. After securing their right flank they would cause a diversion in the Arakan to tie down the British 15th Corps and then launch a major offensive across the Chindwin, with the aim of capturing Imphal and its large supply depots and advancing over the Naga Hills to capture 14th Army's base area at Dimapur, which extended for ten miles on both sides of the railway. The Japanese could not carry enough supplies with them to sustain their offensive and they had no air supply capability; they would have to take what they wanted from the British supply depots. Thereafter the victorious Japanese could continue on into northern India where they hoped to be greeted as liberators by a population who wanted to see the back of the British.

Operation 'Ha-Go' was launched in the Arakan on 4 February and a month of bitter fighting followed. Operation 'U-Go' began on 7 March when three Japanese divisions (15th, 31st and 33rd) crossed the Chindwin and headed for Imphal, Kohima and Tiddim. Wingate had correctly assumed that a Japanese offensive was on the cards and he was right. A week after it began he had Mike Calvert's 77 Brigade established at White City and Joe Lentaigne's 111 Brigade was in as well. If 16 Brigade could take the all-weather airfields at Indaw, the 36th British division could be flown in, or so Fergusson thought. General Slim was

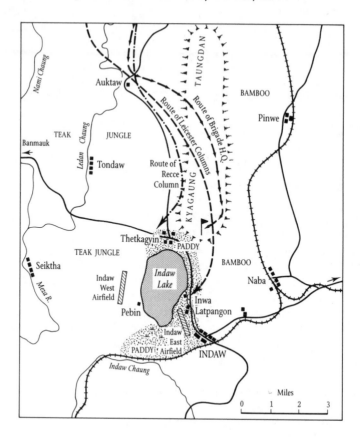

16 Brigade's advance on Indaw.

aware that the Japanese logistic system was in poor health and the further he could stretch it the better. He planned to retire in good order on Imphal and fight the Japanese on ground of his own choice. There would be plenty of work for the Chindits. Not only could they cause chaos in the rear areas of the enemy divisions facing Stilwell, but they could perform the same service against the rear of the divisions invading India as well.

On 23 March Wingate flew into Aberdeen and discussed the plan of attack on Indaw with Fergusson. Four columns would attack from the north while two others would work separately, one blocking the road from Indaw to Banmauk and the other circling round Indaw to attack from the south. The Leicesters were already in the forests north of Indaw and they would lead the attack. The Queen's were at Aberdeen and Fergusson would have liked to have used them together with the Leicesters, but that would have meant that 45 Recce would have to be sent off to carry out the two independent tasks and they had still not reached Aberdeen. Therefore the two Queen's columns were sent off to the west and south. 45 Recce would attack Indaw with the Leicesters.

Wingate's plan was for the attacking force to approach Indaw along the Kyagaung Ridge, which ran north to south. This might avoid the main defences and bring the attackers straight to the town and one of the two airfields. Wingate insisted that the attack went in right away. There were already two or three thousand Japanese in Indaw and the surrounding area and to rest the columns for a couple of days might allow more reinforcements to arrive. The main assault would therefore be carried out by 1,800 men who had just completed a march of 400 miles without even a day's rest.

Fergusson was faced with a dilemma. Despite Wingate's plan to approach Indaw along the Kyagaung Ridge, the area through which the four attacking columns must march was as dry as a bone. There was water in the Ledan Chaung a couple of miles to the west of the ridge, and water in Indaw Lake. Fergusson decided to attack Indaw from the Ledan, the nearest water to his objective. However, the Japanese were waiting for them. Two columns from another brigade had passed through the area a couple of days previously and had informed the locals that they were planning to attack Indaw. They said this to disguise their real destination, in ignorance of 16 Brigade's plans. The Japanese were also well aware that the area was bereft of water and deployed their troops accordingly, in two villages to the north of the lake and around its shores as well. When 45 Recce and the Leicesters reached the village of Auktaw, they bumped the Japanese and a fire fight began. The Leicesters cleared the village and then turned left, heading for the Kyagaung Ridge and thence to Inwa by the lake. 45 Recce was sent straight ahead to pass through Thetkegyin, reach the lake, water themselves and then join up with the Leicesters. Fergusson pulled back his Brigade Headquarters of sixty mules and 200 men and the battle commenced. The story of the next few days is told by some of those who were there.

John Knowles can still recall the long walk into Burma with 16 Brigade. He was an American citizen who went to Canada in June 1941, six months before Pearl Harbor and just after his eighteenth birthday, to join the Royal Canadian Air Force. Sent to India as a pilot officer in March 1943 he flew Hurricanes until December when the call went out for RAF volunteers to join Special Force as air liaison officers. Attracted by the sheer adventure of the thing, he volunteered and was given the good news that he would be promoted to Flight Lieutenant. The bad news, although he did not know it at the time, was that he would have to walk a thousand miles to earn it:

'I was posted to the 2nd Battalion, the Queen's Royal Regiment (Royal West Surreys) to replace a drop-out, a fellow RAF officer who could not cope physically due to a wound he had suffered in the Middle East. We were trucked ninety miles down the Ledo Road, from which we kicked off, on foot, over what the lads ever afterwards referred to as "them fuckin' hills". General Wingate personally saw us off with a prayer service and led a couple of rousing hymns. We were the only brigade that marched, or more precisely, climbed, slithered and generally struggled our way in, the other brigades being flown in a month later by the Air Commandos.

'I was with 22 Column and we only really engaged in one major battle. We were pretty thoroughly exhausted physically. It was, above all, the three-week slog through "them fuckin' hills" that did it. Having carried up to 100 pounds through 400 miles of the worst conceivable terrain, we were walking skeletons, without reserve energy and subject to hallucinations; in my case, aural, in Brigadier Fergusson's case, visual. He told me when I visited him in New Zealand in the late 1960s, where he was Governor General, that he saw the trees in the forest all decorated and lit up like Christmas trees!

'Our one big battle took place on 26 March, a couple of days after Wingate's death, which was unknown to us at the time. It was at Milestone 20 from Indaw, on a major highway leading west to the front at Imphal. This was a great place for an ambush. A hill sloped down, at about a twenty-degree angle to the road, which ran parallel to a river, separated by perhaps a hundred yards of flat, relatively open country. At the road, the slope of the hill ended in a short bluff – about a three-foot drop. Our soldiers were spread along approximately 1,000 yards of the road, on the uphill side, and our engineers mined the opposite side of the road, with trip-wired hand grenades, to greet any of the enemy who ran in that direction. "Lifebuoy" flame throwers were stationed at both ends of the ambush to trap any vehicles caught in between them and to prevent them from escaping in either direction.

'The morning before we sprang the ambush, and while we were still getting into position, a solitary saloon car drove through, heading from Indaw towards Imphal. The soldiers on watch allowed it to pass unmolested and were subsequently much criticised by Lieutenant-Colonel Terence Close, the column commander. It was reasoned that the car could have been carrying a senior Japanese officer, the bagging of whom would have been quite a prize. At the same time, it could have been a decoy, deliberately sent to trigger off the trap into which, a few hours later, a large Japanese truck convoy was to fall. It must be borne in mind that our strongholds were all established, that the whole area was crawling with our columns, that the Japs knew this, and accordingly had become extremely nervous about the likelihood of running into ambushes, especially on a major supply route like this one.

'After the passage of the vehicle, we took up our final positions. At about 0230 in the morning of 26 March, I was awakened by gunfire and hastily pulled on my boots, which, against orders, I had removed. A long convoy of Japanese military lorries was moving through our 1,000-yard ambush area, heading for Imphal. The first couple of vehicles had been allowed through, before the main body of lorries arrived. The first of these was incinerated by a flame thrower, the others, crowding up behind, were trapped by similar burnings at the eastern (Indaw) end of the ambush. As I recall, we caught some twenty-five or thirty vehicles in the trap. The enemy soldiers apparently jumped from the trucks and headed for the other side of the road, into the area mined by our engineers. While lots of small arms fire was exchanged, we took no casualties, as best I can recall, during this first phase of the action. As for me, I crept as close as I could get to the road, while still under cover, to try to get a fix on what was happening. Although it was a very dark night, there was some light from the burning vehicles. A comrade, Lieutenant Walker-Brash, slid over to me and proposed that we go to the western (Imphal) end of the ambush and see if we could do any damage. Having reached our objective, we heard Japanese soldiers calling to each other in the darkness, obviously trying to regroup. I pulled a pin and threw a number 36 Mills bomb right into the centre of where the voices were coming from. Unless it hit some luckless Jap on the head, it didn't do any harm. I waited for the 'BOOM!' but it never came. Walker-Brash then threw a grenade with a much more satisfactory result.

'Things quietened down as the Japanese survivors withdrew. At first light we inspected the site. There were many dead Japs but no casualties on our side. At least one of the lorries was a Pay Corps vehicle and we picked up wads of worthless Japanese occupation currency, printed in English, with the words "The Japanese Government" prominently displayed. At about 0900 hours the expected enemy force arrived. We were well entrenched on the hill and repelled a number of attacks. Our soldiers were dug in as well as they could manage, in some depth, in the undergrowth along the line of the road. Each time their attacks were repelled, on a number of occasions the Japanese soldiers retreated across the relatively open area between the road and the river, and our Bren gunners had a field day, shooting them down like clay pigeons. It was in the course of one such Japanese fall-back that Lieutenant Harry Sparrow was killed, while trying to lead a charge against the retreating enemy. I did not personally witness this, and believe the facts may have been hushed up for obvious reasons, but I was reliably informed by several Chindits who took a direct part in that particular action that Sparrow had jumped up from a concealed position, intending to drop to the road, just as a Bren gun was fired from his rear, and that he took a full burst in the back, killing him instantly.

'At this time many of our officers, and a number of other ranks, were stretched out prone in a line along a ridge at the top of the hill. The column commander was six or seven bodies to my left. Before us was a stretch of about twenty yards of exposed twenty-five-degree slope, without cover to speak of, while most of our force was dug in and fighting from positions in the brush along the roadside at the bottom of the hill. The Japanese managed to get at least one sniper, armed with a machine-gun, up one of the tall trees facing us at the bottom of the hill, making it somewhat difficult and dangerous to cross the open area between our command position and the bulk of our soldiers. One of our chaps, Private "Chippy" Woods, was wounded down near the road, and a call went up for an aid man to come to his assistance. I called to the column commander asking for permission to go after the wounded soldier. The word was passed down the line that I was to remain where I was. I pretended to mishear the order, called out "Thank you Sir!" and flew down the slope. Unfortunately I had overestimated my strength and underestimated both the weight of the wounded man and the steepness of the hill. I could not carry him on my back and had to take his left arm around my shoulders and try to support and walk him up the hill. It was a slow and agonising business and there were quite a few bullets flying about. I don't know why we were not hit, unless the enemy had uncharacteristically taken pity on us. Once at the top we discovered that he had been hit through the middle and, to try to cheer him up, I told him how lucky he was to catch a "Wingater" a word play on the name of our great General and Chindit slang for a wound light enough not to be fatal, but serious enough to require evacuation to hospital – thus "winning the gate!" In fact, he not only had the death pallor on him, but also knew himself that he was finished. He tried to smile at my fatuous attempts to comfort him and towards the end I had the strangest feeling that, dying as he knew he was, he was trying to comfort me! A short while later he was gone.

'Leaving this battle area was remarkably easy. During a lull in the fighting, at about noon, we buried our six dead and simply walked away into the jungle. Another Chindit column took up the same position some weeks later and found that our dead had been exhumed, suspended by the feet and used for bayonet practice by the Japanese.

'I must also pay tribute to two other RAF officers who were with us. The other Queen's column was number 21 and my equivalent was Flight Lieutenant Gillies, a famous character who hailed from Doncaster and had won the Distinguished Flying Medal as a sergeant-pilot in the Battle of Britain. Out on patrol with an infantry platoon one day, they wandered into a village which contained several huge Japanese supply dumps. Taking careful note of their location, they then withdrew. He then arranged for two Hurricane aircraft to be flown in to Aberdeen. In one of these he flew over the area and, in the "Pathfinder" fashion, pinpointed the supply dumps for the attacking American bombers, who had specifically been called up for the purpose, and who successfully blew up the lot. It was learned after the war that this was the main supply of munitions stores for all of the Japanese forces attacking Imphal and Kohima and that its loss was a total disaster for them. "Gilly" was awarded the Military Cross, but never got to wear it. It had been decided to keep the Hurricanes at Aberdeen and a few days later "Gilly" took off in one and disappeared, down somewhere in the jungle. Our brigade squadron leader took off a day or two later in the second Hurricane and disappeared in the same way. I have often wondered if, when ordered to supply two Hurricanes for these operations, some very clever bastard saw it as an opportunity to get rid of a couple of clapped-out old bangers. Both "Gilly" and the squadron leader were top quality pilots – it had to be the machines. I could only hope they would not send in yet another one and order me to fly it.

'After a few more weeks it was apparently decided, at the highest level, that we were too exhausted to be an effective fighting force, and we were accordingly flown out from Broadway to Comilla the night of 18/19 May, just before Broadway itself was shut down.'

Sergeant Joe Adamse was in charge of the mortar section in the support platoon in 22 Column. They were armed with two three-inch mortars, two Vickers machine-guns and four flame throwers. The mortars were carried by two mules, 'Gert' and 'Daisy' who could not be separated; they later learned that they had previously been paired pulling a wagon. Joe also recalls the terrible hills:

'The hills were so steep that all the equipment had to be passed up hand-to-hand and then the mules and ponies led up. It was so steep that the engineers had to cut steps in the hillside in order that we could get a footing. The gradient in places was one in one. One memory of the climb over the Naga Hills was the rain, terrific heat and then we bedded down on the hillside and woke next morning covered in frost.

'On the march one of my men twisted an ankle while crossing a chaung (dry river bed). I helped him along, but we gradually dropped behind the main column. We marched until it became pitch dark and I felt it would be prudent to bed down for the night and carry on next morning to catch up with the column. This was quite an awesome experience – every jungle sound kept you on edge, so sleep was out of the question. After lying quietly for some time, a torch suddenly shone on us and two rifles pointed at us, a truly heart-stopping experience! Fortunately it was one of our own officers and a Sergeant who had also been left behind – a great relief, believe me!

'While marching we had a ten-minute rest in each hour – to say that we were ready for it is an understatement. At one such rest period there was an uncanny silence and everything seemed to stay still, even the mules. Suddenly a whirlwind hit us, breaking branches off trees and blowing foliage all around. This only lasted for about thirty seconds, but it was quite scary.

'We reached the Chindwin on 29 February after 110 miles. Gliders flew in and landed on a sandbank in the middle of the river. The tall trees on each side made this a very hazardous operation. One of the gliders was flown in by Jackie Coogan, ex-husband of Betty Grable. They brought in boats which were used to take equipment over, while the men and mules swam the 300 yards across. The gliders were picked up again by plane. A tow line was slung from a tree at each side of the river and connected to the glider. A Dakota then flew down the river valley and hooked on to the tow line, pulling the glider up into the air again and towing it back to base.

'The food rations were mainly American K rations, an individual pack for each day, supplemented at times with bully beef. Many of us found that until we got used to them, we had diarrhoea; for some it seemed to last for a long time. I personally found them enjoyable and of course the five cigarettes they contained were most welcome. After several months of these rations we had what some pundit called a luxury drop of supplies, which included fresh bread and bacon. After a good feed of this, many had upset stomachs.

'The treatment to counteract malaria was a daily dose of mepacrine tablets for everyone and every seven days a crash dose of, if I remember correctly, three tablets. These had the effect of giving one a yellow complexion. Of course they did not stop you getting malaria, but suppressed its effects until you ceased taking them, so when we eventually returned to base it was into hospital and then the full effects of the malaria took its toll. In all, in my service in Ceylon, India and Burma, I had malaria six times. While I was recovering from one bout in the hospital in Chittagong I helped some of the unfortunates whose nerves had been badly affected and could not hold a spoon to feed themselves. I often wonder if they ever recovered. I recall while we had one brief skirmish with the enemy one of my soldier friends, who had been in Singapore when the Japs invaded and eventually escaped with some others in an open boat, went completely to pieces and had to be assisted to continue the march. Fortunately it was a temporary effect and in fact he visited me after the war and thanked me for the help given to him at the time.

'On 26 April, the brigade was ordered to return to India, so the march of fifty miles to Broadway began. A lot of exhausted and many sick men were pleased to be on their way out, but still had to climb the 3,000-foot hills. The journey took seven days. On 3 May we reached Broadway and some were flown out each night to Comilla. A lot of the men went straight into hospital with fever, malaria and sores caused from insect bites. It is ironic that, having endured and survived the long march and the fighting, one plane crashed and an officer and several men were killed.'

Joe returned to England as an instructor at 206 OCTU in Derbyshire, but still had problems shaking off the jungle:

'The method we used for awakening the men in the jungle was to shake their foot, as this seemed to rouse them quietly without a sudden jump or shout. My wife soon learned to do this when I got home, after experiencing my sudden and aggressive attitude when aroused by shaking my body. Some nightmares were the norm for quite a few months and on one occasion I had grabbed my wife around the throat and almost strangled her. Fortunately she managed to wake me, but she was terribly shaken.'

The other Queen's column was number 21, tasked with circling around to the south of Indaw. One of its objectives was the jail, which was said to contain British prisoners. Various historians have alleged that the column 'was ambushed and as a result the unfortunate Colonel Metcalf lost all his radios'. A very indignant signaller, Mr George Hill, would like to set the record straight:

'On the evening of 25 March, our column commander, Lieutenant-Colonel John Metcalf, had intended to set up night bivouac immediately after crossing a river called the Sedan Chaung, which we reached just before dusk. The chaung flowed into the southern end of Indaw Lake, which lay just off to the north-west of Indaw itself. However, it was found that the banks were very steep and the river deeper than expected and with darkness falling it would have been impossible to get the whole column across before nightfall. The CO decided to turn back from the river and ordered the setting up of night bivouac.

'What seems not to have been noticed was that the HQ section of the column, including the signals detachment, was actually straddling a track which cut across our line of march at right angles. We were at that point in the most vulnerable position in which it was possible to be, so I suppose what followed was inevitable. Perception, no doubt, had been blunted by being at the end of a very long, arduous and tedious day's march – we were making all speed possible to get to the south of Indaw – and the morale-destroying problem of having been without water for almost a day and a half. In Burma this could, in itself, have created fatal results within a short period of time. One could argue that the cards were most definitely stacked against us on this occasion. Our HQ section of the column would normally be in the centre of a circle and protected by perimeter guards, but our 400 men and 100 mules were still in single file behind us and it takes a considerable length of time for the "tail of the snake to coil around its head".

'Our Corporal was on the far side of the track, hurling our forty-foot open aerial up over a tree branch and our other two signals men had off-loaded the wireless equipment from the mules and were starting to unpack. I was slumped with my back propped against a tree, wondering whether I would ever get to my feet again, – and not much caring one way or the other. Suddenly I heard the Colonel yell "My God, stand to!" Three trucks, loaded with Japanese troops, had arrived along the track, smack in the middle of us, and nobody had heard them coming. Within seconds all hell was let loose, with bullets flying around and ricocheting off the trees all over the place. Our Corporal arrived back like a scalded cat – he hadn't carried his rifle! Grenades then started crumping and the Japanese set up with their usual unnerving screaming, which they kept up for most of the night, somewhere away in the jungle. Shortly after the action began, by which time it had gone dark, I heard someone shout "The CO's been hit!" He had, but luckily not fatally. He was evacuated shortly afterwards and Major Clowes took over. A little after this someone realised that the signals section was where it ought not to have been, except on the march – right up front! We were told to pack up and get back to the river. This was where I confirmed what I had already suspected; that it is just not possible to load a mule from one side only. Nobody wanted to be on the side from which the bullets were arriving! When we got to the river, we found that it was still too dangerous to try to cross and, by the way, where the devil was every-one?! Apparently the order to disperse had been given in the meantime.

'We moved back to the area in which the fighting had started, to find only a group of abandoned mules. What the hell to do now? Fortunately we shortly ran into a body of our own men and followed them, crossing over the river in a much safer place than before. Later the following day we were joined by the dispersal group under the command of the cipher officer, Lieutenant Phillips, and with which group we should have been. This group had lain "doggo" all night around the initial battle area. Phillips was a very worried man, believing that the whole signals detachment had possibly "bought a packet" and that all the wireless equipment had been lost. If we had not met up with the other dispersal group he could well have been right!

'The high tension under which we were all living twenty-four hours a day manifested itself later the same day. A shot was suddenly heard and within seconds the whole column had disappeared from the track! Obviously everybody thought that the Japanese had found us again, but it turned out to be one of our own men jarring his Sten gun climbing over an obstruction across the track. This was a fairly common problem with most of the earlier Sten guns.

148

'I never found out the extent of our casualties, although a figure of thirty was mentioned. We did, however, lose a lot of mules together with the heavy equipment and ammunition that they had been carrying. A little later on I witnessed the largest defaulters parade I ever saw while in the Army – around sixty to seventy men drawn up in three ranks in a clearing. These were men who had lost weapons, equipment or animals in the skirmish. What punishment they received I have no idea.

'By the morning of 27 March we were in position to the immediate south of Indaw, waiting only for the order to go in. It never came. Whether we were in any fit state to do so is very much open to conjecture. Not only had we lost a large amount of equipment but we were in a parlous condition, not having had any respite from marching for anything other than an overnight bivouac since leaving Hkalak Ga more than five weeks previously. We continued on to Aberdeen, arriving there on 10 April. Eventually we were flown out of Broadway.'

Signaller Philip Sharpe was part of Colonel Cumberlege's headquarters group when 45 Column led the Reconnaissance Regiment into its first action. It was Sunday 26 March, the forty-third day since the start of their trek into Burma:

'As we pressed on towards Thetkegyin there was an air of foreboding. All was quiet around us and as the tension increased, the only sounds were the hoofs of the mules as they scuffed the hard-baked track, and the odd nervous remark. The scrub became more sparse, the sun became unbearably hot and our shirts were sodden with sweat. No orders had been given about the scarcity of water and many began to drain their water bottles to quench a mounting thirst.

'After two hours we halted in the scrub on the edge of an expanse of paddy. We could see a dirt track road about thirty yards ahead, the main road between Indaw and Banmauk. At the other side of the paddy we saw the huts of the village of Thetkegyin. Almost at once, sporadic firing broke out to our left and within minutes this became a fusillade of shots with long bursts, as machine-gun fire was exchanged with the Japs holding the village. Mortar bombs began to fall behind us; one exploded as it hit the treetops overhead with a deafening roar. Branches, leaves and shrapnel showered down around us. A hail of bullets whistled fan-wise overhead, ricocheting off the trees. One mortar bomb exploded between our two signal mules and one was torn apart by the blast, the blood splattering all around us. Our wireless set was reduced to pieces of torn metal. Simultaneously, two yellow lorries pulled up in a cloud of dust no more than fifty yards away. How the Japs failed to see us was amazing, because we were not in solid jungle. They ran into the thickets behind us, presumably to encircle the rear of our column. I vividly remember that some had machine-guns

149

and all were wearing white vests, jungle green slacks and soft PT shoes. They were huge fellows, nothing like the Japanese we had expected.

'We felt doomed and without direction, when in the next few seconds there occurred probably the most fortunate moment in my whole life. Unbelievably, across the other side of the road Colonel Cumberlege was leading a group of men parallel to us away from the battle. We tore across the track to catch up with the fast disappearing huddle of men with the column commander.'

Colonel Cumberlege led the men away from the battle in a westerly direction through a thickly wooded teak forest and after a short march they halted in a shallow depression. As other small parties arrived, Sharpe realised that the location was the RV chosen by the Colonel before leaving Auktaw that morning. It was five o'clock in the afternoon, two hours after their first brush with the enemy and 45 Reconnaissance Regiment had ceased to be commanded and no longer existed as an integral unit. Apparently Cumberlege had decided to disperse his column, but only sixty out of the 450 men in his column arrived at the RV, leading one to assume that either the rest did not hear the dispersal order or found it hard to comply due to the fact that the area was swarming with Japanese. The junior column, 54, under Major Varcoe, remained largely intact. All were now fighting for their lives. Captain Peter Taylor was the recce platoon commander of 45 Column, but he and his men found themselves acting as the defence platoon for Column HQ as soon as fighting broke out.

'When we bumped the enemy they were surprised and the company under Major Ron Adams achieved some success. However, as no recce had been organised nor any admin area selected, they were equally unprepared and attacked while still wearing their heavy packs; the Japanese on the other hand appeared to be in PT kit. After a couple of hours, or possibly less, I cannot remember, the CO ordered First Dispersal and our group set off for the RV, at the mouth of a small chaung where it entered the lake high up on the north-east shore. The RV was in enemy hands, so the CO chose another RV and sent me with three men to find the other groups. This was a fairly tall order as the groups knew they had to arrive at the original RV by circuitous routes, but it was clear that the CO was absolutely exhausted and unable to think properly. He was a very good officer, very keen to leave the staff in Delhi and get to the war proper. He was just over the maximum age of forty allowed for people joining the Chindits. He would not ask his men to do anything he could not do himself and for most of the march he refused to adopt the standard and well understood practice for column commanders to have their packs carried on a mule, so they would be in good shape for sizing up situations and taking the necessary action. Off I went with Sergeant Morris and two others and we soon located Major Adams and his men. He had refused off his own bat to allow his company to be broken up into smaller groups for dispersal, with a view to having a proper fighting force with him. We searched for other groups but were seen by a Jap patrol and had to run for it. We followed the trail made by Ron Adams until we lost the Japs, then lay down for some sleep.

'Early next morning we caught up with the company as they approached a collection of huts on stilts. My Burmese talked to the inhabitants and discovered that there was a stream a few yards ahead and that Japanese troops were in the lantana on the east bank, covering it. This I passed on to everyone as they filed by, but the overwhelming desire for water overcame common sense and mules and men rushed to the stream and started to drink. They did not stay a moment when the enemy opened fire. Ron ordered everyone to get back into the cover of the thick lantana behind us (we had crossed the stream) while he, myself, and I think, Lieutenant Dudley Wynter gave covering fire. Quite soon we were on our own and withdrew to join the rest, but Ron was wounded and unable to move. He told us to get out and he was last seen propped up firing away, a brave and intelligent man with a high moral sense who would have been an influence for good had he returned to civilian life after the war. I found a dozen men in the scrub and organised them into a section of sorts. They were very shaken, but we, or rather I and one other, kept on shooting at the enemy whenever he got close. In a short while they broke off the action and we, still very thirsty, withdrew into the thicker scrub and lay up until nightfall. We then slaked our thirst in the stream which must have been used as a lavatory for a hundred villages upstream and set off for Aberdeen.'

Lieutenant Roger Brewer was with 13 Troop, 54 Column and noted in his diary the events of 26 and 27 March:

'Today and the following days I shall never forget as long as I live. How good it is to be alive to write. We were leading troop and set out at six a.m. to go down the road (madness) to Thetkegyin. We moved off and marched for an hour – awful strain – never knowing quite what was going to happen. Finally saw Jap prints followed by naked feet. Must have been close then. First shot fired about ten a.m. and then things happened quickly. Bill Langley wounded. Gave him morphia but he died later. Pearce in good position and sounded as if he was doing good work. Tried myself to get round to the left flank but they had us absolutely beat. Once we were in position we dare not move for snipers. Managed to get Jimmy on wireless. He went round to the right and did good work. Finally got to top of hill. Killed and wounded about twenty Japs. Very pleased. Dying of thirst. No hope of water. Stayed in position until four p.m. and then moved round to bivvy.

'Had fairly peaceful night, but first thing in the morning they attacked. Vickers machine-gun was wonderful. People now starting to drink own urine. About ten a.m. John (Burma Rifles) found water by digging in chaung. He definitely saved the column. Had to go and guard water point and drank myself stupid (mostly sand). Moved at about three p.m. and were attacked again. 15 Troop held position while we got out. Awful time looking after sick and wounded. Got onto ridge and again were machine-gunned and mortared. John hurt but Japs were very inaccurate. Sergeant Poole put out their mortar and we settled down for our night vigil. Thought they were certain to attack us, but we were lucky and they did not. The column is in pretty poor shape. Twenty killed and twenty wounded.'

The next morning they moved out back towards Aberdeen. Captain Jimmy White was waiting for Roger Brewer and his men when he finally got back to Aberdeen on 1 April. He had been in the thick of the fighting. While 45 Column disintegrated after their commander decided to disperse his men, 54 Column stood and fought. When interviewed by the author fifty years later, Lieutenant-Colonel Jimmy White, now chairman of the Chindits Old Comrades Association, commented: 'I don't remember 45 Column taking part at Thetkegyin and I was fighting there all day and lost a lot of soldiers.'

The riflemen of 54 Column spent the best part of that day killing Japanese soldiers and being killed themselves. Five times Jimmy White ordered his men to fix bayonets and five times he led them forward. For his actions that day he was to receive the Military Cross. 54 Column Headquarters was some way behind them, but not far enough away from the fighting for their own safety. Cyril Baldock was the animal transport officer: 'Suddenly there was chaos and fire everywhere. The Japs had hit the lifebuoy fuel for the flame throwers and it blew up, setting fire to the mules and the jungle around us. Terrified, burning mules careered through the jungle setting the tinder-dry trees alight. Ammunition began to explode as the fire took hold.' Jimmy White was told over the walkie talkie that Column Headquarters was about to pull out to try to find water and to evacuate the casualties. He pulled his rifle company back and joined up with them, moving three or four miles eastwards in an attempt to get to high ground. There they found a dried-up chaung, where a lot of digging produced a tiny amount of water which they gave to the wounded.

When the battle began, Number 10 Troop under Lieutenant Tony Musselwhite circled around to the right flank. Sergeant Ernie Rogers recalled:

'Going up the hill we spotted some Japs moving across the ridge. Sergeant-Major Parker came up and said, "Those Japs aren't second-line troops as our intelligence would have us believe, they look tall enough to be Imperial Guard." We arrived at Column Headquarters where Major Varcoe had been attacked; there were lots of dead Japs about. We laid up with the Japs attacking us. Paddy Flynn was on the Vickers, covering a path along which the Japs were trying to encircle us, and he would not be relieved. He was later awarded the Military Medal. Our mortar platoon was called up to fire mortars at close range with very high trajectory; the bombs were going straight up and straight down again. When the column pulled out in late afternoon, my section was the rear guard, obliterating tracks. We went the wrong way and passing along a dry chaung we looked over the edge to discover that we were next to a Jap lorry park. We hid up for the night and in the morning the eight of us set off for Aberdeen.'

Another member of 10 Troop who had a lucky escape was 5677328 Roy Vine, the troop sergeant:

'My memories of Thetkegyin are somewhat hazy, as I was suffering from malaria and pneumonia at the time. We killed a lot of Japanese and eventually they broke it off. When the fighting stopped, I went round the bodies and recovered their water bottles for the doctor to distribute to the wounded. While I was collecting the bottles I heard a "BANG" and as I put them down, blood poured from my arm and I realised that I had been hit with probably a grenade. The wounds were not serious and I dressed them with Jap field dressings taken from the dead.

'Somewhat later we were ordered to withdraw and my troop was designated as rear guard to the column. They moved off and somewhat later we left too, but went the wrong way and bumped into the Japs. After a bit of a skirmish we got through without losing very many men and headed for the hills to lay up and recover for a while. We could see Indaw Lake and later made our way down and got some water. We decided to march by night, with me leading with a compass. During the night I slipped down a rock bank into a dry stream bed and my hand went into a pool of water. The others came down and we all filled up and drank the water from the pond. When it was time to move on, I found it impossible and after a lot of arguing it was decided that I would be left. One of the chaps, I think his name was Gardener, stayed with me.

'When we awoke in the morning we found the water we had drunk was from the previous monsoon and was purple where vegetation had rotted, and it stank. How long we were there I don't know, but I decided that if I did not move I would lie there and die. We moved off and were later found by the Leicesters. Their doctor took my temperature and said "105.4. Can you march?" I said "Yes" and off we went. I remember saying to the chap in front "I'm going", and I was gone. When I came round, I was on the back of a pony, with my hands strapped to the saddle. I said to the chap with the pony "I'll get down and let someone else get up here." He said, "You have been up there for four days. You stay there." Later they got three light planes in and I was flown out to Aberdeen and back to India. I met the medical Sergeant afterwards and he told me that if they had not got me out that day, they were going to dig a hole for me.'

The morning after the battle, Major Varcoe produced a map and showed Captain White the route that he proposed to take to find water and get back to Aberdeen. It led through a narrow ravine. The Japanese were now on their trail again and Jimmy White was told to take five men and fight a rearguard action until the column was clear:

> 'As I lay in the defile firing at the Japs, I had my pack blown off my back by an exploding mortar bomb. I was very upset; it contained a brand-new four-ounce tin of tobacco sent to me from England by my girlfriend. It was blown to bits. Eventually we had shot off all of our ammunition and with the Japs now behind us we had to withdraw in the opposite direction to the column. The Japs followed in hot pursuit, guided towards us by the loud cracking of the dry teak leaves as we ran through them. We came to a dried-up chaung and I told the men to lay down and cover themselves with teak leaves. I said that we must be very tough mentally and not panic no matter how close they came to us, because our lives depended on it. We lay there for two hours and the Japs came within ten yards, but didn't find us. As we continued our journey, one of my men was coughing and in a poignant display of human nature one of the others said, "Sir, his coughing is going to give us away to the Japs. We have to kill him or they will hear us." I can still see the man's face as he waited for me to answer. I told them that we had come in together and we would go out together. Two days later we walked into Aberdeen.'

Captain Peter Taylor continues:

> 'At Aberdeen the CO and Major Varcoe were both flown out. Major Ted Hennings took over and the much depleted columns were organised into two companies; I was made company commander of the mainly 45 Column men and Captain Jimmy White remained commander of the other. Later Lieutenant-Colonel George Astell of the Burma Rifles was appointed commander. He was not a regular soldier and his tactical sense was almost non-existent, but he was an exceptionally brave man and a morale booster.'

A boost to morale was most certainly needed. Many brave men had died at Thetkegyin. Colonel Cumberlege had eventually scraped together two platoons of men and moved off to find the Leicesters. He linked up with them a couple of days later as they withdrew from Inwa. The rest of his column had broken up in disarray and 54 Column had been left to their own devices. Perhaps if he had summoned the powerful might of the Air Commandos, it might have been a different story. As the weary survivors struggled back to Aberdeen, little did they know that even heavier fighting lay ahead of them.

Only one battalion achieved its objective in the fight for Indaw and that was the 2nd Leicesters, commanded by Colonel C. J. 'Jack' Wilkinson. As they advanced they reached the village of Auktaw, defended by some men of the Burma Traitor Army and a few Japanese. The Leicesters cleared the village with the bayonet, but Jack Wilkinson was shot through the arm. He told the author in 1995:

'One should not talk about one's wounds, but mine always seemed of technical interest to doctors. Radius and ulna were both smashed, leaving a gap across which the bones had to re-grow. My medical officer, in the jungle with the kit he had on a mule, set my arm and put on a plaster so that I could continue in command of my battalion for the next five days. Everyone who knew the form said that when I got back to a hospital it would have to be re-broken and re-set. But my MO had done such a good job that the arm did not have to be touched until it had mended three months later. Eventually I played polo again. I cannot say, when I led the 2nd Leicesters south from Auktaw towards Indaw, that I was aware of the importance of those airfields. At the time there was much confusion of intentions by brigade and battalion officers, partly due to Wingate's sudden death and to a general break-down in communications. As the commander of the leading battalion I was never properly in touch with Fergusson after crossing the Chindwin, having, after Auktaw, to rely on messages by liaison officer. I understood my task was to block the road north through Inwa, which was being used by the Japs, and so help Calvert and Stilwell. This we did, I believe, most effectively, until ordered three days later to pull out. This small action convinced me that our organisation, equipment and training in 2nd Leicesters were satisfactory, as was our ability to use the support of No. 1 Air Commando.'

Lieutenant George Grossmith was a member of the Royal Engineer platoon that went into action with the 2nd Leicesters:

'We fought our first skirmish of the campaign at Auktaw and it took us a couple of hours to clear the place, costing us about ten casualties. The following morning, at 0200 hours, the fighting group of both columns, comprising the rifle companies, commando and support platoons, pushed off at high speed and in complete darkness down the Auktaw–Thetkegyin road, the first road we had seen since Namyung. The soft elements of the battalion were left behind to build a light plane strip and evacuate the wounded. Captain Hindmarch and myself were now completely respon-sible for our commando platoon, as Brown had been evacuated.*

'We carried on down the road until about an hour after dawn when we branched off into the hills to the east. The country here was very difficult, not the old densely covered mountains, but steep low hills covered with

* Each of the two columns had a platoon of Royal Engineers, known as the commando platoon (Wingate's designation, not really appropriate) and a platoon of Royal Artillery – support platoon, armed with Vickers MMGs and mortars.

high teak, mostly without leaves at that time of year. Also the hills were very dry, there being no perennial streams east of the Ledan Chaung. Our battalion must have looked a queer sight to any neutral observer, the Colonel in the lead with his arm in a red-stained sling, and his face as usual, grim and set, followed by 500-odd sweat-soaked soldiers toiling over those parched hills, each with a sixty-pound pack on his back. By this time a lot of the mules were in bandages too, as many had saddle galls, legs cut by sharp bamboo and many other infirmities. We were also feeling the effects of marching through 300 miles of country over which no organised army had ever campaigned before.

'About six miles after leaving the road we reached the end of the Kyagaung Range on a spur overlooking the south-eastern shore of the Indaw Lake, including the mouth of the Indaw Chaung, Letpangon and Inwa villages and Indaw West airfield. Indaw town itself was hidden by another spur, and lay to the south-east of our position. Our objective was Inwa village. The Leicesters were to come down from the hills, surprise and occupy Inwa on the Indaw–Thetkegyin road, and advance along the road north and south. 45 Recce Regiment was to advance down the Auktaw–Thetkegyin road, occupy Thetkegyin and drive on down the road on the east side of the Indaw Lake, thus sandwiching and annihilating the Japs between Thetkegyin and Inwa and eventually meeting the Leicesters advancing north from Inwa.

'The Leicesters arrived on the spur at about 1600 hours on 26 March. Here I was reminded that the fighting spirit of British troops cannot be rivalled by any other army in the world. We had not touched any source of water since leaving Auktaw, and every man had a healthy thirst and an empty water bottle. The only water in the area was Indaw Lake; between us and the lake was the Indaw–Thetkegyin road, Inwa village and the Japs. If we could not penetrate to the lake that night, our fighting capability would fall very rapidly to nil. From now on we operated as a battalion, and not by columns. The Colonel called his two company commanders together and gave his orders. Zero hour was 1700 hours and the platoons detailed for the attack moved off silently down the hill, not knowing whether they were going to bump an enemy platoon or a brigade. With a parting hail to those of us being left to guard the hill – "Don't worry boys, we'll have a drink waiting for you before you've got time to unpack your mugs" – they advanced down the hill. They knew the issues at stake: they had to capture water for their battalion, and capture it they would.

'They did. After a short brisk engagement they occupied Inwa, and secured beaches on the Indaw Lake and Indaw Chaung. The surprise was complete. An officers' mess was captured intact, also a Japanese imprest account. The Jap officers took to flight in a couple of canoes and put out on the Indaw Lake. Unfortunately for them they came very nicely into the arc of fire of a couple of Vickers machine-guns, mounted at the top of the hill by 17 Column to support the attack. A couple of very well directed bursts from these capsized the canoes and the occupants were not seen again.

'The following morning, 27 March, the Colonel decided to send a patrol to the east to reconnoitre a good mortar position overlooking Indaw town itself and to report on Jap activity in that area. We were asked to provide the patrol, so Captain Cann, the commander of the other RE platoon, Captain Hindmarch and myself, with a party of some twenty-five sappers, set out. We had gone about a mile and a half when the patrol came under fire from two Jap machine-guns, one firing down the track and one across it. I was near the tail of the patrol, while Cann and Hindmarch were just behind the point section. In an ambush like that you are likely to lose about ten men within seconds of fire being opened and I expected to find them all dead. As I crawled forward I found Cann and he ordered a withdrawal of all uncommitted men to a ridge about fifty yards back down the track, leaving Hindmarch and his section to extricate themselves as best they could. Hindmarch eventually turned up with two men short and ordered me to take four men and locate them. We found one sapper who had rolled clear with a bullet in his shoulder, but the other man, the Bren gunner, was dead and lying in full view of the Japs. There was no undergrowth to conceal us, just high teak, and we must have been clearly visible as we crawled closer. We got within about thirty yards and Sapper Terry ran up and got down beside the body as the Japs opened up on us. How they could have missed us from that range I'm hanged if I know, but miss us they did. I decided to get as close to the Japs as possible and then go in with the bayonet. I shouted my orders and we sprinted for a piece of dead ground about halfway to the Jap machine-gun post. The Japs started throwing hand grenades at us, but they were badly aimed and quite ineffective. I was getting my own Mills 36 grenades ready when I was hailed from behind and a Corporal gave me verbal orders from Hindmarch to withdraw immediately. I was somewhat relieved. We did not know how many Japs were in the position or if they were covered from further back. Hindmarch had realised that it was not worth incurring more casualties to recover one dead man and we returned to the battalion position.

'When we got back we found Sergeant X waiting for us. He had disappeared from the patrol as soon as fire was opened, made his way back and told the Colonel that we were pinned down, cut off and needed assistance to extricate ourselves – all completely untrue. He was charged with desertion in the face of the enemy and spreading false information of a grave nature and causing alarm and despondency. He was eventually brought before a Field General Court Martial convened in the jungle by officers serving with the battalion. He was reduced to sapper and transferred to a column of 2nd Queen's. The sentence was subject to confirmation and whether or not it was so confirmed at a later date, I do not know. About halfway through the afternoon of the twenty-seventh the Jap made his first determined attempt to kick us out. Their attack was pressed home hard, but our Vickers machine-guns proved their worth and we held them until dusk. All that night we were on tenterhooks expecting attack at any moment, but it was not resumed until the following day. The whole of that day we were heavily engaged. Inwa changed hands several times and our water point was cut. We lost many mules and a number of men who were watering them. Thereafter we had to draw all our water from the Indaw Chaung and even that was very hazardous and water parties were restricted to two a day to reduce casualties to a minimum. Later in the afternoon we got some fighter-bombers to soften up the Jap positions, which they did very effectively. Although the enemy was only about fifty yards away from our own forward troops the aircraft only caused one minor casualty to us. The air support just about saved the day. The troops' morale was bucked up enormously to see that they were not entirely on their own. We had seen nothing of the brigade for some time and had a rather desperate feeling of isolation.

'It was now our third night in the position and our mules were kept saddled in case we had to make a rapid departure. Our last mortar shell had been expended in trying to silence a Japanese machine-gun that had caused us many casualties and our ammunition was nearly exhausted. Wilkinson, despite our deteriorating position (and, incidentally, his broken arm) was determined to hold on to the last.

'Meanwhile Brigadier Fergusson was getting worried. The Recce Regiment had failed to achieve their objective, having been ambushed and scattered at Thetkegyin. They filtered back to Aberdeen in small groups, with the exception of two platoons under Lieutenant-Colonel Cumberlege who set out to find us. The Queen's were south of Indaw and one column had been forced to disperse and were out of wireless contact. We were the only battalion to achieve its objective and were holding the fort all on our own. On the morning of 29 March Fergusson ordered us to withdraw.

'That morning we pulled out by dispersal groups to an RV in the Auktaw area. Just as we were pulling out we were met by Cumberlege and his two platoons, who although very tired and battle-shaken had gallantly come to our assistance. As we moved back we had no interference from the Jap – I don't think he even knew we were going. Five minutes after our rear guard pulled out the aircraft came over again and gave him another pasting. We were not pursued.'

Brigadier Fergusson's plan to capture Indaw was probably doomed to failure from the start. In his book *The Wild Green Earth*, Fergusson mentions that after the Leicesters and 45 Recce began their advance, for three days and nights his 200-strong HQ column 'had continual thunderstorms and we were virtually deaf and dumb', a rather puzzling statement as he was only a couple of miles from the two battalions and their areas were as dry as a bone. What cannot be denied is that he was out of radio contact with his columns and also with Special Force HQ, which had moved out of Imphal to Sylhet as the Japanese advanced into India. At this most crucial time in the battle for Indaw, 16 Brigade was leaderless. Although it was hardly Fergusson's fault, his men were in desperate need of a good rest. There was no time to give the reconnaissance platoons the ten or fifteen miles' start they required, although short-range reconnaissance would have helped the Recce Regiment at Thetkegyin. Fergusson's biggest mistake, however, was that he had obviously forgotten Wingate's dictum 'Concentrate, concentrate, concentrate'. He had no reserve that he could use; the two Royal Artillery columns were days away, returning from Lonkin, and the two Queen's columns were involved with enemy forces in their own areas and could not assist. The Recce Regiment was scattered after a fierce fight at Thetkegyin, leaving the Leicesters to attack Indaw on their own. Perhaps if another battalion had joined up with them, it may have been a different story. Fergusson wrote later that if he had stuck to Wingate's original plan and sent both battalions down the range of hills called the Kyagaung Range, 'we might have pulled it off'.

Chapter 11

Death of a Warrior

Early in the morning of 24 March, Wingate flew into Broadway in an Air Commando B-25 Mitchell bomber. He boarded a light plane and flew on to see Mike Calvert at White City. They discussed the defences of the block and Wingate told Calvert that he had been awarded a bar to his DSO. 'Let it go to your heart and not your head.' When he left he said, 'Be of good heart. I will see that you lack nothing.' It was the last time Calvert would see his friend.

Thereafter Wingate flew on to Aberdeen and spoke to Lieutenant-Colonel Green of the Black Watch, who had just arrived by Dakota with some of his men. Fergusson was not there of course, he was on his way to attack Indaw. Then Wingate flew back to Broadway where his B-25 was waiting for him. While Wingate was touring his strongholds the pilots of the aircraft asked to see Lieutenant-Colonel Claude Rome, the commander at Broadway. 'They told me that they were not happy about the aircraft's serviceability. An engine was not developing its proper power. They asked me to persuade Wingate to wait for a relief aircraft, which they would call for. They were obviously rather in awe of Wingate and pretty worried young men.' However, Wingate would have none of it and the plane eventually taxied for take-off. Rome later recalled: 'As the chocks were pulled away, I caught the eye of the pilot on the near side of the cockpit. I smiled at him and gave the "thumbs up" signal. I remember very clearly his giving me a wave but no smile, and he made a grimace at me, pulling down the corners of his mouth. The aircraft fairly staggered off the runway, using every inch of it, and climbed very slowly. I thought he was flying one wing low.'

Wingate had an appointment with Air Marshal Sir John Baldwin at Imphal and after an uneventful flight he landed on time and had an amicable discussion, mainly about communication with 221 RAF Group headquarters now that Special Force headquarters had left Imphal. Afterwards Baldwin watched Wingate clamber into the co-pilot's seat of the aircraft, two journalists joined Wingate's staff in the belly of the aircraft, and they took off, heading for Assam. It was just after five p.m. A couple of hours later Wingate's aircraft crashed into the ground near the village of Pabram in the hills west of Imphal, killing all on board.

Two days later a search party reached the area and found the wreckage of the B-25. Nearby they found Wingate's Wolseley helmet and also a revolver belonging to his ADC George Borrow, which was bent in a complete semi-circle. Baldwin, who had left Imphal in his own aircraft and saw Wingate's B-25 flying on a level course up to six minutes before the crash, had his own explanation for the disaster. The pilot may have left his aerial trailing out of the aircraft in flight and the static electricity that it would have gathered may have shocked him into unconsciousness when he switched on to speak to Sylhet. He knew of similar cases. With the body of the pilot slumped over the controls, Wingate would not have been able to regain control and the co-pilot would not have been able to come forward in time to help. Perhaps with hindsight, Wingate should have been in the back of the aircraft, leaving the pilot and navigator to fly the plane, but who would have told Wingate no, had he insisted on a seat in the cockpit? Baldwin discounted weather conditions as a factor in the crash, but there had been a problem with one of the engines at Broadway. Could sabotage have been responsible? It was very unlikely, although one of Wingate's close friends, when asked by the author, suggested that there were one or two in Delhi who would have organised the demise of Wingate if they felt they had reason enough to justify such a terrible deed.

General Slim wrote an appreciation of Wingate after hearing of his death, which included the words: 'Genius is a word that should not be easily used but I say without hesitation that Wingate had sparks of genius in him. Someone has defined genius as "an infinite capacity for taking pains". Genius is not that. People who have an infinite capacity for taking pains are not geniuses. They are routine men fit for minor administrative posts. Wingate was not like that. Real genius has the power to see things more clearly than ordinary men can. This he had.' Prime Minister Winston Churchill went further than Slim in his words on Wingate. In the House of Commons he described Wingate as 'a man of genius who might have become a man of destiny'.

The problem, now, was who should inherit the mantle of the leader of the Chindits? Derek Tulloch, Wingate's Brigadier General Staff, was asked by Slim who he would suggest for the job. Tulloch recommended Joe Lentaigne, the commander of 111 Brigade, and Slim agreed at once. It was a fateful decision. Under the leadership of Lentaigne the Chindit concept of LRP was abandoned and Wingate's guidelines on strongholds forgotten. The majority of the Chindit casualties would occur from this point onwards. From the point of view of Slim and those in India who despised Wingate, Lentaigne was a good choice. Other potential candidates were ignored, including Symes, the original commander of 70th Division and now Wingate's official deputy division commander. He promptly asked for reassignment. When the author asked Mike Calvert why he thought he was not chosen, he said that Slim told him after the war the problem was his 'Mad Mike' nickname. In other words he was too much like Wingate. A tough, brave, resourceful fighter and Wingate's disciple from the beginning, Calvert would have been ideal.

What would Wingate have thought of Lentaigne taking over his job? When Wingate returned from the first expedition he was pleased to see that Wavell had enough faith in his LRP concept to raise a second Chindit brigade, the 111th, but was incensed that Wavell had appointed its commander, a prerogative Wingate deemed his own. Not only that, he had appointed an orthodox Gurkha officer, who was hardly a supporter of Wingate's ideas and methods. Bernard Fergusson later recalled in his book, *Return to Burma*:

> 'Lentaigne remained in command of 111 Brigade and I was sent down to him as second-in-command for two weeks before getting a brigade of my own. My doubts about him began from that moment. I had none about his courage, his skill or his integrity; you couldn't spend half an hour in his company without being sure of those. But he was too forthright to conceal his conviction that Wingate was a mountebank, and his ideas on strategy and tactics lunatic. Wingate had done nothing to make him welcome or to win him over and they disliked each other from the start.'

So what did the future hold for the Chindits? Let us review the state of Special Force at that time.

77 Indian Infantry Brigade had established a stronghold at Broadway and blocked the main road and rail line supplying the Japanese 18th Division facing Stilwell in the north. Two battalions from that division and two railway engineer companies had been decisively beaten and much information had been gained from the sack of Mawlu.

Morris Force and **Dah Force** were operating east of the Irrawaddy against the Bhamo–Myitkyina road. Morris, as the senior Colonel of 111 Brigade, was now promoted to Brigadier, although his forces amounted to only three columns.

16 British Infantry Brigade was about to try to capture Indaw and its airfields. By this time Wingate had little faith in the idea that Slim would fly in a division to take advantage of any gains and in the opinion of Mike Calvert, Wingate was really to blame for the attack failing, because the brigade was hustled into the attack without rest or reconnaissance (see *Prisoners of Hope*, p.94). Fergusson also forgot one of the basic rules of LRP fighting, whereby the columns move like fingers through the jungle, but combine as a fist to strike the target. However, the attack served to occupy Japanese troops who would otherwise have marched to attack White City. In addition, the discovery by one of the RAF officers attached to the brigade of a vast area of stores and ammunition and its subsequent destruction, deprived the Japanese High Command of its reserve ammunition for the division attacking Kohima. Fergusson had also established a stronghold, Aberdeen and the 6th Battalion, Nigeria Regiment was about to arrive as the garrison.

111 Indian Infantry Brigade had been landed on different sides of the Irrawaddy and were trying to regroup. On 27 March they would be directed to block the Pinlebu–Pinbon road, the main line of communication for the Japanese 25th Division.

Bladet Force had blown a bridge on the main railway line, some twenty miles south of Wuntho.

3rd West African Brigade was originally tasked to supply garrison troops for the various strongholds. Its 6th Battalion landed at Broadway on 9 March, but after a night encounter with a Japanese patrol on the way to Aberdeen it dispersed and would not reach Aberdeen until the end of the month. In the meantime the 7th and 12th Battalions were flown directly into Aberdeen and would later proceed to White City to join their brigade commander, Brigadier A. H. Gillmore. He would take over command of the block on 9 April, to leave Calvert free to pursue the enemy outside White City.

23 British Infantry Brigade was earmarked by Wingate to be inserted further south to block the lines of communications to the 31st Japanese Division.

14 British Infantry Brigade was beginning to arrive at Aberdeen and the Black Watch was given the task of blocking the Indaw–Banmauk road, recently cut by the Queen's. The rest of the brigade was to block the southern approaches to Indaw and White City, in place of 111 Brigade.

Across the border in India, 14th Army was reeling under the onslaught of 100,000 Japanese troops and could well have benefited from the activities of five brigades operating in the Japanese rear areas. Instead, they were to be placed under the command of American General 'Vinegar Joe' Stilwell. Leaving aside Stilwell's hatred of all things British, he was in fact in a very difficult position. The one thing that he had in common with Wingate was that they both wanted to get into Burma and fight the Japanese, but Stilwell was short of combat troops. The Chinese Generals had been told by Chiang Kai-shek to ignore Stilwell's orders to attack. Chiang had his own political agenda and it was not until 19 May that he told his Generals to advance. In the meantime, all Stilwell had to work with was the 3,000-strong brigade of Merrill's Marauders, trained by the Chindits but placed under Stilwell's command in January, plus a couple of regiments of Chinese under Stilwell's local command. Stilwell eventually drove his own men to mutiny and made such impossible demands of the Chindits, using them as regular infantry to attack fixed targets without support arms such as artillery, that many a Chindit would have cheerfully shot him on sight. Both the Marauders and the Chindits had been told that they would fight for three months only and then be flown out, preferably before the onset of the monsoon. It was not to be. 16 Brigade was exhausted after its long march and the fighting for Indaw and was flown out first. Calvert would eventually turn off his radios and lead the remnants of 77 Brigade out himself after their heroic fight for Mogaung. The other three brigades would fight through the monsoon, marching less than a mile a day sometimes if the weather was bad, with the men dropping like flies from exhaustion and sickness.

By the end of March the Japanese finally realised what they were up against at White City and put together a formidable force to throw the Chindits out. 24th Independent Mixed Brigade comprised two battalions from Bassein, two from Moulmein and two from Siam, supported by two batteries of artillery. A Chindit patrol captured a Japanese 15th Army order of the day, from General Mutaguchi, stating: 'Enemy moving large forces by air to rear of 18 Division. We will use large counter-attack force. Duty Army Group troops to annihilate enemy. Attack by night and use surprise.' In addition, two new Japanese divisions, the 2nd and 53rd, were entering Burma as reserves for the India invasion. The Chindits would eventually fight units from both divisions and delay their entering the Imphal battle.

On 5 April Calvert brought twenty-six Dakotas into his airstrip, carrying six Bofors anti-aircraft guns and four twenty-five-pounders, together with their crews and an advance party from the 7th Battalion, Nigeria Regiment. A week would pass before the rest of the battalion walked in from Aberdeen. In the meantime, the men of the 7th joined their fellows from the 12th Battalion, which was already in residence. As the Dakotas were landing a Gurkha platoon ambushed a Japanese patrol and papers inside their dead officer's pack identified them as being from the 2nd Division from Malaya. The storm was coming closer to White City. 20 Column Lancashire Fusiliers were also in residence and Bill Merchant of the Commando Platoon recalled their arrival and the events of early April:

'When we got near the block Mike Calvert was waiting for us, complete with his red Brigadier's hat and riding his pony. As he led us into the block we passed the body of a Japanese soldier who had obviously been hit by a flame thrower. One of our chaps went over and went through his pockets. Put me off my breakfast. Our commando platoon was given a position on saddle hill, with bunkers and trenches already dug halfway up facing south-east. Behind us was OP hill with a monstrous sand-bagged front. To our front was a lovely thick barbed-wire perimeter fence, some fifteen to twenty yards thick, sewn with mines and booby-traps.

'It was about the first week of April and I had just returned from a patrol and was starting to brew up for tea when all hell broke loose. Shells came raining in on the block, there was shouting and screaming from the Japs with a bugle blowing the charge. Starshells lit up the whole area, it was like a scene from Dante's Inferno, I thought the whole world had gone mad. Then our own two-inch mortars fired on our positions in error, but fortunately caused no casualties as we were in our bunkers and slit trenches. I had a Sten gun and stood up outside and fired magazine after magazine until the bloody thing packed up. It would fire a few rounds then misfire, so I went back to my rifle. It was one hell of a night. The Japs withdrew about midnight, then just as it was getting light and we were standing to they came back again, probably to carry away their dead. We were shattered as we had hardly had any sleep, but work had to go on throughout the day. Water had to be fetched from outside the wire, bunkers to be repaired, wounded to be taken to the casualty station etc Sleep was at a premium and then there was the bombing.

'One morning twenty-seven Jap medium bombers came over and bombed us. Just outside our position the jungle was on fire and we thought that phosphorus bombs had been dropped, but we had the last laugh as the six Bofors guns, which had only recently been flown in, shot down at least six of the attackers.

'Being on my own I was shifted from pillar to post and in a different position every night. Then Sergeant Harold Bottomly scrounged an EY (Easy Yielding) rifle with all the bits and pieces, discharger cup etc., which could launch a 36 grenade a fair way. Together with Captain Butler I did a recce outside the wire to where the Japs used to form up to attack the block. After a bit of practice I could lob grenades right into the area, so now I had a job to do when the attacks came in.'

The long-drawn-out battle continued from 6 to 11 April and the sequence of attack was the same each night. The enemy would start shelling the defenders at about five p.m., continuing until dusk. Just after last light he would attack the south-east perimeter through the jungle and would be met with a curtain of up to 500 mortar bombs on his forming-up areas. The rest would run into booby-traps and minefields before reaching the outer wire, where they would be lit up by two-inch mortar flares and mown down by the dozen Vickers machine-guns, plus small arms fire and grenades. Suicide parties carrying Bangalore torpe-does–pipes containing explosive–would try to push them into the barbed wire and detonate them to clear a path, but their bravery was in vain. The survivors would pull back and the fighting would die down. Sometimes a second attempt would be made at midnight and the bombardment would continue between two and four a.m. as the enemy tried to recover their dead. During the day the defenders repaired the wire, rebuilt their bunkers, evacuated any wounded and prepared for the next night attack. One daytime annoyance was a six-inch mortar or 'coal scuttle' which launched a shell large enough to penetrate most of the defenders' overhead cover. The shell was five foot five inches high and six inches in diameter. It would take thirty-two seconds from the 'thump' announcing its launch to its arrival. One day a shell burst near Mike Calvert as he threw himself to the ground. He was unhurt except for a cricked neck, but later blamed that on the fact that he threw himself to the ground at such a speed that his head did not have time to follow suit and got left behind.

Just before the Japanese began their attack on the Block Lieutenant John De Quidt took a section of Lancashire Fusiliers north up the railway line to meet their sister column, number 50. On arrival, Colonel Christie told him to escort a party of unarmed sick back to the Block and he was assured that there were no Japanese in the area. De Quidt recalls:

'On the way back we found a couple of railway wagons and, as there was a slight gradient in our favour, we loaded everyone aboard, took the brakes off and rolled gently towards the Block. As we approached it, a mortar bomb landed nearby and then some more. I thought it was our own people in the Block firing on us in error and I remember standing on the roof of one of the wagons trying to signal. It was only when a machine-gun opened up on us, with a different note to ours, that I realised that it was the Japanese firing on us. We promptly disembarked and took to the bush. As three-quarters of our group were sick, progress was very slow and we had to lie up, listening to the Japs searching for us, until night fell. Next morning we tried unsuccessfully to find 50 Column and had to lie up again. I had an uncontrollable fit of shivering which lasted an hour or so, presumably a reaction to stress; I am reassured by the fact that even Calvert has recorded a similar experience.'

Unbeknown to De Quidt, the day he ran into the Japanese on the railway was the day their new offensive on White City began. A few days later his party made it into the Block, but others were not so lucky. Christie's column sent a signal to the Block the day the offensive began, stating: 'Have left seven sick men track bridge BX566 61890491. Please arrange collection by jeep or AT cart.' 20 Column was unable to comply and the party was discovered by the Japanese, who used them for bayonet practice. Only one man survived.

On 11 April Joe Lentaigne ordered Calvert to form a counter-attack force outside the block and attack the enemy. He handed over command of the Block to Brigadier Gillmore of the 3rd West African Brigade and flew out to rendezvous with his new force. The 7th Battalion, Nigeria Regiment under Lieutenant-Colonel Peter Vaughan (35 Column) and his second-in-command Major Charles Carfrae (29 Column), was now assembled a couple of miles from the Block and they met Calvert when he landed by light plane at the rendezvous. Calvert instructed the battalion to establish a base south-west of White City, at Thayaung, from which he would launch the attack. As the various columns arrived at the rendezvous Calvert found he had a formidable force under his command: Tactical Brigade HQ with RAF detachment and defence company; 3rd Battalion, 6th Gurkhas; 7th Battalion, Nigeria Regiment; 45th Reconnaissance Regiment, about 450-strong, and 50 Column Lancashire Fusiliers, making a total of about 2,400 men. Calvert decided to attack Sepein, south of White City and Mawlu, a road and rail junction and headquarters of the enemy attacking White City.

Calvert's first attack went in with the Gurkhas leading and Sepein village was taken. However, they discovered that the main enemy position was beyond the village in the thick lantana scrub, through which the attackers could make little headway. Lieutenant Roddy Wilkins from 14 Troop, 45 Recce: 'Our men were drawn up under cover of lantana bushes with open dry paddy or scrub eastwards. Gillie Scott's troop tried to get across the open, but were repulsed with heavy losses and Gillie was killed. We were giving support with our two-inch mortars, but one of my Sergeants was killed beside me when his mortar exploded.' Calvert eventually withdrew his force with the loss of sixteen killed and thirty-five wounded.

The news from White City was not good. Brigadier Gillmore sent a message to Calvert on 17 April informing him that he could not guarantee to hold out. At this, Calvert decided to move north and attack the enemy from the rear, regardless of cost. Gillmore's conduct was controversial as Calvert's own officers in the Block knew nothing of the signal. True the enemy shelling had been severe and the Japanese had penetrated the wire at OP Hill, now held by Lieutenant-Colonel Pat Hughes's 12th Nigerians, but, the Nigerians counter-attacked and threw them out again. Thereafter many Japanese heads appeared on display in the Nigerians' dug-outs and one man achieved fame by despatching a Japanese soldier with a box of grenades, swung by its rope handle with deadly effect. Not long afterwards Brigadier Gillmore was flown back to India and his place taken by Brigadier Abdy Ricketts.

Calvert, under the impression that he had to relieve the pressure on White City at all costs, decided to concentrate his force and advance with the Reconnaissance Regiment in the lead, then when their advance slowed, to push the Gurkhas around the flank in an enveloping movement. The Lancashire Fusiliers and the 7th Nigerians would play a supporting role. At noon on 17 April the advance began and one hundred Japanese had been killed by dusk, including a large number surprised while bathing in the Mawlu Chaung. They bivouacked quietly for the night, only a mile south-east of White City. No fires were allowed as Calvert planned a surprise attack at dawn on the eighteenth. Captain Peter Taylor of the 45th Reconnaissance Regiment told the author:

'Having been told that we were going to be flown out to India after one further action, we were loaned to Brigadier Mike Calvert to form part of a force to attack the Japanese investing White City. Calvert's plan was for the Nigerians to guard a base some miles south of White City, while the rest of the force was to advance in the far from thick country in single file. 45 Recce was to lead, followed by the Gurkhas, and when we had run into the Japanese we were to hold them down while the Gurkhas executed a pincer movement round either side to sweep them away.

'We left our packs with the Nigerians and set off. My company was leading when in due course we came up against the Mawlu Chaung (water about ankle deep) and entrenched enemy. I was ordered to get across and form a bridgehead, and this I managed to do. However, no one followed me and eventually Jimmy White shouted to me to withdraw to "where the packs are". I heard afterwards that, very much out of character, the Gurkhas broke and ran. We recrossed the chaung as fast as possible as the Japanese were still in the area and in any order. I found myself with about ten soldiers whom I managed to collect and we set off south to the RV. Quite soon we came across a Corporal Brown (I think) giving water to a Sergeant of the support platoon who had been blinded during the action. When one considers the almost *sauve qui peut* atmosphere in the unit when personal safety appeared to come very much first, this was an act of real courage as Brown could have deserted his comrade without anyone being the wiser and I am happy to say that he eventually received the Military Medal for this. When congratulated he merely said he did not know what the fuss was about as anyone else would have done the same.'

Lieutenant Roger Brewer and his 13 Troop reached the edge of the chaung and looked across:

'I saw the Japs before they saw me. Their poor camouflage gave them away; the leaves and branches were drooping. I saw one Jap, fired a quick shot at him and dropped behind an anthill. The chap on my right, also behind the anthill, said, "Sir, I can see them sitting in their dug-out, shall I fire?" He did and there was a long silence. I gave him a cigarette, lit a match and turned to the man on my left. When I looked back he had been shot and killed. Mike Calvert came up and crawled to where I was, waving his revolver. "Where are the Japs?" he said. "They are about five yards ahead of you," I replied. He stood up and looked around, but they must have pulled back by then or he would have been killed. I saw about four or five of my chaps wounded, but there was absolutely nothing you could do for them. I heard that the wounded were well looked after by the Japs. Six months afterwards we got a letter from one of them in Tokyo, saying that he had been well looked after. This was the worst killing area for our officers; we lost ten or fifteen, including my best friend. I was the only subaltern to walk in and walk out again.'

Lieutenant Roddy Wilkins, 14 Troop:

'Suddenly I was aware of a strong blow to my right shoulder. I could no longer hold my rifle as my right humerus was shattered by a Jap bullet. Sergeant Newton slapped on a field dressing and before I knew what he was doing, gave me a shot of morphia. This and the shattered shoulder and arm put me effectively out of action, but at some stage I heard Major Ted Hennings shouting and urging his men forward. I think his column had managed to get closer to the chaung than ours, but he and many others were killed. After what seemed an eternity, on a blazing hot afternoon, the Jap machine-gun fire intensified and we got the order to retreat the way we had come. The effects of the morphia and the wound made me extremely sluggish and reluctant to move, but I was spurred on to run for it when the whole area was sprayed with machine-gun fire.'*

Sergeant Ernie Rogers of 10 Troop was in the thick of the fighting. His troop commander, Tony Musselwhite, had been killed:

'We were firing at the Japs across the chaung when my Bren gunner was hit and died. I think the bullet that killed him, or another one, hit the sight on the Bren gun and a piece of the sight sliced across my throat, but I didn't feel any pain. Corporal Jimmy Parr said, "You've been hit Ern," to which I replied, "Don't be silly, this blood is from the Bren gunner." Jimmy said, "Well it's bloody funny, it's running out of your chin!" Then we had the order to withdraw and I remember Jimmy Parr directing the men out through a gap in the scrub, and I'm yelling "Don't bunch!" Trooper Sutherland was hit in both legs and we carried him back to the RV where our packs were, on a groundsheet stretcher, but he died.'

There were between 2,000 and 3,000 Japanese pressed between Calvert's force and the Block, with little choice but to fight where they stood. The fighting became intense and casualties were mounting. Calvert later admitted that he should have taken two platoons of Nigerians as stretcher-bearers, for many wounded men would be left to fend for themselves that day. The Japs put in a strong counter-attack and the Gurkhas began to fall back, leaving the Recce troopers exposed. Brigade HQ came under heavy machine-gun fire and Calvert lay flat on the ground while three machine-guns raked the jungle a foot above his head, killing the signal section mules where they stood.

---

* Jimmy White recalled seeing Wilkins urging himself on with the words, 'Stick it, stick it. I must get back to my wife.' His determination saw him through and fifty years later he was able to tell the author that his shoulder was now in good working order.

It was now midday and Calvert's cavalry was on the horizon. He had arranged for an air strike by the Air Commandos at one p.m., a very fortunate decision as it turned out. Captain Frank Merchant, flying the lead ship of three B-25 bombers each carrying a full load of fragmentation bombs, spoke into his radio to Calvert's radio operator Mungo Park, and received his instructions. On the ground, the Gurkha mortar crews threw the smoke bombs down their tubes and watched them arc high above the jungle and down into the Japanese positions. 'Bomb at forty-five degrees from the smoke,' crackled in Merchant's headphones and he turned his aircraft and opened the bomb doors. As his aircraft passed over the smoke he released his bombs, closely followed by the others flying in a V-formation behind him. There were no bombardiers or bomb-sights in the B-25Hs, but at those low altitudes they were pretty accurate. Calvert recalled the scene on the ground as the bombs found their mark:

> 'The whole earth quaked under our stomachs as we shut our ears to the roar of the bombs. They landed plumb right. The Reconnaissance Regiment was jubilant, and later stated that the nearest 500-pounder was within fifty yards of them, and on the Japs. We later learned that the Japs were just forming up for a charge and the bombs in the flat jungle killed very many indeed.'

Calvert ordered a general withdrawal and led the survivors of 45 Recce away. They had forty stretcher cases and sixty walking wounded with them. Other wounded had to be left behind in the chaung, as attempts to recover them led to further casualties. Eventually they met up with Peter Vaughan's Nigerians and bivouacked for the night. Their casualties had been heavy: four British officers and sixty to seventy British and Gurkha other ranks had been killed, and a score were missing. Around 150 had been wounded. On the other side of the account, Frank Merchant was later told that the bombing had killed around 800 Japanese. Their final attack on the Block had also cost them 300 to 400 casualties, including the Colonel commanding the 24th Independent Mixed Brigade, and their morale was broken. The survivors streamed away from the White City area.

On 1 May the remnants of the 45th Reconnaissance Regiment began a forty-mile forced march to Broadway from which they were finally to be flown out. Roger Brewer was the only subaltern left. His diary recalls:

> 'Broadway a shambles of smashed-up gliders. Shirt gone and trousers in tatters. Quite a few chaps threw everything away including arms. We really are finished. Threw myself on ground and slept. Woke up and saw sun shining on gold. Had slept on a Jap skeleton all night. God! Flew out in DC-3 which took half of jungle with it. Branches still in wings when we landed at Comilla.'

Of the 800 men who had walked in with 45 Recce, roughly eighty walked out again.

Death of a Warrior

When Peter Taylor and his men began their advance towards the enemy outside White City, they had a party of some twenty-five ill with malaria and sickness who would not be able to march with them. A group was detailed to try and get them to the South Staffords at White City, about ten miles away. Trooper Arthur Withey was with them:

'After moving about three miles, I was in the lead with my Bren gun when we came to a river bed and on the side in a small depression we found a camp fire with three pots of rice cooking. We immediately took up defensive positions at front, left and right. We had come down a small hill and the officer in charge said that the Gurkhas would cover us from the right rear. We don't know where they went, but the Japs came on our rear and we got shot up badly. My pal next to me got shot in both ankles and feet, so we moved him into better cover, or so we thought, but grenades were thrown and we lost sight of him. We accounted for some Japs but we were in trouble. After a day the officer told us of the rough position of the South Staffords block and said, "I'm afraid it's every man for himself." I was appalled by this, but the other members started moving away and the firing quietened down. I held my position in good cover until night fell, then I decided to try for the Aberdeen stronghold. The Bren gun was too heavy and cumbersome so I dismantled it and hid it in various places along the track. The barrel and breech went down an old tree trunk and I kept the firing pin. I had a knife and three grenades, three biscuits and a little water in my bottle. At this point I met up with a Jap. He was more surprised than I was and he came at me with his bayonet and just caught me slightly in the groin, but I was quicker and got him with my knife. I got closer to the river bed and saw that there was a little water in between the boulders, but I held back to make sure that it was all quiet. Then I crossed over and filled up my bottle and moved on. It started to get light so I had to hide up and found a deadened hedge about five feet high and stretching back for about thirty yards. I got down low and crawled in and then turned around and repaired the breakage in the hedge, so it would look as if it was unbroken. About fifteen yards in I came upon a forked tree which was broken down and about eighteen inches thick. I got into the fork of it and it covered me well.

'Towards midday I saw two Japs looking over the hedge, but they went away after a while. When night came and it was dark I came out and started off again. I crossed two paddy fields and came upon a metalled road which I quickly crossed and moved on slowly through the jungle until it got light and I had to hide up again. That morning Jap dive bombers were screaming down and I realised that I was close to the White City stronghold. I ate my last biscuit and when it was dark I moved off again, finding myself at first light on a grassy slope about twelve feet wide with a dip down one side, so I carried on down, keeping a good watch out.

171

I had a feeling that this was it, but I had a hundred yards to go. At the bottom to my left was a cleared area the size of a football pitch and to the left side a partly-covered hill. I knew from its construction it was the stronghold. I could not shout in case Japs were about, but I was carrying a letter which had been dropped to me a month before, so I put it in my hat and prayed and waved it at the hill. After some time I saw movement. They must have had me in their glasses. Then three soldiers came out, marking a path as it was mined, and I walked over to them and nearly collapsed. I had made it. I was questioned by the officer in charge who told me that I was the only one to get through and they said I had done a good job. Then I was fed and watered and given a place to sleep for the night. However, I was now ill with malaria and battle exhaustion and I was flown by light plane back to my own stronghold and thence out in a Dakota to the hospital at Shillong.'*

* By the time Arthur returned to his regiment in Bangalore he had been declared dead and the papers to apply for a widow's pension had been sent to his wife.

A mortar crew adjusting their sights during the fighting for Mogaung.

An Air Commando light plane lands at White City to collect wounded.

It is not surprising that 16 Brigade was exhausted after it had marched in from India to the Indaw area of Burma. Often mules had to be unloaded when the hills were too steep and their loads carried up by hand.

A Lancashire Fusilier commando platoon prepares a railway bridge for demolition.

TOP: Chindits cooking a meal during their midday halt. Lighting fires during the monsoon was another matter.

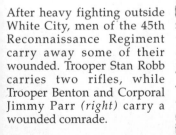

After heavy fighting outside White City, men of the 45th Reconnaissance Regiment carry away some of their wounded. Trooper Stan Robb carries two rifles, while Trooper Benton and Corporal Jimmy Parr (right) carry a wounded comrade.

Brigadier Mike Calvert just after the fall of Mogaung, giving instructions to Major Freddie Shaw of the 3rd Battalion, 6th Gurkhas, while Major Lumley looks on. Officers preferred to carry rifles because side-arms marked them as targets for Japanese snipers.

RIGHT: Major-General Joe Lentaigne, DSO. A regular Gurkha officer who was given command of the Chindits following the death of Wingate.

The commanders put their heads together after aerial photographs showed that the Piccadilly landing zone had been blocked by logs. Around the map from left to right: Colonel John Allison, USAAF, the tall Lieutenant-Colonel Scott of the 1st King's Liverpool, Air Vice-Marshal Baldwin, Brigadier Mike Calvert with map case and Major-General Wingate.

Chapter 12

Ambush and Assault

The 7th Battalion, Nigeria Regiment had been ordered by Mike Calvert to set an ambush south of White City on the Pinwe to Sepein road, and deal with any Japanese transport using the road. They had fluffed an earlier ambush when a soldier had opened fire too soon. Now they were about to get a second chance.

Garaba Gonari was buckling on his equipment when he first heard the distant sounds. 'Trucks coming from de north Sah!' he informed Major Charles Carfrae. They laughed at him at first, but then other Africans began to nod their agreement. A full minute passed before the white officers heard the sound, then they drew their revolvers and began to bark out orders. Lieutenant Denis Arnold stood behind a tree with a signal pistol in his hand. His Africans were spread out around him, nervously aiming their rifles down the road. Dusk had become night and the suspense was almost unbearable as the sound of engines came nearer and nearer. There were five trucks in the convoy and as the first of them drew level with Major Carfrae lying in the leaves thirty feet from the road, Arnold raised his arm above his head.

> 'I fired the Very pistol and all weapons including a PIAT fired at the leading truck. Successive trucks crashed into the one in front and all hell broke loose. I had posted some men with grenades up very high trees overlooking the road. When the first shots were fired they magically reappeared, unharmed, coming through a hail of fire to the platoon. They came down those trees faster than any squirrel could have done! After the PIAT hit the leading truck full of soldiers an officer brandishing a sword rushed towards us shouting – a very brave action, but hopeless. The ambush happened at about six p.m. and all night sporadic firing continued, punctuated with the cries of wounded men.'

As dawn broke Major Carfrae sent Arnold, Dicky Lambert and Tich Cooper, together with thirty Africans, to clear up any Japanese who were hiding in the bushes. Major Carfrae later recalled:

> 'Almost at once rifle shots, grenade bursts and fire from Brens and Japanese light machine-guns could be heard from the undergrowth. I lay on my stomach in one of the scrapes on the perimeter attempting to follow events but saw nothing, though I could hear Dicky's voice shouting

173

commands and ferociously urging on men inclined to hang back. Turning to say a word to the African lying in the scoop immediately to my right, I found he had that moment been shot through the forehead, killed either by a Japanese bullet or one fired by Dicky's Africans. I was sweating with anxiety for officers and men when after half an hour Denis Arnold returned to ask for reinforcements. Unflurried, he might have been taking part in a routine training exercise. "Japs all over the bloody shop, sir, taking pot shots from cover. Mostly wounded from last night. Got the chap next to me clean as a whistle – Shehu Godabawa. One Jap sat up, aimed at me and missed from ten feet! I saw him do it."'

Denis took twenty more Africans and disappeared into the lantana. Eventually the shooting diminished as the Africans stalked the Japanese hiding in the undergrowth. Tich Cooper came back with a smashed elbow where two or three machine-gun bullets had hit him and four or five of the Africans had been killed. Forty-one Japanese dead lay around the scene of the ambush and three wounded prisoners had been taken. There was no way to bury the dead without picks and shovels, so they were piled into one of the trucks, soaked in petrol and cremated.

The author tried hard to track down some of the Nigerian soldiers who served with 3rd West African Brigade, but the search proved fruitless. The daughter of one former NCO offered to produce a video showing old Nigerian Chindits talking about their experiences, but wanted a £4,000 fee for doing so! The author reluctantly declined. Major Carfrae, who commanded 29 Column with the 7th Battalion, Nigeria Regiment, recalled one of the Africans under his command:

'I recommended Sergeant Umoru Numan for a Military Medal, which he was awarded, not so much for any particular individual action, but for many in which he distinguished himself. Besides being an excellent platoon sergeant – Denis Arnold, his platoon commander, and he were a first-class combination – he took part in many other column operations, such as acting as rearguard at Ywathit, going on dangerous patrols, for which he was automatically first choice, and so on. He was always willing, indeed eager, to "have a go" but at the same time possessed sound military judgement. Probably we relied upon him too much, taking advantage of his leadership, courage and good sense. Nonetheless he survived without a scratch! Umoru Numan was a Christian, unusual for a northerner, and genuinely and deeply religious. He always carried a bible and read it, I believe, daily, though reading was a bit of an effort! He was absolutely straight and honest and would never have complained about anything, however justified. He later became RSM of the 1st Battalion, Nigeria Regiment after independence.'

Ambush and Assault

Doctor Leslie Wilson served with the Brigade Field Ambulance and was asked by the author to describe the Nigerians, both in their attitude to life in general and life in the jungle in particular:

'There were instances of breakdown in the face of the terrible conditions among British, American, Chinese and Japanese troops and I doubt if the incidence was any greater in our West Africans. My own impression was that if they did not have the long military traditions of, say, the Black Watch and the Leicesters, they fought bravely and well. This was all the more commendable since most would have had no idea, when they enlisted, that they were due to go overseas, and most had only a vague idea of the larger purposes of the war.

'Could they simply give up the will to live? Charles Carfrae, in his book *Chindit Column*, describes an apparently healthy man dying under a Ju-Ju curse. I had heard of such curses, but never came across one. A few were highly suggestible. Rarely, if one had to give an intravenous anaesthetic, the mere approach of the needle could send a man into a hypnotic sleep and one could proceed with minor surgery without the injection. Our Hausa infantrymen had a fatalistic, not pessimistic, outlook on life, believing that everything that happened, or would happen, was the Will of Allah. The southerners tended to live for the hour: "Why worry about tomorrow?" Our staple diet was the American K ration; the rich corn pork loaf, the processed cheese, the richly compressed fruit were not to British taste and was one factor in most of us losing a lot of weight. But my medical muleteer, John Bull, actually grew fat. Before the column was due to march, he would be lying on the ground, hands behind his head. When I shouted to him to get the panniers loaded, he would grin from ear to ear and say, "What Sah, you want me die for work!" But we always got away in good time.

'They had an enormous sense of fun. In Nigeria they would sing, leader and chorus, as they marched. They would drum and dance to exciting rhythms. They were acutely perceptive of, and greatly amused by, their officers' eccentricities, and in private would delight in mimicking them without actually losing respect. At the same time, they became angry and bitterly resentful if they felt any injustice had been done. They were endlessly curious and inquisitive, examining new and unfamiliar objects intently and finding names for them. They loved a bit of drama. My Tiv stretcher-bearers (clecher-bellas) had listened to my lecture on security with rapt interest. During a stop at a railway station in India, I spotted some of my men in an excited huddle on the platform. I got them disengaged to find a bewildered Indian gentleman. My NCO explained, "He be spy, Sah – he ask if we be West African!" But in general, they were friendly and sociable. When we first met Chiang Kai-shek's troops, individual Africans and Chinese sat on the ground and communicated with each other for long periods by sign and gesture. They indulged in a lot of harmless fibbing.

Having seen my clecher-bellas enjoying a good tuck in, I would ask the NCO the routine evening question, "Have your men fed?" He would assume a pained, martyred, expression: "No Sah, we never chop since morning." He knew perfectly well that I knew he was fibbing, but it was worth a try.

'In the campaign, disease and the monsoon took a much heavier toll than enemy fire. Malaria, dysentery, leg sores and jaundice were prevalent. Some of the columns slept in huts which were found to be infested with the mites carrying scrub typhus. Victims, white more than black, were laid low by fever, delirium, depression, and severe loss of weight. Several died, but those who survived eventually made a good recovery. To have served with Nigerian soldiers was a rare privilege. The key to relations was simple: if we liked them and were scrupulously fair, they would like us. If one had been away, and came back in the half dark, scores of little lights would appear – the gleaming of African teeth.'

Towards the end of March as the fighting died down at White City the Japanese prepared to assault the stronghold at Broadway. By 11 March, the troops allotted to the defence of Wingate's first stronghold were in place. The 3rd Battalion, 9th Gurkhas commanded by Lieutenant-Colonel Noel George were to garrison the base while the two columns of the 1st Battalion, King's Liverpool were to act as floater columns, circling the stronghold at a distance, ready to fall on the rear of any attackers. A troop of twenty-five-pounder field artillery also arrived, together with a troop of light anti-aircraft artillery with their Bofors. Colonel Claude Rome was in overall command of the stronghold.

On 13 March the Japanese air force finally arrived and twenty Zero and Oscar fighters began to strafe and bomb the ground installations, light planes and glider remains. They were unaware that six RAF Spitfires had arrived the previous day and five of them immediately took to the air. Four of the enemy were shot down for the loss of one Spitfire and damage on the ground was slight. It is interesting to note that when the Spitfires found themselves in trouble, they would fly over the Bofors positions to allow the gunners on the ground a good shot at their pursuers. The Japanese air force returned again and again and eventually the surviving Spitfires were withdrawn. The Bofors, however, were having a field day and the battery which provided anti-aircraft cover for Broadway, White City and later Myitkyina was credited with shooting down more aircraft than all the anti-aircraft regiments in India put together. In addition, while the Japanese air force was engaged in attacking the Chindit blocks and strongholds, it deprived the forces attacking Imphal and Kohima of half of their air support.

At four p.m. on 26 March, a Kachin scout reported that a battalion of the enemy had crossed the Kaukkwe Chaung and was moving towards the airfield. Rome sent Major Astell of the Burma Rifles with a mixed platoon of thirty men to locate them. He found them at dawn the next morning, still in bivouac, and attacked them with his small force, killing and wounding a number of Japanese. He lost two of his own men in the withdrawal.

Around 10.45 p.m. the storm broke on Major Irwin Pickett's 'D' Company, 3/9th Gurkhas. They were supposed to have been used as the floater company for the airfield, but were in fact placed in static positions along the northern edge of the clearing. The reason for this is unclear. If they were supposed to have been used in defence, they would have been better used inside the perimeter. If their role was attack, then they should have been mobile and well clear of the perimeter. One cannot help but think that a tactical mistake had been made somewhere along the line. The result of this was that the three platoons and company head-quarters were overrun one after another. After heavy fighting Major Pickett was killed and the survivors of his company dispersed into the jungle.

Just after midnight the Japanese attacked the main perimeter, but they were beaten back with heavy casualties. At first light the survivors of 'D' Company tried to regain the perimeter and Major Reggie Twelve-trees took out a platoon from his 'A' Company and escorted them in. They carried Irwin's body with them. In keeping with the custom of his men, he had the top of his head shaved, with the exception of a small area right at the crown where the hair was grown in a long tuft. The men believed that when they were killed in battle, the tuft would enable the gods to snatch their soul into heaven. Irwin was buried with his men and no doubt their souls met again in heaven.

The enemy attacks continued over the next few days, mostly at night. Captain Bill Towill, the Gurkha intelligence officer and later adjutant, had a lucky escape:

'One night there was an electrical storm of an intensity I don't think I have experienced before or since. There was continuing incessant thunder and lightning with the rain bucketing down almost as if you were under a waterfall. As if this were not enough, the Japs attacked under cover of a massive mortar bombardment. I decided to go and see how my own lads were getting on and was crawling on my hands and knees along a shallow and narrow communications trench and putting my head up from time to time to look around, because it seemed to me that the Japs were likely to get through the wire and come flooding over us at any moment. In all the noise and tumult it was quite impossible to hear a mortar bomb falling, as we usually managed to do. As I stopped and raised my head to look over the top, two mortar bombs landed absolutely simultaneously and within three feet of me, on either side of the trench. I felt a crashing, stunning blow across the top and back of my head, as if some giant hand had taken a mighty swipe at me, which knocked me violently face down in the mud at the bottom of the trench. A split second later and the whole of my head would have been in line with the explosions, and I just don't see how I could have survived. I found myself retching uncontrollably and many minutes passed before I managed to continue. I must have been suffering from concussion and shell-shock, but in the relief of my still being alive, was soon able to shake off the after-effects, although it has left my hearing impaired.'

Despite the ferocity of their attacks, the 2nd Battalion, 146th Infantry Regiment never managed to breach the perimeter. Fighting patrols were sent out to take on the enemy and recover the bodies of those killed earlier on. Seven Gurkhas were found, stacked in a pile two or three feet high as if they were a pile of logs. They had been taken prisoner and butchered. Other headless bodies were found, used for practice by sword-wielding Japanese officers. A request for assistance was radioed to the two King's columns, but Lieutenant-Colonel Scott's column could not be reached. Major Gaitley, the commander of the other column, sent a company led by Captain Coultart and on the afternoon of 29 March they assaulted the Japanese positions. However, there were simply not enough of them and three dozen of the King's were killed and wounded. Among the dead was Captain Coultart.

Colonel Rome planned to attack the Japanese on 31 March with one company of Gurkhas and Major Gaitley's 82 Column from the King's. He very sensibly arranged for an air strike by Air Commando Mustangs just prior to the attack and the enemy started to withdraw in disorder. As soon as the last fighter pulled off the target, the Gurkhas and King's fixed their bayonets and charged. The Japanese put up little resistance and fled. Thereafter the stronghold was not attacked again. The Japanese battalion was from the 18th Division, which had White City as its first priority. Broadway was finally evacuated on 13 May and the two battalions marched away to join up with 111 Brigade.

One disgraceful postscript to the fighting at Broadway was brought to the attention of the author by Joe Milner CBE, formerly a NCO with 82 Column. When he returned to Broadway nine months later with a graves registration unit, he discovered that no attempt had been made to inter decently the bodies of his fallen comrades. Their rifles and identity discs had been taken, so eventual identification prior to burial proved difficult. The senior officers of the column and indeed those command-ing at Broadway should bear responsibility for this omission.

When we last left Morris Force, Peter Cane, the commander of 94 Column, and two platoons with the river-crossing equipment had gone ahead to the Shweli River to find a crossing point for the force. Colonel Morris and 49 Column set off to follow them, but within a few miles of leaving Chowringhee to scout ahead, the reconnaissance platoon got itself lost and Morris and the rest of the force continued on without it. Then, to make matters worse, Morris and the rifle platoons set off at such a pace that they left the transport section of the column behind – a hundred mules, all the equipment of both columns, and with just a rearguard platoon as protection. They were only ten miles east of the airstrip.

Two days later the mules and equipment finally joined up with Morris at the RV by the river. By now they were all behind schedule and should have been across the river in time to meet a pre-arranged supply drop. Some of the men, particularly those on the advance party, were running out of food and a request was radioed to headquarters for a supply drop and additional river-crossing equipment. Within two hours the reply came back from Wingate himself: NO SUPPLY DROP UNTIL YOU HAVE CROSSED THE SHWELI. There was no mention of the extra river-crossing equipment. The signal galvanised Morris into action and he declared that the river must be crossed that night, a difficult task with only four lilos and a few lifejackets between the lot of them. Fortunately sense prevailed when it was discovered that there was no nearby jumping off point as the river banks were twenty feet high. The crossing would begin in the morning.

The same day, 12 March, Lentaigne's 111 Brigade HQ and the two columns from 3rd Battalion, 4th Gurkhas were having similar problems crossing the Irrawaddy. The majority of the mules would simply not cross the river and so much time was lost that he decided to leave 40 Column behind, together with many of the mules and much heavy equipment, and march the rest of his brigade on without them. 40 Column was told to turn around and try to catch up with Morris Force. Almost two months would pass before they joined them. Wingate sent a signal to the Prime Minister the same day, stating confidently that '111 Brigade is now crossing Irrawaddy to attack roads and railway. Two columns (Morris Force) now crossing Shweli to east to block Mandalay–Bhamo communications. A special patriot force (Dah Force) is raising Kachins around Broadway, thence east to Bhamo area. Situation most promising *if exploited.*' While one can understand that Wingate wanted to send a confident signal to Churchill that all was going well, particularly in order to secure his continued patronage, he was being rather economical with the truth. 111 Brigade was in disarray and would spend the next two weeks marching north, to link up with the battalions which had landed at Broadway. Dah Force had never been tasked to raise Kachins in the Broadway area and was, in fact, still in India. They would not reach their operational area until 22 March. And as for Morris Force, it was split into three groups, each out of touch with each other, with the main body considering crossing the river with four lilos and a few lifejackets.

Fortunately for Morris Force, some of Peter Cane's men came across them at the river bank and the crossing was eventually made using the proper equipment. The river stuck in many Chindits' memories; it was four hundred yards across and a swift five-knot current was running. But it was also blue, rather than the usual muddy brown colour. Colonel

Morris was also anxious, directing his RAF section to request continuous air cover during the crossing, a rather unnecessary, and of course unfulfilled, request. The signallers used the 1086 radio and were frustrated at their inability to contact base with their 22 set, as it was out of range. Rear HQ sent one signal to the columns insisting 'The 22 set can, has, and will operate at 300 miles' range. Experiment with the length and position of your aerials.' An exasperated Peter Cane candidly replied, 'Have experimented with every length and position except one position. Leave that experiment to you.'

Finally 94 Column got across and were about to head for the site of the supply drop when Morris ordered them to stay there and protect 49 Column as it crossed and then wait behind to cover their rear, as they headed for the DZ. It was an unpopular and unnecessary decision. The supply drop did not go well. The clearing selected was only four hundred yards long, so Pat O'Brien set up the six signal fires accordingly. Colonel Morris, however, insisted 'Fires must be set out the regulated distance' with one hundred yards between each and as a result two of the fires were set up in the dense jungle and that is where many of the parachutes eventually landed. When Morris heard the noise that was being made as the supply drop party began to chop down trees to get to the suspended parachutes, he ordered the work stopped at once. Half of the supplies remained in the trees and 94 Column went hungry for a further week.

As for the wayward reconnaissance platoon, they reached what they thought was the correct RV by the river, waited two days and then crossed, thinking they had missed the rest of the force. By the time they were discovered by Kachins and reunited with their comrades they were all in. The platoon was later disbanded, their morale shattered, and some were sent out prematurely. And there was still no sign of the Japanese. As the two columns marched separately on their way, they discovered that the Japanese had heard of their landing and had sent out pairs of Shan spies to watch each village. Half a dozen were soon captured by the Gurkhas, one of whom was the Thugyi of Kwehaungdon on the Shweli, who was responsible for rounding up old Burrifs and survivors from Wingate's first expedition. They tried to escape by bolting downhill, but the Gurkhas raced after them and killed five of the six with their kukris. The men learnt a hard lesson at a village called Sintha, where they were befriended by the inhabitants. A Japanese spy informed the local commander and the five head families of the village were taken to Bhamo and executed. Thereafter all strangers in the villages were taken along by the Gurkhas and ten were later shot as spies.

On 29 March, while the columns were preparing their separate attacks on the Bhamo–Namhkan road, 94 Column passed through Majigunj where the friendly Kachins delivered to them two men left behind by Ken Gilkes' 7 Column when they marched out through China in 1943. Private Critchley and Corporal Jones of the 13th King's were overjoyed to see their countrymen. Sadly Jones died of typhus a month later.

In the meantime, Dah Force was in trouble. Involved in raising the Kachins north of the Taiping River, Japanese spies had discovered its base at Nahpaw and twice the force had been broken up. Bert Reeves was a Royal Signals radio operator who volunteered to serve in the Independent Companies, the first of the Army special units and the brainchild of Sir Winston Churchill. He then spent two years with 2 Commando before moving to the Chindits, joining Dah Force. He told the author:

'I was Fish Herring's wireless operator and as I was the most experienced operator within the signals section I took over completely the constant installation and operating as we moved around. An interesting anecdote: the aerial for the transmitter was just a long wire and in order to get it as high as possible I used to tie a stone to the end and lob it as high up in a tree as possible. Usually a gentle pull would free it, but on this occasion it had become twisted and there was nothing for it but to climb up and free it. I had succeeded in freeing the tangle when I found that I had become the target for some ferocious red ants, dozens of which got inside my open collar shirt and started to bite. I got down the tree five times faster than I went up and had there been a theatrical agent there he would have booked me on the spot, as the best contortionist he had ever seen. No wonder Fish Herring thought I was worth a Mention in Despatches.

'The battle at Nahpaw is one of those wartime incidents that remain in one's mind for a lifetime. In my case the reason was that it was a time when I was very, very cold that night and many after. Up in the mountains the temperature could reach above 100 degrees Fahrenheit and plunge to below freezing during the night. Fort Nahpaw was a large steep hill with an old tumbledown fort perched on top. I did not have the radio fitted up because we were expecting an attack from the Japs some time that night. We were informed by the Colonel that in the event we were attacked a long blast on the whistle would be the signal for all to retreat to a given rendezvous where the mules and equipment were already loaded for a quick getaway. It was a moonless night and a very dark one. After positioning one of the signal section lads, I think his name was Whitely or Whitelaw, some yards in front of me, I settled my groundsheet on a grassy patch and sat down. Presently I noticed that it had become quite cold and I wrapped my lightweight blanket around myself. It was very quiet. Some hours passed by as my mind fed itself on memories of things past.

'Suddenly the "withdrawal" whistle was blown and a quiet withdrawal took place. I laced up my pack and slung it over my shoulders, then I remembered Whitely was in front of me and I had not heard him go past. I decided to leave my blanket and groundsheet where it was and collect it on the way back and set off in a forward direction. I must have gone forward some fifteen yards. It was still dark and there was not a noise to be heard. I decided that he must have passed me after the whistle went and went back for my blanket and groundsheet. I could not find them and decided it was time to make my way down pronto. I arrived at a path at the bottom of the hill which was being used as a collecting point and met my signals officer Captain Treckman. He said he was becoming worried about me and had I seen Whitely? I told him that he was nowhere to be found and presently we plodded on through the night to a safer area.

'After we had put a few miles between ourselves and the Japs we moved off the trail and spent what was left of the night in the jungle. The next day we arrived at a small village and rested up. The following day we learned from a Kachin from the Nahpaw area that the Japs had gone and that Whitely had been found alive but very seriously wounded. He had been found by a Kachin woman who had raised the alarm and then carried him back to her local village where she tended him and stuffed chewed leaves of an antiseptic nature into his large and many open wounds. We immediately sent a party with the MO to bring him back by stretcher so he could be operated on and a bamboo operating table was built out in the open awaiting their return. Whitely had been bayoneted several times as he lay on the ground and had received a final sword slash across his back as a Japanese officer passed. He was left for dead. The MO stitched his wounds and the next day he was carried to a light plane strip a few miles away. I also heard that a British Sergeant and Corporal, probably from the 1st South Staffords defence platoon, had been taken prisoner by the Japs and were last seen by the Kachins being marched away with heavy boxes of ammunition tied to their backs.'

Lentaigne ordered Morris Force to proceed north at speed to assist Dah Force. The two columns set off at a cracking pace and 94 Column marched day and night with only two four-hour stops. At the end of it they captured the town of Moyothit, which hit the headlines five months later when Stilwell's Chinese finally reached it. Some of the marching was purgatory: on the night of 4/5 April they marched for three hours from 2,000 to 6,500 feet up a bleak, bare hillside in three-quarters moonlight, with half a gale blowing. After crossing the Taiping River, Morris Force heard that Dah Force was re-forming after its flight from Nahpaw. They also heard that Morris had been promoted to Brigadier in Lentaigne's place, so the long-suffering Ted Russell became the new battalion commander. However, Morris was to stay with the force, a decision hardly greeted with enthusiasm by his junior officers.

One outsider who was in a unique position to observe the activities of Morris Force was Captain Bill Howe of the Special Operations Executive. He and his two Karen signallers were flown into Broadway and joined Dah Force in the field, courtesy of two New Zealand pilots who flew their light planes onto a dirt road that even the Air Commandos refused to land on. One of the planes lost its tailwheel on landing, but Bill and his men held the tail off the ground while the pilot revved the engine before accelerating back down the road and into the air again. Some of Fish Herring's Kachins were waiting for them. Bill recalls:

'It was agreed that I should join Morris Force and Fish took me there next day. As we were just getting back to his HQ, I remember saying, "Well everything is quiet and peaceful here" when all hell broke loose. In spite of Fish's precautions the Japs had found us and in fact walked right into our camp. We had a pre-arrangement of where to disappear to and where to reassemble, so I rushed off, grabbed my radio and beat it rapidly into the jungle with my boys. It took a couple of days to reassemble and I don't think we lost many chaps, although the Japs looted our stores.

'After each day's march we used to harbour, generally on top of a hill where there was some water. The mules had to be watered first and when they had churned the water up we were allowed to fill our water bottles and chagules (canvas water bags) and that was all we had to drink, brew up and wash. On the second day's march I emptied my water bottle at the first stream we crossed and told my boys to do the same and fill them with clean water. That night I was told off by Brigadier Morris for breaking column discipline! I told him that if his column carried on drinking the muddy water stirred up by the mules, he very soon would not have a fit man. He was not amused and told me if all the column stopped at clean water we would provide a soft target for the Japs. I took his point, but where were the Japs? I am afraid I was a very undisciplined soldier and reckoned that common sense should override orders. I reckon I was proved right because by the time we were told to attempt an attack on the Japs at Myitkyina, we could hardly muster a fit platoon, there were so many men down with malaria, scrub typhus and tummy trouble!

'Once in harbour my chaps had to get the radio going while I had to encode and decode the signals using a microscopic "one time pad" that you had to use a magnifying glass to read, this frequently in pouring rain with only one groundsheet to try to provide some shelter. My radio was very good and I frequently passed signals from Brigadier Morris to my HQ to pass on to the Army when his radio could not make contact. In harbour everyone had to creep around and talk as quietly as possible in case the Japs were around and could hear us. This used to seem a nonsense to me because the "chore horses" were belting away to charge the radio batteries and could be heard miles away! I had a hand charger for my radio, and a contraption like a bicycle that we had to take turns to ride.

'During my time with Morris I never really gathered what we were supposed to be doing. I think that Pat O'Brien's book *Out of the Blue* leaves one with the same doubts and uncertainties. Shortly after I joined the column we were bumped by the Japs. We were fired on by a mountain gun and the order came down to "dig in". I don't know what with because we had no shovels or entrenching tools. The Brigadier sent a section of Gurkhas with a British officer to attack the gun. They scrambled up the hill and when they could see the gun position the officer told them to charge, but was shot and killed. The Gurkhas retreated back down the hill. They buried the unfortunate officer, the Japs withdrew and as far as I am aware we made no attempt to follow them up! This episode did not inspire me with much confidence.

'The rains had set in and we were soaking wet and cold all day. Supply drops were more difficult, food was often short and at night we laid down as we were, but happily I can sleep anywhere and I stayed fit. We marched up and down hill tracks every day. They were frequently muddy and very slippery and churned up by the mules. We had two big Argentinian mules to carry the RAF radio and they were absolute buggers on the steep hills. They would pull away from their drivers and go charging up the hill, scattering everything and everybody.

'We frequently passed Kachin villages and I always hoped that the Brigadier would harbour in the village, where we might get a night's sleep in the dry and perhaps a little different food, but not a hope. Once again it would have provided a soft target for the Japs, but where were they? To be fair to Morris he was living in exactly the same conditions as the rest of us.

'The nearest I came to being hurt was one evening when we had harboured. As usual it was on a hill and I had camped on the side of the hill and just got a small fire going to try to make some sort of warm meal. Unfortunately a Gurkha further up the hill was trying to clean and prime a hand grenade. It was all greasy and slipped out of his hand, rolled down the hill and into my fire! Half a dozen of us were standing around the fire and the grenade exploded of course! The blast went down and blew quite a hole, but the only person hurt was a little Gurkha who was bending over the fire to poke a few more sticks in. There was a temporary panic in the column because the immediate thought was that it was a Jap mortar!

'On another occasion we had to cross a very rickety suspension bridge. My mule, whom I had christened Topsy after my sister, just was not having any. We pushed, pulled but she just would not cross the bridge. So we got a large bamboo, got it under her rear knees and then with two of us on either side we lifted her hind legs off the ground and she just had to move forward on her front legs!'

Operating independently from Morris and 49 Column, Peter Cane's 94 Column discovered that the key point on the Bhamo – Myitkyina road was the village of Nalong. It was halfway between the two towns and was being used as a permanent staging post and road maintenance centre. His column attacked and burnt the village and then tried unsuccessfully to entice Morris to bring the rest of his force down to try to block the road permanently. Cane reckoned that they could cause a landslide which would have dropped the entire road down a steep cliff, but Force Headquarters would not drop the required equipment to them. He also asked for direct air support on 27 April, when 135 Japanese lorries drove into Nalong from the north. None materialised. 183 more lorries arrived, bringing the total to 318. A once in a lifetime opportunity for the Air Commando Mustangs, but none arrived. In the end, 94 Column used what explosives they had to blow the road and withdrew. It was in use again thirty-six hours later.

On 17 May, after a fifty-mile trek through mountainous jungle, the three battalions of American troops comprising Merrill's Marauders captured the airfield at Myitkyina. Stilwell was jubilant and announced to all that 'Myitkyina has been captured.' Unfortunately his men had captured the airfield, but not the town, and the 3,500 Japanese defenders were to keep 30,000 of Stilwell's Chinese at bay for another three months. Stilwell put Brigadier-General Boatner in charge of the 'Myitkyina Task Force' and he had as few ideas of practical warfare as Stilwell. The three battalions of Morris Force, 40 Column having joined up with them on 3 May, were put under Boatner's command and squandered in an attempt to do what Boatner's twelve battalions of Chinese could not. The inability of Stilwell's men to throw the Japanese out of Myitkyina caused the Chindits to be kept in Burma much longer than planned and their casualties soared as a result. Morris Force was the first unit to suffer. Bill Howe again:

'We were ordered to advance on Myitkyina to help the Yanks pushing down from the north. We did a night approach march which was absolute hell. We could not see any track, it was muddy and slippery and the mules were difficult to control. It was cold and we had to cross several small streams often four or five feet deep, so we were soaking wet. Early the next morning we joined a good track and the jungle was fairly clear. Morris called an "O" Group meeting, so we had all the section COs in one spot. I suggested to Morris that if the Japs were near we would make a wonderful target for a mortar attack. I had hardly spoken when there was a bloody great bang just ahead of us – a Jap mortar! We rapidly dispersed to a more sensible and safer spot. I did not see any Japs, but there was a good deal of firing ahead. I saw the Doc trying to cope with a Gurkha who had copped a burst of machine-gun fire across his tummy and was practically holding his guts in with his hands. He was cursing like a trooper and I remember the Doc saying that as long as he could curse he would be OK – I hope he was.

'I don't know what we achieved and eventually we retired to a safe

185

harbour up in the hills where we had left the sick men and the soft part of the column. Soon after, I left the column with my boys and a party of sick and found an American light plane airstrip. I called up two Dakotas to take us out, but they were reluctant to land on the soft ground. I reassured them that it was OK and they duly landed and flew us to Assam. I shudder to think what would have happened if they had sunk in the soft ground and had not been able to take off again. I presume I should have had two planes debited to my pay book and would still be paying for them!*'

After Bill and his men had departed for India, the rest of Morris Force continued to try to do Stilwell's bidding and attack the Japanese around Myitkyina. The American commander had little understanding of the role of the Chindits, nor the fact that they were lightly armed and without artillery. Indeed he probably did not care. The Chinese continued to drag their feet, while Merrill's Marauders were driven into the ground by a callous and ruthless commander who ordered his hospital scoured for men to be thrown back into the meat grinder.

Morris Force put in attacks against the villages of Waingmaw and Houla in the suburbs of Myitkyina during the first weeks of June, with some success. However, casualties were mounting and in the early hours of 10 June, as 94 Column put in another attack on Houla, the rest of Morris Force ran into a number of Japanese patrols from nearby Maigna. Major Donald McCutcheon was there when Lieutenant-Colonel Monteith, the commander of 40 Column, was killed:

'I well recall the death in action of Ian Monteith since it affected me personally. 40 Column was moving in column snake of battle groups preparing for an attack on Waingmaw. Ian was with the second group with Column HQ and I as second-in-command was with the last group. We were about to shake out into formation for the attack when he was called forward by Brigadier Morris for final orders. As usual he went with his escort of one rifleman and shortly after leaving their group they were jumped by a Jap patrol. For some reason they were unprepared and their weapons were not cocked. He fell seriously, if not mortally, wounded by light machine-gun fire and was decapitated by a sword-wielding Japanese officer. I was then called forward to take over and left with my escort going from group to group, passing the site of Ian's encounter. We had no need of a reminder to be alert. We saw the same patrol just a split second

---

* Bill Howe was very unhappy about what was happening in the Kachin Hills after the departure of Wingate's men. The tribesmen were defenceless and at the mercy of the Japanese who would kill anyone suspected of aiding the British. In December 1944 the SOE parachuted him back into the same area, together with two bombers full of weapons and ammunition. As he stood on the ground watching the stores containers float down around him, one container, whose parachute had collapsed, hit the ground ten feet from where he was standing. It was full of grenades, but luck was with him that night. Within weeks he had his own private army operating in the area, but that, as they say, is another story.

before they saw us and hit the dirt, opening up with grenades and our personal weapons. For a lifetime I shared a bush with a Jap, but a grenade from my escort ended day's play and they withdrew. The grenade was rather too close to me for my own personal comfort, but it did the trick. Later we recovered a sword from a dead Jap officer, which is now with our heirs in 4th Gorhka [current spelling] Rifles in the new Indian Army.'

Morris sensibly withdrew his force and later turned his attention to Maigna, which Cane, McCutcheon and their men almost captured on 19 June. However, without any supporting fire to deal with bunkers and pillboxes there was little chance of overrunning the well dug-in Japanese positions. Dah Force was evacuated on 22 June, leaving behind a dozen Kachins, two British officers (medical, signals) and Bert Reeves as radio operator. Their job was to gather any British missing from the current or past operations and brought in by the Kachins. On 17 July, those of Morris Force still on their feet were relieved by the Royal Sussex Regiment and flown out of Myitkyina airfield back to India.

Chapter 13

All March North for Blackpool

After the decimation of the Japanese 24th Independent Mixed Brigade, a period of relative calm descended on White City. General Takeda wisely decided to wait until the whole of his 53rd Division had been assembled before attacking the block again. In the meantime Lentaigne, Slim and Stilwell were discussing the fate of the Chindits.

In order to carry out their obligations to Stilwell, the Chindits had to continue to block the Railway Valley. However, the strongholds at Aberdeen, Broadway and White City could not hold out during the monsoon. There were no resources to convert their airstrips to all-weather fields and resupplying the brigades solely by air could not be guaranteed because of the low clouds and poor visibility that would accompany the monsoon rains. The only way out of Burma for the Chindits was to march North, to link up with Stilwell's Chinese. Stilwell was reluctant to take the Chindits under his command, but when he finally relented it was as though a death warrant had been signed for hundreds of Wingate's men. Fifty years later one of his Chindits gave an opinion on the change of commanders: 'Lentaigne was a disaster. Together with Slim they gave us to Stilwell who hated "the limeys" and 77 Brigade was slaughtered like sheep at Mogaung, not having been relieved before then to recuperate. We in the Commando Platoon (Lancashire Fusiliers) survived because we went to Tapaw Ferry, missing a lot of the terrible fighting up to and at Mogaung.'

The new orders for the Chindits were thus: 111 Brigade was to establish a new block in the area of Hopin, forty miles north of White City, supported by floater columns from 14 Brigade and the 3rd West Africans. 77 Brigade was to take up positions east of the railway and the Namyin River, opposite the new block, and protect it from that side. Fergusson's weary 16 Brigade was to be flown out. The biggest problem was evacuating White City under the noses of the Japanese. Brigadier Gillmore worked out the detailed plans, which involved using 14 Brigade to occupy the enemy outside the block, while the defenders pulled out. The 7th Leicesters would relieve the South Staffords, who would then march north, together with the Fusiliers, while the heavy equipment and guns were flown out from the White City Dakota strip, protected by the

York and Lancaster columns. The Black Watch would block the tracks east of White City and the Bedfordshire and Hertfordshire would put in a diversionary attack on Mawlu. Thereafter both 14 and 3rd West African Brigades would march north and take up positions in the mountains west of the railway corridor close to Hopin and near the Kyusunlai Pass through the Bumrawng Bum.

Jack Masters and his 111 Brigade had a head start on the other brigades and they set off at a fast pace to establish the new block near Hopin. The grand plan of Lentaigne's hinged on the block being protected by the other brigades. What his planners had not taken into account, however, was the effects of the monsoon, due to burst on the Chindits in mid-May. When Masters finally established his block, he found he was on his own.

23 Brigade would not be joining the rest of the Chindit brigades. They had been placed under Slim's command, a fate which almost befell 14 Brigade as well. At that time, Wingate's plan was going well. Calvert had blocked the enemy's main line of communication to the north and was holding it against all comers. However, the Japanese had crossed the Chindwin in force and were advancing into the mountains of Manipur as exposed Indian formations were fighting their way back to the plateau about Imphal. Wingate was determined to prevent his force being diverted elsewhere and commented: 'If we aren't careful, the rats will get at us.' He resolved to send 14 Brigade into Burma as soon as possible.

The 2nd Battalion, Black Watch were alerted on the evening of 22 March and the first Jocks flew into Aberdeen the day after. Their two columns were numbered 73, commanded by Colonel Green, and 42, under Major David Rose. Two Black Watch officers had been on Wingate's first expedition: Major Bernard Fergusson, who later commanded 16 Brigade, and the unfortunate Lieutenant Duncan Menzies, who had been captured and bayoneted to death. Fergusson was able to advise the battalion on what to expect of the new form of warfare.

On 9 April, 42 Column carried out its first attack with the new technique of direct air support. The objective was a Japanese supply dump in the small village of Singgan. As the column attacked, the 1st Air Commando Group Mustangs and Mitchell bombers bombed the dump and soon it was ablaze. The column suffered five casualties, including its commander, Major Rose. He was hardly amused as he had been shot in the shoulder, in almost the same hole as had been made in Somaliland nearly four years before. The bullet was removed, but he refused to be evacuated and continued fighting for two more months before he succumbed to his wounds and sickness and was flown out by light plane.

The 2nd Battalion, The York and Lancaster Regiment was also a part of 14 Brigade. Its commander, Lieutenant-Colonel Graves-Morris led 84 Column and his second-in-command, Major Downward, led 65 Column. They flew into Aberdeen on 2 and 3 April to join the rest of 14 Brigade, tasked with acting as marauding columns south of Indaw. 111 Brigade would be carrying out a similar task to the south-west of Indaw. The first task given to the battalion was the destruction of railway communications running south from Indaw, but after they crossed the Meza River they found the area to be completely waterless and abandoned the plan to destroy the railway bridges north of Bonchaung. Instead they turned south towards the bridges in Bonchaung Gorge. Between 12 and 15 April they had a number of skirmishes in the area of Bonchaung, but finally destroyed the bridge and station.

On 19 April the battalion moved to the area of Gahe to prepare for a second co-ordinated attack on Indaw by 16 Brigade (less 45 Recce) from the west and 14 Brigade from the south. The attack was once again met with heavy resistance and the brigades withdrew. However, a number of large enemy dumps were found and destroyed. Lieutenant John Salazar, a platoon commander in the Bedfordshire and Hertfordshire Regiment, disposed of one of them. His diary recorded:

> 'On patrol, four miles. Ambush on Nannaung–Indaw road. Two Japs come along road, I shoot the leading one and Lance-Corporal Phipps brings down the second. Both are dead very soon. I collect cap badges and chevrons for identity. I take Corporal Lane's section and go north. Spot a dump of drums of what looks like petrol or oil. Fire four incendiary bullets. The first forty-gallon drums go up in flames. As we retire quickly hear more explosions and a thick column of smoke rises high in the air.'

Four days later Flight Lieutenant Yorke, their RAF officer, was flown out to guide bombers on to the targets pinpointed around Indaw. However, at the end of the day, the capture of Indaw and its airfields would have been for nought. Slim had no intention of flying in additional troops and the plan had died with Wingate.

In the first week of May the Black Watch was given the task of diverting the attention of the Japanese while White City was evacuated, and was soon to fight its first major engagement in Burma. On 5 May, three platoons of 73 Column were sent to prepare an ambush on a track that the enemy were known to use at night to bypass the White City block and rejoin the railway further north. Piper Bill Lark was one of the men chosen to go:

> 'The first I heard of it was when they needed a mule to carry the hand grenades – four boxes. Katina my mule always carried the medical kit, but since we were in a "safe area" and Thrushy Joe, Menzies' mule, wasn't well with his usual complaint, I took on the job. Well, it was only rumoured that Japs were marching along a back road through the jungle to strengthen their forward troops. It would surely be another wasted effort. Still, it had to be done!

'It was evening when we arrived at the track. The men lined one side of the track and the mules with wireless, ammunition, etc. were among the trees about twenty yards behind the men. We unloaded the mules and settled down, as I thought, for the night. The moon was shining through the trees when about eleven p.m. the fireworks started. A large body of Japanese troops was marching up the road with an officer riding a white horse at their head. When they reached the last man in the ambush he fired the Bren gun, but nothing happened. He tried again – still no joy. He changed the gas port and finally threw the tool to signify that the enemy had reached him. Then it all started. Private McLuskie shot the Jap officer and everyone else opened fire. The horse ran off up the road; the Japs were shouting and screaming. I stood by the mules with my Sten gun at the ready. There was a crashing through the trees; here they come, I thought. Good job I didn't pull the trigger as it was our own lads changing position. This happened about three times and I was a nervous wreck. When things quietened down they bought in our lad "Boozy Broon", a Dundee chap, badly wounded. We made a bamboo stretcher and retired to our column.

'The next morning a patrol went out to survey the scene. The dead bodies were lying around all with their right hands cut off. It was believed that they were cremated and the ashes returned to their families. The officer's papers were captured, plus rice and money which the men on the ambush shared out.'

A similar but larger ambush was laid on the night of 7 May, on the same track but south of Nathkokyin village. The ambush force was to consist of six platoons, roughly 200 men, and Colonel Green himself would be in command. The night wore on but no enemy appeared. At 4.50 a.m. the ambush force fell in on the track and started to march back to their safe harbour. Thirty minutes later a breathless runner came back to report that a party of Japanese had been seen fifty yards ahead of the lead scouts. Green quickly deployed his platoons; Lieutenant McGuigan's platoon would lead the attack, supported by two platoons on the left of the track and two on the right. The Jocks began their attack, but soon discovered that the party of Japanese was approximately 1,200 strong and a sharp fire fight began. Their initial rush had given them certain advantages of ground which enabled them to stem a series of bitter counter-attacks, but platoons became isolated and the number of wounded steadily mounted. After five hours of fighting, Green decided to break off the action and withdraw. The bugler sounded the dispersal and that was the last anyone heard of the Colonel and the main body for the next twenty-nine hours.

Lieutenant 'Gory' Anderson and most of his platoon were the first to arrive back at the safe harbour, together with three wounded. They had been separated early from the main force and had fought on alone, completely surrounded by the Japanese until they broke out with the bayonet. Major Fraser arrived next with a larger party. Colonel Green and his men rejoined them at three p.m. the following day. He had found himself with 105 men, including eleven wounded, two of them officers. Lieutenant Scott-Hyde had a bayonet thrust in the thigh while Lieutenant Richmond had been shot through both ankles while standing to attention addressing the Colonel. Finding the enemy still between them and the safe harbour, the Colonel's party had laid up in the jungle, watching an endless procession of Japanese carrying dead and wounded. It took four hours before the last had passed and it was obvious that there had been a great killing. Thereafter progress was slow because of the wounded, two of whom died on the way and one, with a broken femur, was left behind and never heard of again. Out of the 200 men in the ambush party, twenty-six were killed and thirty-five wounded and a couple were missing. Lieutenant McGuigan had been killed together with Lieutenant Douglas Nicoll who had been wounded in the head and bandaged, then killed by a sniper at fifteen yards' range while speaking to the Colonel. Two days later the wounded were flown out by light plane and the battalion marched steadily northwards to join the rest of 14 Brigade.

Thirty-seven Dakotas landed at White City on the night of 9 May and took out all sick and wounded, surplus mules, thirteen artillery pieces, ammunition and stores. The following morning the Leicesters and Nigerians melted away into the jungle, leaving White City a death trap of mines and booby-traps. Two days earlier, Jack Masters had reported that he had reached the Hopin area and was preparing to establish his block, initially named 'Clydeside' but changed to 'Blackpool' after the codename was compromised over the radio. He had the Cameronians and King's Own with him and the 3/9th Gurkhas would follow as soon as the evacuation of Broadway was completed, on 13 May. The two columns of the 1st King's, acting as floaters around Broadway, would leave earlier on 3 May and march direct to the new block.

Brigadier Mike Calvert sat in the hills of the Gangaw Range, east of Blackpool, and rested with what remained of his brigade – the South Staffords, the Lancashire Fusiliers and the 3/6th Gurkhas. Calvert was far from happy. He bitterly opposed the evacuation of White City after all the blood spilt holding it. He also felt that his brigade should be flown out, having lost forty-six officers and almost 1,000 other ranks killed, wounded or evacuated sick. His new position, between the Namyin River and the mountain range, facing Blackpool with the Japanese behind him, was also unsound. He also received bad news from India. Colonel Richards of the South Staffords, Paddy Ryan and Paddy Dermody, his groom, had been in the Special Forces Hospital in Sylhet under Matron

McGeary, undergoing penicillin treatment. As penicillin was not available in India – it was being stockpiled in Europe ready for the D-Day invasion – they were obtaining supplies from the Americans. However, soon after Wingate's death the hospital was closed and the three were moved to Dacca, which had a bad reputation as a death centre, and there, taken off penicillin, they had all died. The death of Wingate had also been a deep personal loss and it rankled to see his friend's plans changed or discarded. His signals to Lentaigne grew more insurbordinate and on 8 May Lentaigne made one of his rare visits to the field and summoned Calvert to meet him at Broadway. There he explained that there were no fresh troops to relieve 77 Brigade and the Chindits were obliged to continue to block the railway valley for Stilwell and his reluctant Chinese. He did not want to lose Calvert, but if he continued to object to the plan he would have to be relieved. Calvert later wrote that he 'came to his senses' and returned to his brigade. Lentaigne was fortunate to have retained Calvert's services; he was the best brigade commander in Special Force. He was also correct in his opinion on the removal of the White City block; a fortnight after its evacuation and the establishment of Blackpool, the new stronghold fell.

The night after his meeting with Lentaigne, Calvert sat with his officers around a roaring fire and opened some bottles of rum. They sang the old 'Calcutta Cholera Song' which ends with the words, 'Here's a toast to the dead already, and here's a toast to the next man to die.' One tall Gurkha officer told them that he had booked a houseboat in Kashmir for his leave when he came out. He was immediately toasted as 'the next man to die'. Of the officers present, he was.

The 14th and 3rd West African Brigades were on the march towards the mountain overlooking Blackpool from the west. If the plan worked, ten battalions totalling almost 5,000 men would be in position, ready to fight the Japanese 53rd Division. However, the monsoon intervened. Calvert later wrote: 'The weather was now appalling, with thunderstorms roaring and flashing around us in the hills with very heavy rain. The battalions had great difficulty getting their animals and weapons down the slopes, and the South Staffords had to manhandle their heavy weapons down 3,000 feet as the mules kept slipping and rolling with them.' The Namyin Chaung was soon flooded and there were no boats with which to cross over and assist 111 Brigade, which had come under attack almost as soon as it had arrived. One or two officer patrols managed to swim across, but they could achieve very little. One officer was so badly covered with leeches that he needed a blood transfusion when he got back. Lieutenant David Wilcox managed to blow the railway line on one occasion and almost bagged a train: 'Crossing the river at Blackpool took three consecutive nights. During my reconnaissance patrol we had walked in daylight across the chaung, but when trying to get across later that day the monsoon had flooded the river and we had to swim across, using ropes to get the non-swimmers over. The land between the river and the railway was flooded and we were wading very noisily until we reached the railway embankment itself. Our contact detonators failed to go off when a train ran over them, some two hours after we had laid them, but the time fuses worked and we heard the explosion as we were recrossing the river early the next morning.'

The block at Blackpool was not truly a block across the road and railway, but overlooked them at about a mile's distance. The block was also overlooked itself to some extent and its forward slopes were very vulnerable to artillery fire. Unlike White City, it was very accessible to the Japanese, who could bring up troops and artillery without hindrance. It was too close to the Japanese front lines and they had troops, guns and ammunition in abundance. A Dakota strip was carved out of the paddy, but the enemy later brought up anti-aircraft guns and rendered it inoperative. Perhaps with hindsight, it would have been better to forget about a new block and revert to traditional Chindit warfare to wear down the Japanese and disrupt their lines of communication. Masters later described Blackpool hill as

> 'looking something like a sharp-spined animal, say a boar, lying with head down, forearms and legs extended sideways, and short tail outstretched. The area between outstretched members constituted defilade (shelter) from enemy fire, from three directions in each case. The Namyin Chaung curved in round the animal's left forefoot and then on past its nose. Our water point was sheltered just inside that forefoot. The airstrip extended along the animal's right side, the near edge about one hundred yards away from the tips of right forefoot and right hind leg. The tail joined another hill feature, which was not part of the block. To left and straight ahead were tangled hills, split by streams and gorges and folds, all heavily forested.'

As Masters prepared his defences, he allocated cricketing names to the various positions and strongpoints, such as Cover Point, Midwicket, Deep etc.

As the men of 111 Brigade began to dig in and prepare for glider loads of earthmoving equipment to arrive, with which to construct their Dakota strip, Calvert was ordered to take his brigade north-east and capture Mogaung. To the west of Blackpool both 14 Brigade and the West Africans struggled through the monsoon towards the block. By the time they got near, it would be too late.

Lieutenant Geoffrey Straight of 1st Battalion, The Cameronians, was hungry. For a full month before his battalion flew into Broadway they had been on one continuous exercise, living solely on K rations and then a score of them, including Straight, were found to be suffering with jaundice:

'The whites of my eyes turned brown and I was passing what looked like strong tea. I tried to eat, but everything placed to my mouth totally turned my stomach. The only item I could eat for a fortnight was the fruitbar in the breakfast rations. It was a bad fourteen days; the only advantage was that my pack was carried on a mule for that period.

'We marched and marched – I reckon we could have covered 700 miles, but this may be an overestimate. 90 Column had a few brushes with the enemy, nothing very complicated or serious. Doc McFie of 26 Column spent the whole of three ten-minute halts trying to extract a back tooth from a suffering Jock without anaesthetic. They had a more exciting time than us, contriving one highly successful ambush of a column of vehicles, marred sadly by a supposedly dead Japanese suddenly arising to shoot the officer in control of the ambush as he inspected the damage that had been caused.

'We of 90 Column called in at Aberdeen for a rest, then pressed on to our final objective – Blackpool. As we neared the block our mules were taken away from us and as we moved down a ridge to take up our position near the bottom we passed two or three light artillery positions. The gunners told me that they had a fine field of fire, but I thought they had very little cover or protection. After the first Japanese bombing I repassed their position on the way to report to Column HQ and there was no sign of them, or their weapons. Either they had been moved or they had been wiped out – from the smell that was developing the latter seems most likely.

'We dug our various holes in the ground and had just a little while to take in our situation. Blackpool was far from being a conventional road block sitting athwart the enemy lines of communication. It was sited on raised ground and the road and railway were more than a mile away on flat ground stretching from the block. The intention was that we would be able to prevent movement by gunfire from four twenty-five-pounders and various light artillery weapons. The airstrip that was vital to us for the landing of supplies and evacuation of the wounded was sited outside the perimeter and completely vulnerable to ground attack. Hindsight may well be that the block was ill-conceived, poorly sited and unsustainable once the use of the airstrip was neutralised. Night after night their attacks would go in at the north end of the block, followed by short lulls and succeeded by final attacks that lasted for little more than a quarter of an hour. We guessed that these secondary attacks were mounted so that they might retrieve some of their dead and wounded. In the rest of the block life continued relatively quietly; shells were lobbed over from time to time, disconcerting to experience, but achieving little. Food, stores and ammunition could be retrieved from the airstrip and sick and wounded could go out.

'We had things to watch. A bomber flew low and slow along a ridge to our left front, leaving in its wake a series of twenty parachute bombs. This provided a heavyweight fireworks display when they all exploded just below tree level. The routine continued until the fifth or sixth day when the enemy introduced the "whizz bang" gun into the attack. This created a far greater sense of urgency than had the previous high trajectory shelling and one of my slit trenches took a direct hit which killed a couple of very good riflemen. At about the same time the nightly onslaught on the northern end of the block ceased. The airstrip soon became unusable and enemy anti-aircraft fire caused the supply planes to drop from such a height that most of the parachutes fell into enemy hands. We were moved to a ridge overlooking the strip and one night saw a convoy of vehicles moving up the valley from the south towards us, with headlights blazing. Because of the ridge our artillery could not be brought to bear on them and in any case our twenty-five-pounders had suffered considerable damage to guns and personnel. We could only sit and watch.

'The next night my batman, a stocky 5'6" Geordie, and I were in a slit trench peering out towards the enemy. I asked him to change places with me, and to illustrate how important split seconds can be, as we did so a bullet passed through the very top of his steel helmet, doing little more than gently parting his hair. If I had still been standing there I would have received the bullet at about eyebrow height.'

One rifleman who was wounded and lived to tell the tale is Brian Soppitt. Fifty years later he told the author:

'I served in 26 Column under Major T. Brennan, who, it seemed, never appeared to duck when the lead was flying. He installed great confidence and trust among us, a great leader. I was in 7 Platoon, led by a Captain Beasley who, with his batman, disappeared completely while acting as liaison between a road block and the "safe harbour" in the Banmauk area. He got us lost a number of times and his favourite saying was "I see no ships".

'Sergeant Donald took over the platoon. He was a first-class man and soldier, quietly spoken, exuding confidence within the platoon, and was later awarded the Distinguished Conduct Medal for his actions at Blackpool.

'Up until about 15 May, the King's were holding the Deep. It seemed to be a main fronting position for the Japs and very many of them died there. Our column took up positions there to give the King's a rest. We were continually shelled and mortared day and night with dawn attacks on the Deep. Our little airstrip was shelled continuously, but there was a "Cochran's Circus" man there, driving a small bulldozer, who had a charmed life as he drove around filling in the holes in the strip as they appeared. I never knew his name, but he offered to swap my stinking shirt for his clean camo-jacket.

'The hills around us provided good OPs for the Japs and we suffered for it. Our four twenty-five-pounders were quickly silenced as soon as they were sited. On 19 May, about 4.30 a.m., a heavy barrage was laid down by the Japs and my foxhole was hit. I was blown out of it, a piece of shrapnel entering my head just below my right eye. I could not see or hardly hear. Sergeant Donald dragged me into his cover and gave me morphine. When the shelling eased I was taken down to the First Aid Post (FAP), bandaged up, examined and labelled for evacuation. My worst moments were lying on my back in a large open trench at the FAP, expecting every shell and mortar was for me. I was flown out about 2.30 p.m. the same day to Shadazup, which was now a US hospital.'

Joe Milner, of 1st Battalion, The King's (Liverpool) Regiment, was one of Scottie's men who fought at Blackpool. He wrote a fictional account of the battle at Blackpool in his book *To Blazes With Glory* (Gaskell, 1995). Joe wrote to the author:

'I doubt whether any of the rank and file, or many officers, really knew whether it was intended to be a road and rail block or a stronghold. As a block it was well over a mile from the road and railway, and broadside on to mass attacks, which the enemy could marshall and concentrate out of sight and range of any effective harassment. As a stronghold it was too close and accessible to the Japs' forward reserves. Masters was, of course, ordered to establish Blackpool in that area, but the precise siting was his choice alone.

'A few miles south he could have established it in the valley, straddling the road and railway at Hopin. True the enemy could have attacked up the road and railway from both sides, but their supply route to the north would have been strangled. Their attacks would be on a narrow front, across a mile or so of open "killing ground" surrounding the block, and vulnerable to both the defenders and to Mike Calvert's brigade on the mountain to the east. The West Africans and 14 Brigade could have swept down from the south-west. The Japs' concentration areas would have been exposed to aerial attacks. Once the rains set in, flooding the valley, the dry season road would have been impassable, leaving only the one-metre rail track available to tanks and heavy guns etc. and requiring a massive sampan navy to mount any offensive in strength. The weather would have been our ally instead of the Japs'. Retreat, if necessary, could have been over the east to Broadway, a tiring trek, but by no means as punishing as that from Blackpool to Mokso Sakan. Although by then closed down, it would have been an infinitely healthier evacuation and regrouping area than the Indawgyi Lake. During the Blackpool siege, men constantly voiced the foregoing beliefs.

'The withdrawal from Blackpool was not, as some war reports state, well planned and conducted, but a chaotic rout of exhausted troops without any clear orders or known destination. It was completed more due to the toughness of Wingate's training, the leadership of unit officers and regimental *esprit de corps*, than to any professed planning and skill of Brigade HQ that carried the survivors to Mokso Sakan.'

The battle for Blackpool reached its climax on the night of 23 May. The Japanese fought their way into the eastern side of the block and overran the field gun and Bofors pits. A counter-attack by the King's Own failed and the mortar crews were almost out of ammunition. Resupply from the air was now impossible due to enemy anti-aircraft fire, and of 14 Brigade there was no sign. Jack Masters reluctantly gave the order to evacuate the block. Lieutenant Straight describes the withdrawal of the Cameronians:

'Pressure mounted throughout the night. The Japanese were beginning to re-occupy Pimple from which they had been ejected earlier by an assault bravely led by Sergeant Donald of 26 Column. Mortar bombing intensified. Finally, early in the morning, word was passed down the line to abandon our ridge. The higher part of it, nearest to Pimple had already been evacuated and there were groups of dead and wounded where mortars had taken their toll. I sent my batman on ahead and he scurried across the gully to the other side. I stood for a moment at the top of the steep twenty-five-foot slope for a last check on the nearby slit trenches and they appeared to be empty. Small arms fire was crackling through the air quite near. It occurred to me that if I walked down the slope I could easily become a target, so I let myself go and rolled down to the bottom. There I lay still for a few seconds, hoping to convince any observing Japanese sharpshooter that he had claimed another victim. Then I got up and ran as fast as I could to the other side of the gully.

'When I reached Geordie we heard a shout from behind and there was rifleman Drysdale scrambling down the far slope carrying a Bren gun. We urged him on, but he fell into a hole. The Bren became hopelessly entangled in some netting and had to be abandoned. The three of us carried on up the ridge. Machine-gun bullets spattered the path a yard or so in front of us, so we descended a little way down the far side of the ridge where, for a short while at least, we had adequate cover.

'At the top of the hill our battalion commander Bill Henning was there to meet us. I told him there were a number of wounded in the dip between the two ridges. Could we do anything about them? The Japanese were already to be seen in numbers on the far ridge. He pondered the matter for a moment or two. "No," he said, "we must get out." A heartbreaking, but in the circumstances a correct, decision. And so we began the slow walk out through the block. The pace was dictated by the many walking and stretcher-borne wounded at the head of the column. On we shuffled, but once again were brought to a halt by the main dressing station. Every book written on Blackpool carries a description of the slaughter and destruction caused by mortar bombs. Sufficient to say that to stand there for five minutes was a horrifying and unforgettable experience. The passage of time has blurred the edges, but the ghastly memories linger on.'

The main dressing station was already filled to overflowing with the wounded and dying when two enemy shells scored a direct hit, adding to the misery. Among the carnage worked Doc Whyte, the senior medical officer:

'In some 60 minutes, 300 shells exploded within the block perimeter, wreaking havoc among men and animals. We dug ourselves out of the mud to rescue what we could and to find that the jungle birds had burst into song after the din, a strange contrast. I believe I heard a hill mynah. The adjutant informed us that fifteen enemy planes had carried out a bombing raid during the shelling. Our four field guns had been knocked out and our sole Bofors gun lay at an absurd angle, fought to the end by the detachment of gunners, not a single member of whom survived. We now had a full view of the enemy, carefully creeping on to the airstrip, covered by field pieces, machine-guns and mortars. The main dressing station was becoming unmanageable with helpless wounded, some critical; and we blessed the inventor of tubunic morphine, the quick-ampoule injection. I was ordered to withdraw north through the attacking force by any means available, the scene within the hospital area now being difficult to put into words. In the din of battle and flying metal orders were impossible. I assembled the medical team from their posts, placing the walking wounded in sections under NCOs with orders to meet me at the map reference.'

Jack Masters was now faced with one of the worst decisions of his life. Nineteen men lay on stretchers on the track, each and every one a hopeless case. Thirty others might have a chance of survival, but there were not enough men to carry them all. The dying would have to be left, but they should not be left alive for the Japanese to torture and butcher. Masters sent the stretcher-bearers on ahead to carry out the other wounded, nodded his agreement and walked away. As he gave orders to the rear party to retire in five minutes the sound of single carbine shots rang out behind him. Doc Whyte continues:

'We carried the remainder, one helping another, up the muddy hill. The shells were tearing men and animals apart; two men disappeared as I tied up the shoulder of a third. There was a furious rearguard action, of which we were now a part. Enemy snipers had taken up positions on either side of the only track possible. As we stumbled and slithered upwards, the

199

blinded men tied in a line by lengths of cloth, my ear rang as a shot hit the tree beside me. Heavy monsoon rain was falling. I half spun round as a bullet went through my medical pack, scattering my string of casualties. The shelling eased, the machine-guns, mortars and rifle fire continued. We made the first ridge and somehow got over the top, awaiting the inevitable attack from the enemy. Why the Japanese failed to follow up and finish off the remainder of our force remains a mystery.'

One of the stretcher-bearers was Norman Campbell, one of the Cameronian cipher operators:

'I took the front end of the stretcher and we set off down the track behind Brigade HQ. The track was wet and muddy and we slithered along rather than walked. Some distance along I saw what I thought was a West African soldier, who was taking a breather from carrying a Vickers machine-gun, which stood on the track alongside him. I began to lose my grip on the stretcher handles and called for a halt. As we crouched down to lower the stretcher I heard a bang up ahead and felt something hit my face. I wiped my hand across my face and it came away bloody and I thought I had been hit. I looked down the track and the soldier was no longer there. The Vickers was still there, so were the soldier's boots with his feet inside them, and his head lay on the track. He must have suffered a direct hit from a shell or mortar bomb. We came down off the hill and on to the flat. In front of us lay a stretch of flat open ground, perhaps half a mile wide, hardly a tree or cover whatsoever. Beyond the flat, the ground started to rise into hilly, well-wooded ground and we had to get there for cover. We moved as quickly as we could, with an occasional "splat" as a bullet hit the wet ground. Just in front of the tree line we came across a lot of trenches which had been occupied by the Japs. Why they pulled out and had not re-occupied the trenches when the big onslaught began was a mystery. Had they done so, every Chindit on Blackpool would have been killed or captured.'

Campbell and his small party got separated from the main body and struggled for five days over the hills without a scrap of food to eat. Finally they found the rest of the battalion and Captain Neil McLean kindly cut his blanket in half and gave Campbell a piece. He also gave him some of the very small amount of food he had. He was still hungry, but he was alive.

Jack Masters was the last man in the last column to leave the block. Behind him stood Lieutenant-Colonel Scott of the 1st King's with about seventeen men, left holding the upper slopes of the eastern face. Joe Milner's section was detailed to form a rearguard picquet astride a stream about a mile outside Blackpool. They bypassed the retreating Cameronians with Masters around the water-hole. Not being encumbered with wounded they were able to take a direct route via nullahs and wildlife tracks. They reached the picquet point to find Scottie already there, calmly squatting on a boulder as though resting on a Sunday stroll. An orienteer *par excellence*, he had found a more direct route. For one reason or other, those with Masters had been forced to take a very circuitous route and it seemed an age, and spells of murderous gunfire, before he reached the picquet. By then Scottie was leading earlier columns of men uphill, leaving Milner with a map reference for an RV to pass on to Masters. The other survivors of the brigade dragged themselves up the slippery slopes rising over 3,000 feet and began to wade through the mud, taking their wounded and dying with them. They were cold, hungry and mentally and physically exhausted. It took them four days to reach Mokso Sakan where the Gurkhas of 30 Column and huge Africans from 6th Battalion, Nigeria Regiment awaited them.

Chapter 14

Indawgyi Lake and Mogaung

The wooded valley in which Indawgyi Lake lay was worked by a British timber firm before the war. Its natural outlet is to the north, by way of the Indaw Chaung to the Mogaung Valley, and it is shut in by the Kachin Hills on the south, west and east. The east flank was the most dangerous, since there are passes over the hills giving access to the railway only twelve miles away. The easiest pass to march through was the Kyusunlai Pass, whose summit is fifteen miles south-east of the southern end of the lake.

With the establishment of Blackpool, the Japanese sought another route by which they could send reinforcements to Kamaing to fight the slowly advancing Chinese, and this route lay through the Kyusunlai Pass. 14 Brigade was instructed to seize the pass before the Japanese. Major Jeffrey Lockett's column of the 7th Leicesters were determined to occupy the pass first and by some fast marching arrived there on 20 May, just in time to beat off the enemy. When Blackpool fell, it was important to hold the pass to prevent the Japanese interfering with the evacuation of casualties from Indawgyi Lake.

Struggling through the mud and rain towards Blackpool, the two columns of the 2nd Battalion, York and Lancaster Regiment were turned around as news reached them that the block had been abandoned. 84 Column was now ordered to put a block on the Zigon track to the east of the pass, while 65 Column was to march to the lake. March, of course, was a mere figure of speech. On 27 May the whole bivouac area of 65 Column was flooded by raging torrents of water from the swollen chaungs. Much kit was lost and even Bren guns were buried in an avalanche of rocks and sand. One group just escaped death when a large tree crashed to the ground beside them. The men spent a miserable night, soaked to the skin and swathed in their dripping groundsheets. The tracks and paths turned to quagmire and the men were lucky to travel a mile per day.

A couple of days before the York and Lancs were directed towards Zigon, a member of the 1st Battalion, Bedfordshire and Hertfordshire Regiment won the Military Medal there. His name was 3656585 Private Robert Boyd, and he told the author:

'We did a platoon attack late in the afternoon of 24 May and captured about twelve ponies loaded with supplies. As I was leading one back to our base I came across a dead Jap, an officer or an NCO. When we got back to base I mentioned it to our officer Mister Salazar. Trust me to open my big mouth. I was told to show another patrol where the dead Jap was. By now it had started to get dark and I handed my Bren gun to my number two and took his rifle instead. We were ambushed and the patrol leader was shot in the legs. How the hell they missed me I'll never know. All I could see was three, maybe four of them and I opened fire and kept firing; I must have killed a couple of them. I tell you I was feared to death and it was only due to training that I got out alive. I made one mistake: I never checked the ammunition in the rifle and I ran out of ammo. I was feared all right, feared they would shoot me, so I kept on jabbing with the bayonet and also using the butt of the rifle as a club. It was a fearful thing to happen to me that night, but looking back I think someone was looking after me.'

Captain Shadbolt, Royal Engineers, was with 2nd Black Watch who were guarding the pass above Indawgyi Lake while the sick and wounded were being evacuated by flying boat:

'Two fighting patrols had been sent out, but none returned. I volunteered and after some hesitation the CO sent a message "accepted". I was detailed with some fifteen men to follow the same route, along a ridge with a steep drop to one side. We proceeded for some four to five hours, when going down a steep incline a machine-gun opened up on the other side. It was, fortunately, on a fixed line, fired over my head and killed five men immediately behind. We broke right, down the precipitous slope, through some trees and made our way back to the column. Subsequently we discovered the Japs had evacuated the position.'

Lieutenant Denis Arnold of the 7th Nigerians walked up the slope and stopped dead. Five paces ahead of him in a slit trench sat a handful of Japanese with a machine-gun, covering the track. He slowly exhaled as he realised that they were asleep, then quietly retraced his steps to his platoon of Africans:

'I had been sent to the Kyusunlai Pass with my platoon and met Jeffrey Lockett DSO, a famous Chindit from the first expedition. Now commanding a Leicesters column, he was soaked through, wearing his famous waistcoat complete with oiled silk-lined pockets in which he kept his snuff, from which he would take a pinch, leaving a brown stain all down the front. His lack of teeth also gave him a raffish brigand kind of appearance, but he was brave and resourceful.

'I had great difficulty getting to my new position up on a ridge with a track on which the Japanese moved from time to time. My job here, with my platoon, was to control the track and follow a telephone wire which had been found earlier by Captain John MacFarlane when they had killed a Japanese soldier. The wire followed the path along the ridge towards the pass and we were in no doubt of the Japanese presence here. We had gone some way when I was aware of a widening of the path leading towards rising ground to a hill feature. Our lead scouts were sure there were Japs on the hill and I wanted to get on, so felt a personal recce was necessary. After finding the sleeping Japs I carefully withdrew and outlined a plan to attack immediately, having forgotten about my orders to locate and observe the enemy and report back to my CO. One half of the platoon would go left under Sergeant Umoru Numan, MM, the other half under Sergeant Keevil would go right. I advanced up the hill again, with the flank parties in line with me, and found the Japs still asleep. I opened fire with my American Remington 300 rifle and followed up with a grenade for good measure. At the same time my men charged up the hill firing and shouting as they ran. The Japs responded with customary vigour and we were hard put to drive them out. Afterwards we were very pleased with our action, although I lost one of my excellent Tiv men who I was very attached to. My CO thought the day's activities merited an award and my receiving an immediate MC was a most agreeable and surprising end to the day's action.'

Lieutenant Kenneth Kerin, mortar officer, 6th Nigerians:

'We were somewhere in the hills in the vicinity of Nawku, in the heights overlooking Indawgyi Lake, towards the end of the campaign when the rains had started. We came across a very slippery and steep section of the track and the muleteers were forced to offload the mules and lead them down individually. I took it upon myself to carry the muleteers' rifles, which were an encumbrance in their task. When I started on my descent I had about three rifles on each shoulder and being otherwise heavily laden commenced to slip. I had almost fallen when I felt a steadying grip on my upper right arm, and turning found myself gazing into the seemingly understanding eyes of a mule, whose teeth were firmly clamped on my biceps. As I recovered my balance he released me, and the amount of pressure he had exerted had in no way hurt or damaged my arm, being just sufficient and no more. I may be imputing a human characteristic to an animal where it did not exist, but I would swear that this mule was trying to help.'

The three brigades, the 3rd, 14th and 111th, were now located to the east of Indawgyi Lake. To the north lay Kamaing and to the north-east Mogaung. The monsoon was now in full swing and at the lakeside waited hundreds of sick and wounded Chindits. How to get them out? Squadron Leader 'Chesty' Jennings, the 111 Brigade senior RAF officer, had an idea: flying boats. The lake is sixteen miles long and five wide at its broadest point and would be no problem for the two Sunderland flying boats *Gert* and *Daisy* who were given the job. Two evacuation stations were established on the lake: 'Dawlish' at the north end near 111 Brigade and 'Plymouth' at the south, near 14 Brigade. The

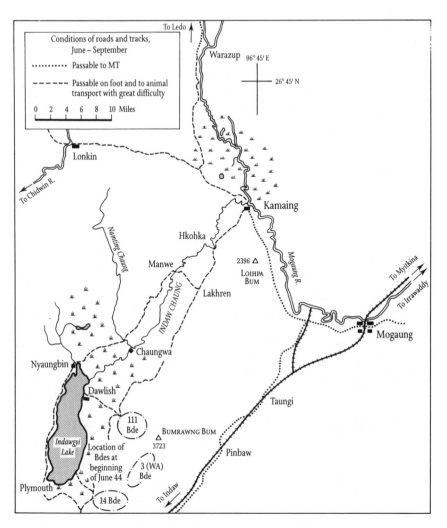

Indawgyi Lake and the river evacuation route.

Royal Engineers were given the job of preparing for their arrival: constructing jetties, hospital accommodation, marking a 2,000 by 100 yard landing strip with buoys, and various other tasks. Major Kenneth Robertson of 54 Field Company, Royal Engineers was the senior engineer with 14 Brigade. He recalled:

> 'Work started after a large supply drop. Ammunition, food, medical supplies, petrol and RE stores landed in clouds of spray and mud in the marsh. Among things collected, or rather salvaged, were buoys and

anchors to mark the landing strip, ten rubber "Ranger" boats and five Johnson outboard motors. Two jetties were made; one was a trestle affair made from jungle timber and bamboo lashed with parachute rope, the other was a half-floating bay supported on local canoes. A squall swamped and sank the latter right in the middle of the first embarkation. The hospital accommodation was the pride of a West African sapper platoon. Experts in the use of bamboo, they soon had a very creditable casualty reception station organised in the buildings of the nearby village. A "Ranger" boat has plenty of buoyancy, but little room inside it, especially for lying cases. Consequently four rafts were made, each supported on two boats and powered by one motor. With a crew of two and fourteen sitting or six stretcher cases, its speed was roughly three knots.

'Bright and early on 3 June the flying boat appeared through a break in the clouds. For a few breathless seconds she skimmed along the surface before settling down in the water and coming to rest safely. Rafts were called forward, each to a particular hatch for loading. To load four parties of troops through four separate doors with a squall blowing at the time produces a result like Piccadilly Underground in the rush hour! Forty men were loaded aboard before she left. She made two more trips to "Plymouth" and took forty out each time. On the last visit only eighteen minutes elapsed between the motors stopping and re-ignition for take-off.

'In the middle of June, 3 and 14 Brigades moved northwards towards Kamaing. It was therefore decided to close "Plymouth" and combine both stations at "Dawlish", with command of the latter being taken over from 111 by 14 Brigade. Around the same time, Stilwell's forces captured Kamaing and this meant that the only enemy between Stilwell and ourselves were isolated and scattered parties from Lonkin and Kamaing. For various reasons the flying boat service had been withdrawn, so the decision was made to transport the remaining 400 casualties in the lake area to Kamaing. The Indaw Chaung flows from the north-eastern corner of the lake to Kamaing, thirty miles away as the crow flies. By boat, however, it is around fifty miles and many of those miles are choked with weeds and underwater obstacles. It is no place for a frail hull. We decided to build what we called "dreadnoughts". These were large rafts built primarily for ferrying mules over broad and fast rivers and all but one of their essential components could be dropped from the air. The exception was the frame, which would be built from bamboo and wood obtained locally. Two similar flat bamboo frames were made, and between them were lashed five "Ranger" boats. The hull was wrapped in a forty by twenty foot tarpaulin to give it a better "streamline" and a little extra buoyancy. A deck was made from bamboo matting, such as abounds in north Burma, where whole villages are principally made of it. Between two and four Johnson outboard motors were fastened to the stern by a frame designed to take their weight, thrust and torque. A timber cut-water was desirable to cut down excessive bow wave and to strengthen the blunt inflated bow. Any superstructure, such as canopies, were added as required. When finished a dreadnought was thirty-seven foot overall and twelve foot in the beam and when fully loaded the draught was about fifteen inches. The minimum crew was four men: captain, two motor-men and a deckhand, and thirty-five fully equipped men could be carried. Construction of the "Indawgyi Grand Fleet" took place at the end of June and ten dreadnoughts were laid down: *Ark Royal, Vindictive, Valiant, Vanguard, Revenge, Renown, Resolution, Barham, Benbow* and *Blenheim.*'

The next two weeks were hard work for all concerned. Although all 400 men and ten dreadnoughts cleared the lake and reached Chaung-wa, roughly a quarter of the way along the chaung, they were informed that Kamaing could not receive all the casualties and three-quarters of them had to return to the lake. Eventually three more flying boat visits were made before one of them was sunk by a squall as she sat in the Brahmaputra River in India, and the other was withdrawn. Some time passed before all remaining casualties reached Kamaing, but even then their troubles were not yet over. At the end of July, Kamaing was still principally supplied by air and American resources could not cope with the numbers of sick. Most would have to be transported forty miles further north, up the Mogaung River, to be flown out of Warazup. Instead of the dreadnoughts, American M2 boats were used, which carried a dozen men at a time and the round trip could be made within a day. During July and August, 1,800 men were taken up to Warazup in this way. By the end of August the main line of communication was firmly established by air to Myitkina and by rail from there to Mogaung and the south, so that traffic on the river route practically ceased.

A brigade was approximately 3,000 strong, so roughly three-quarters of a brigade was evacuated in this manner. The total does not include those killed, died of sickness, or evacuated by other means.

EVACUATION FIGURES

DATE	METHOD	NUMBER.
June	Flying boat to India	240
June/July	From Indawgyi Lake to Kamaing aboard dreadnoughts manned by 54 Co. 60 miles	400
July/Aug	From Kamaing to Warazup for evacuation by air to India. In US assault boats manned by 54 Co. 45 miles.	1,800
Total		2,440

While the bulk of Special Force was embroiled in and around Blackpool, Mike Calvert's men shouldered their packs and set off for their own date with destiny. Some of them recalled the march to Mogaung.

John Chesshire, medical officer, South Staffords:

'On the march from White City to Mogaung there were few opportunities to evacuate the wounded. They had to be carried with us forward, sometimes well behind the column. One day a man was wounded near the track, a bullet wound in the shoulder. I sent my casualties on to try to keep up with the column. It was dark and raining hard and we had no chance of keeping up with the column, so we moved off the track into the jungle. I lay down with the wounded man under my blanket and woke up to find him dead beside me. I don't know why he died. We buried him and managed to catch up with the column next day.'

Bert Gilroy, Lancashire Fusiliers:

'One night our platoon was put on guard just outside a village where there was a watering point. Our position was on top of a bank about ten feet high, overlooking the watering point. During the night we heard voices and saw some Japs approaching. There must have been about six of them. Our Sergeant and a Corporal lobbed some grenades and shortly after there was quite a commotion and screaming. Obviously the Japs had casualties and quickly withdrew. When we moved on in the morning, our platoon was leading and we had only gone a hundred yards when we were fired on. We all took cover and saw there were two tracks ahead, one left and one right. Sergeant Tommy Maloney crawled forward and saw a slight movement from the track junction. He threw a grenade and when we advanced we saw a dead Jap on his back. His chest had been blown open and we could see his intestines like you would see in illustrations in medical books. I can still see that sight as if it were today. We searched the dense undergrowth and killed three more Japs who were well camouflaged and dug in at ground level.'

Lieutenant John De Quidt, Lancashire Fusiliers:

'After leaving White City I have various disconnected mental pictures of the move north with the monsoon starting. We had no air drop of rations for about six days and by the time we did get a drop we were very tired and lethargic. A free fall bale of mule fodder landed on one side of a tree while I was sitting on the other side. It would have been an undignified way to be killed. Mostly I remember scrambling up and down muddy tracks, sometimes hanging on to the tail of a mule, sometimes falling down on my face. Once I picked up an apparently discarded groundsheet by the side of the track and found that it had been laid over a dead Fusilier, killed in one of the encounters which we had with the Japs on the way to Mogaung. I remember one occasion when we were mortared in rather open ground, which was frightening, and another when we charged up a short bare slope at the Japanese in the trees at the top, after intensive fire from our Vickers MMGs. Several years later I told some officers who had served in a machine-gun battalion in the desert how we had used Vickers at a range of fifty yards to rake the jungle. They were very shocked and thought this most unprofessional, almost improper. It was one of Wingate's ideas and it was very effective.'

While 77 Brigade marched towards Mogaung, the 1st Battalion, King's Liverpool left Broadway to join 111 Brigade at Blackpool. However, the Japanese were moving their 53rd Division towards Blackpool from White City and the jungle south of Mogaung was swarming with them. The two columns of the King's, comprising A and C companies in 82 Column under Major Dick Gaitley and B and D companies in 81 Column led by the battalion commander Lieutenant-Colonel Walter Scott, moved cautiously as they approached the road and railway which ran up to Mogaung. 81 Column crossed safely and moved on towards Blackpool, but 82 Column ran out of luck and bumped into an enemy unit, suffering heavy casualties. Ken Davenport recalled:

'It was dark when our column reached the road. We took up our positions and let the ponies with the sick and wounded and the mules cross. Then, as our section waited as the rest of the column passed through, we heard the sound of marching feet only a few yards away. Our Sergeant-Major shouted "Halt!" three times and then all hell broke loose. Part of the column went back into the jungle with the Japs on their heels, the rest, including Corporal Bibby and myself, crossed the road safely and continued on to Blackpool. He was later killed by a mortar bomb – he was from Blackpool and he lost his life in the battle for Blackpool.'

A later enquiry held Major Gaitley responsible for the disaster and he was sent home. The survivors of those who failed to cross, numbering around a hundred men, including Captain Fred Freeman, made their way to a predetermined rendezvous where they joined up with Mike Calvert's 77 Brigade and later took part in the battle for Mogaung. Freeman told the author:

'The specialist troops such as machine-gunners, mortar crews and wireless operators joined Brigade Headquarters. The remainder, consisting of two platoons, were known as the "King's Company" and were attached to the Lancashire Fusiliers. The officers included Captain George Morrow, MM, from Belfast. He had been flown in as a reinforcement officer after the glider casualties and became the company commander. He had served with Wingate in Abyssinia, where he had been a Company Sergeant-Major with the 2nd Ethiopian Battalion, largely made up of local tribesmen. On one occasion, when all the officers in the battalion had been killed or wounded, he signed a message to Wingate as "CSM o/c 2nd Ethiopian Battalion." This bizarre situation, of a battalion with no officers, tickled Wingate's sense of humour and he sent back a message stating that "under King's Regulations non-commissioned officers commanding battalions should designate themselves 'i/c' (meaning in charge) not 'o/c' (meaning officer commanding)".

'Another reinforcement officer was Captain Ollie Evans, who was from the Welch Regiment. He requested to be allowed to serve as a platoon commander, as he did not know any of the men and he had had no training in Wingate's long-range penetration warfare. He was an extremely brave soldier and should have received a high decoration for gallantry at Mogaung. In fact, like many unsung heroes in the Chindits, he received no recognition.

'The hills leading to Mogaung were very steep and slippery. We had a number of men wounded during the advance and transporting them was a tremendous problem. It frequently meant carrying men on piggy-back. In my mind's eye I can still see Mike Calvert, who was very strong, personally carrying a wounded man on his back up one particularly steep hill.'

It was 3 June, ten days after Blackpool had fallen. Brigadier Mike Calvert stood at the top of the 1,200-foot-high ridge and looked through his field glasses towards the town of Mogaung, two miles away. It had been a long trek from White City and the fighting had not been easy; the previous day's fighting had cost him five dead and twenty-six wounded. As the Dakotas began a supply drop to the east of the ridge, Calvert pondered his next move. The Lancashire Fusiliers were with Brigade HQ at Loihinche and the South Staffords and the 3/6th Gurkhas were nearby at Lakum. To the rear, the two commando platoons of the Lancashire Fusiliers under Captain Butler had captured the Tapaw Ferry on the Mogaung River, providing a back-door escape route for the brigade if it was required.

Mogaung was a difficult place to attack. To the west was the flooded Wettauk and Namyin Chaungs and to the north the Mogaung River, which flowed in a semi-circle round to the Tapaw Ferry and on to the Irrawaddy. The river was crossed at Mogaung by a damaged girder railway bridge, which carried the rail track from Rangoon towards Myitkyina. One direction of approach was from the south, along the line of the railway, from Loilaw to Ywathit, but that was the direction from which the Japanese would expect them. Calvert decided to advance from the south-east, crossing the thirty-yard-wide Wettauk Chaung over the bridge near the village of Pinhmi. Here Calvert made one of the worst mistakes of his career.

Up until now, the brigade had mostly faced Japanese defences at platoon strength or less and they had been overcome by aggressive assaults. After capturing Pinhmi village, the Lancashire Fusiliers moved up to the bridge and waited for orders. The Japanese were in excellent concealed positions high up on the 15 foot embankment leading to the far side of the bridge, surrounded by a sea of marsh and mangrove swamp. On the Fusiliers' side of the bridge, the road from the village was raised several feet above ground level, with a ditch on one side and dense jungle on the other. At first a platoon tried to work its way along the ditch towards the bridge, but it was overgrown and the water too deep and they could not place effective fire on the Japanese bunkers. About six p.m. the Brigadier arrived and decided to send two platoons straight down the road, across the bridge and into the Japanese positions. He later admitted that he should not have given the order. One platoon crouched in the ditch, the other lay down in the jungle, while the mortars laid down a barrage across the bridge. The faces of the men were tired and grim and some of them pressed each other's hands for reassurance. One of the mortar bombs fell short and wounded Lieutenant De Quidt and his Sergeant. The Fusiliers fixed bayonets, pulled themselves up on to the road and charged.

The Lancashire Fusiliers were sitting ducks. The Japanese machine-gunners waited until they reached the bridge, then opened fire. For several minutes the men tried to get across the bridge, so that they could throw grenades into the bunkers, but the fire was too heavy and they had to retreat, losing more men on the way back. Major David Monteith, the company commander who had led the attack, miraculously escaped injury and that night he visited the wounded as they lay in huts in Pinhmi village. The next morning he returned to the road near the bridge to try to get a better view of the enemy positions. He was shot by an enemy sniper and died soon afterwards. The following day, the Gurkhas forded the chaung south of the bridge and fell upon the Japanese from the rear. They were led by Captain Michael Allmand, who would win the Victoria Cross before Mogaung fell.

The delay in taking the bridge had been costly; 130 casualties had been incurred and in the meantime two more Japanese battalions had arrived to reinforce Mogaung, making a total of four. 77 Brigade would destroy itself defeating them. The next day saw the Fusiliers across the bridge and fighting in the Courthouse Triangle, an area bounded by the Pinhmi road, a cart track and a stream. At the same time, the South Staffords were sent in to clear the area between the Mogaung road and river and thus secure the right flank of the brigade. Lieutenant David Wilcox and his platoon were in the lead when they ran into stiff resistance and the new company commander, Major Archie Wavell, came up to see what was happening and was shot in the wrist at twenty yards by a sniper. He had been ill when his battalion went into Burma, but joined the South Staffords as a replacement after a company commander had been killed on the way to Mogaung. Wavell remained where he was and briefed Wilcox with further orders before, holding his damaged hand with the other one, he went back to the Regimental Aid Post. That night Chesshire took off the rest of his hand. Captain John Chesshire was usually too busy tending the sick and wounded to get to Mike Calvert's 'O' groups, but he recalls one that he did attend. Calvert said, 'When you think you are beaten the other chap is probably worse, so have another go.' His men did try again and they did win. One other indicator that the men looked for was the appearance of their Brigadier. If he was wearing his blue pyjamas at night, they were safe. If they saw him wearing his red Brigadier's hat they knew battle was imminent.

The two companies of South Staffords were under heavy pressure and snipers were everywhere. It was getting dark, but before they could pull back there were still the wounded to recover. They seemed to be covered by two snipers, so David Wilcox stationed himself where he might be able to get a shot and someone else began rustling the bushes nearby. The Japanese soldier moved and, standing up, Wilcox shot him, at the same time getting a graze under his chin from the second sniper's bullet. However, Wilcox had seen him as well and was able to fire quickly enough to get him too. It was a very courageous action which enabled the wounded to be carried back to cover. Joe Bate, medical orderly:

> 'I have some special memories of Mogaung. One of course is of assisting Captain Chesshire in amputating Archie Wavell's shattered hand. We were working in a basha raised on stilts some feet off the ground, with the wounded lying in the hut around us. We were both kneeling in the centre of the hut beside him, when I said to Captain Chesshire; "We are being fired at!" He replied, "Nonsense." But then he saw another row of holes appear in the wall each side, so we finished the task lying flat on the floor. What in fact was happening was that we were getting the "overs" from a battle going on for the nearby bridge over the river. One chap I knew quite well figured in an amazing incident. His name was Sam Adey and he was a runner in 10 Platoon, 38 Column, South Staffords. Everybody carried grenades in the pouches at the front of their webbing equipment and Sam received a hit which exploded a grenade in one of his pouches. Amazingly the blast all went outwards and, though his webbing and clothing were blown off, Sam was virtually unhurt. I believe the Brigadier came to see him shortly afterwards and said, "You must be the luckiest chap in the world, Adey!" I was told that Sam was the calmest man there until reaction set in later and he was then trembling violently.'

A couple of days later, Calvert received a signal from Lentaigne to the effect that 'unless Archie Wavell is evacuated immediately, you will be dismissed from commanding your brigade'. Apparently a message had been sent to his father, Field Marshal Wavell, now the Viceroy, informing him that his son was dangerously wounded and he had flown to Assam to meet him when he was evacuated. However, Archie saw that there were far worse cases than his awaiting evacuation; in fact Chesshire had 200 waiting to go out, but the light planes were under Stilwell's control and the pilots took a dim view of the waterlogged strip where they had to land. A light plane kept coming back to fetch Archie, but he was adamant and nearly sixty men had been evacuated before Calvert arrived to force him on the plane. Later Squadron Leader Thompson dreamt up the idea of building a ramp at the end of the light plane strip, to help the pilots get airborne. He decided not to tell the pilots that the ramp underneath the coconut matting was made up of unexploded mortar bombs.

David Wilcox then received his fourth wound of the campaign and when Calvert saw him lying on the ground with his scalp ripped open, he thought he was finished. A couple of days later, he reappeared with his scalp sewn up. He was the only surviving subaltern from the South Staffords who had originally flown into Broadway and he had taken part in fourteen separate platoon attacks. Calvert ordered him to be flown out immediately. He would later be awarded the DSO and American Silver Star. Weeks later, back in India, he was combing his hair when the comb grated on something in his scalp. Chesshire later removed the Japanese bullet while Wilcox asked him how it had been missed in the first place!

The day after Wavell was wounded the Gurkhas took over and fought their way to the river. The railway bridge was now only 800 yards away. On 13 June, all three battalion commanders went to Calvert and told him that their men were exhausted and they could only muster one company of fit men each. Only 550 men were left out of the brigade and many had been wounded at least once and nearly all were suffering from malaria, trench foot or jungle sores. The next day Calvert sent Captain Andrews of the Burma Rifles across to the north bank of the Mogaung River with instructions not to return without at least one Chinese regiment. The six-foot-four-inch, black-moustached officer saluted and trotted off with his men.

At that time the survivors of the brigade were being shelled daily from a village called Naungkyaiktaw on their left flank. Calvert planned to capture the place and eliminate the forty or fifty Japanese believed to be there. The village was at the end of a peninsula of jungle jutting out into the paddy. Calvert's plan was to place a company of Lancashire Fusiliers across the isthmus leading to the peninsula to block any escape, while other Fusiliers, together with the King's Company, would attack across the paddy at dawn. The assault force would be accompanied by Captain Stewart Binnie, formerly with Bladet Force, and his flame thrower detachment. Half an hour before dawn on 18 June, the mortars opened fire and 400 bombs fell on the Japanese positions in ten minutes. Bert Gilroy lay in the jungle with the blocking company of Fusiliers:

'We were to kill any enemy retreating that came our way. There was a mortar barrage by our people and unfortunately some of the mortar bombs fell short and killed some of our chaps and injured others. This error was rectified and the attack went in, assisted by the Bladet Force of flame throwers which had been flown in to help in the attack. The Japs were forced out and we had a period of firing on them as they escaped across the open paddy towards the railway. They must have lost quite heavily.'

Lieutenant John De Quidt was with the assault force, advancing across the paddy: 'A very unpleasant occasion. The flame throwers attracted a lot of enemy fire and I admit that I tried not to spend too much time next to any of them. I picked up another minor wound there from a grenade.' Captain Fred Freeman of the King's was also wounded by the Japanese grenades, which left a trail of sparks from the fuse as they were thrown through the air. Stewart Binnie was more seriously wounded by a grenade and lost an eye. By the end of the morning the village had been cleared. There were actually twice as many Japanese in the village as expected and half of them were killed during the fighting, the rest escaped back to Mogaung. Friendly casualties were sixteen dead and thirty-seven wounded.

At five p.m. that afternoon, Captain Andrews appeared at Calvert's shelter and announced that he had a Chinese regiment waiting on the other bank of the Mogaung River. The 1st Battalion of the Chinese 114th Regiment began to cross over that night and the Hong Kong Volunteers came into their own as interpreters and liaison personnel. Four days of sunshine passed, during which the Chinese moved into the area and made some half-hearted attacks on the Japanese around Mogaung. They did not believe in direct assaults, rather they preferred to shell the enemy out, leaving them a back door through which to escape if they wished. One can understand their lack of haste; they had been fighting the Japanese for years and were in no hurry. They were also inveterate looters and thieves and considered anything floating to earth during a supply drop to be fair game. Colonel Li, their commander, later shot one or two who had run off with some money that had been dropped for the Chindits. An American Lieutenant-Colonel also arrived with the Chinese. He, like his master, Stilwell, knew little about fighting, but he was a great blusterer. Calvert took a dim view of the Yank sitting in his shelter, spitting on the floor to show he was tough, while calling the Chinese cowards and urging the Chindits to attack. Eventually Calvert took him out to an exposed position near the Courthouse Triangle, where they stood while Calvert discussed tactics and the enemy positions. The American made a much larger target for a Japanese sniper than the Brigadier, but none of the snipers would oblige.

Calvert knew that with the sickness and shelling he would soon have no one left with which to attack Mogaung and made his plans for the final effort. He had 110 Lancashire Fusiliers and King's, 180 South Staffords and 230 Gurkhas. The Gurkhas were to push in from the direction of Natyigon as far as the railway bridge. The South Staffords were to cross the 400 yards of paddy to the railway embankment. The Fusiliers would remain in reserve. If all went well, they would hold the railway line from the station to the bridge and could then continue into Mogaung. The attack would go in during the night, after seventy air strikes had been flown against the town. A barrage of a thousand mortar bombs would take place between 3.00 and 3.15 a.m. At 3.10 the South Staffords would begin to advance across the paddy. Everyone was tired and jumpy and the men prepared for the attack with an air of resigned fatalism. Private Tom O'Reilly later wrote:

> 'Even though I had been in attacks before, I had an awful feeling in my stomach and I am sure everyone felt the same; we were no longer fit to fight such odds. The Brigadier came along and said, "Well lads, we have had a very rough time and I am sorry, but I have had orders to capture Mogaung and if we can do so, this is our last battle." We looked at each other and then realised our commander had tears in his eyes. For many of us it would be the last battle one way or the other. We had no heavy support or tanks to fight our way past concrete pillboxes, thick sticky mud and strong defences. I was put in Sergeant Asher's platoon. He said to us, "Right lads, we will cover the heavy mud in the darkness, then at dawn we charge the railway line and over to the pillboxes and beyond into the houses, as far as we can go. Good luck." '

Although there was a moon it was fairly dark when the mortars began their barrage and the men began to trudge forward, weighed down by extra ammunition and grenades to use on the bunkers. The Japanese began to reply with artillery and their own mortar bombs began to fall on the forming up places and start lines. The South Staffords moved faster, close up behind their own barrage, so that when it stopped they could be in among the enemy before he had time to come out of his shelters. On the right and centre they successfully reached the railway line, but as dawn broke they came under concentrated machine-gun fire from a previously unknown Japanese strongpoint in a house at the junction of the Pinhmi road and the railway. The gung-ho American Colonel had wrongly informed Calvert that the Chinese had occupied the railway station. Now their left flank was unprotected. Calvert brought up the Fusiliers and mortars, machine-guns and Piats were all directed against the house. As the flame throwers began to work on the strongpoint, the surviving Japanese fled. By now there were sixty dead and 100 wounded, half of them caused by that one position. Tom O'Reilly found himself on his own:

'The lad with the flame thrower shot flames into the nearest pillbox and you could hear the screams and smell the burnt bodies. However, the lad who was using the flame thrower was hit and was on fire himself and was running around in circles screaming. There was no hope of saving him, so he had to be shot. I ran across to where Sergeant Asher lay, but he was dead and there were many more as well. I just wanted to kill as many Japs as I could before I went. There were about five left out of the twenty-eight of us in the platoon, so we joined on to Major Hilton's men. He went over to what I thought was a dead body, pointed his pistol at it and said, "Get up or I will kill you." It was one of our blokes whose nerve had gone. He got up and joined the rest of us, then we went into the houses after the Japs. We threw grenades down the foxholes and into the rooms. There was a lot of hand-to-hand fighting. I jumped over a small fence and almost on top of a Jap. Being quicker than him I ran my bayonet into his body. As the enemy was running away Major Hilton shouted, "Don't chase them, just pick them off." '

A very weary Tom O'Reilly ended up with a party of Gurkhas on the bridge over the river:

'I noticed there was no officer with them, only a Jap prisoner. They told me that Major Stagg, our liaison officer with the Gurkhas, had been killed. The Jap jumped up to attack me. Although there were about ten Gurkhas in all, he must have thought I was their officer. However, the little brown men grabbed him by his arms and legs and threw him into the Mogaung River. We heard his back crack as he struck a girder on the way. The battle must have stopped because there was just the odd shot now and then. We were sitting drinking tea when the Gurkha on look out shouted and began pointing. It was not Japs, but Chinese troops who were coming to help us. But the fighting was over.'

To the right of the South Staffords, the Gurkhas attacked towards the railway bridge over the Mogaung River. During the next couple of hours the 3rd Battalion, 6th Gurkha Rifles was to earn two Victoria Crosses. The citations for the awards tell their own story:

10119 Rifleman Tulbahadur Pun:

'On 23 June 1944, a battalion of the 6th Gurkhas was ordered to attack the railway bridge at Mogaung. Immediately the attack developed the enemy opened concentrated and sustained cross fire at close range from a position known as the Red House and from a strong bunker position two hundred yards to the left of it. So intense was this cross fire that both the leading platoons of "B" Company, one of which was Rifleman Tulbahadur Pun's, were pinned to the ground and the whole of his section was wiped out with the exception of himself, the section commander and one other man. The section commander immediately led the remaining two men in a charge on the Red House, but was at once badly wounded. Rifleman Tulbahadur Pun and his remaining companion continued the charge, but the latter too was immediately badly wounded. Rifleman Tulbahadur Pun then seized the Bren gun, and firing from the hip as he went, continued the charge on this heavily bunkered position alone, in the face of the most shattering concentration of automatic fire, directed straight at him. With the dawn coming up behind him, he presented a perfect target to the Japanese. He had to move for thirty yards over open ground, ankle deep in mud, through shell-holes and over fallen trees. Despite these overwhelming odds, he reached the Red House and closed with the Japanese occupants. He killed three and put five more to flight and captured two light machine-guns and much ammunition. He then gave accurate supporting fire from the bunker to the remainder of his platoon which enabled them to reach their objective. His outstanding courage and superb gallantry in the face of odds which meant almost certain death were inspiring to all ranks and were beyond praise.'

Rifleman Tulbahadur Pun received his Victoria Cross from His Excellency the Viceroy, Field Marshal Lord Wavell, at a special parade held in Delhi on 3 March 1945.

Lieutenant (Acting Captain) Michael Allmand: Volunteered for service with the Chindits from the 6th Duke of Connaught's Own Lancers, a cavalry regiment of the Indian Army. He had participated in a number of actions before that fateful day, as the citation described:

'Captain Allmand was commanding the leading platoon of a company of the 6th Gurkha Rifles on 11 June 1944 when the battalion was ordered to attack the Pinhmi road bridge. The enemy had already succeeded in holding up our advance at this point for twenty-four hours. The approach to the bridge was very narrow as the road was banked up and the low-lying land on either side was swampy and densely covered in jungle. The Japanese who were dug in along the banks of the road and in the jungle with machine-guns and small arms were putting up the most desperate resistance. As the platoon came within twenty yards of the bridge, the enemy opened heavy and accurate fire, inflicting severe casualties and forcing the men to seek cover. Captain Allmand, however, with the utmost gallantry charged on by himself, hurling grenades into the enemy gun positions and killing three Japanese himself with his kukri. Inspired by the splendid example of their platoon commander, the surviving men followed him and captured their objective. Two days later Captain Allmand, owing to casualties among the officers, took over command of the company and, dashing thirty yards ahead of it through long grass and marshy ground, swept by machine-gun fire, personally killed a number of enemy machine-gunners and successfully led his men on

217

to the ridge of high ground that they had been ordered to seize. Once again on 23 June, in the final attack on the railway bridge at Mogaung, Captain Allmand, although suffering from trenchfoot, which made it difficult for him to walk, moved forward alone through deep mud and shell-holes and charged a Japanese machine-gun nest single-handed, but he was mortally wounded and died shortly afterwards. The superb gallantry, outstanding leadership and protracted heroism of this very brave officer were a wonderful example to the whole battalion and in the highest traditions of his regiment.'

Captain John Lucas won the Military Cross in the same battle that saw Mike Allmand win his VC. Lucas was probably the last man to leave White City, weeks earlier. He had been suffering from sand fly fever, with symptoms akin to malaria, and had been left behind in his foxhole. Fortunately the Japanese left the area alone for a few days and the following morning, feeling much better, Lucas climbed out of his hole, shouldered his pack and marched on to join up with his Gurkhas. Now, sick and exhausted, he recalled the early days when Allmand joined them as a reinforcement: 'We were sleeping in a village and the huts were infested with fleas. In the morning Mike discovered that his shirt was full of them and I remembered seeing him mincing down the path holding his shirt at arm's length, heading for the MO to get it fumigated. We wondered then, "What kind of chap have we got here?" Well we soon found out.' Captain Allmand was just twenty years old when he was killed. At an impressive and moving ceremonial parade held at Cassino Lines, Hong Kong on 22 July 1991, the Allmand family presented to the regiment the Victoria Cross won by their brother.

Calvert had gathered his Brigade Defence Company and HQ animal transport personnel under Major Gurling and sent them across the railway line. They advanced 400 yards into Mogaung and spent an uncomfortable night under enemy fire. The following morning the Lancashire Fusiliers moved up on Gurling's left and the Chinese finally captured the railway station and joined up with the Fusiliers. That evening, as the Japanese shells fell around them, Calvert's men heard on the BBC news that the Chinese-American forces had captured Mogaung. They were furious and soon tracked down the source of the news to the American Colonel and his direct line to Stilwell. In typical Calvert fashion he sent a signal to Stilwell, which read: 'The Chinese forces having taken Mogaung, 77 Brigade is proceeding to take Umbrage.' Stilwell's staff searched in vain to locate Umbrage on the map.

However, Mogaung was not yet taken. On 25 June, Calvert's men moved forward again to discover that the surviving Japanese had pulled out under cover of their last artillery barrage. Mogaung had finally fallen and was the first town in Burma to be retaken. Captain Chesshire recalls that the day after the final capture of Mogaung Calvert started to throw his weight about. It was a reaction to all he had been doing and so they gave him a paperback book and half a bottle of brandy and suggested he had a rest. Reaction had set in and made him keep looking for something to attack. He was all right the next day.

Initially Stilwell tried to persuade Calvert to send his remaining 300 'fit' men down the railway towards Hopin. Calvert reminded him they were promised that they would be flown out after Mogaung was taken and enquired, 'Do you want me to form the King's Royal Staffordshire Gurkha Fusiliers?' Eventually, orders were received instructing Calvert to march his brigade to Myitkyina for evacuation to India. Calvert was concerned that his men, who had suffered so much, might be thrown into the battle for Myitkyina. His brigade had suffered seventeen officers and 238 other ranks killed and thirty officers and 491 other ranks wounded since the beginning of the Mogaung operation. That does not include the very many sick and those who died later in India. Enough was enough. Now that the tension had ceased, reaction had set in and men were going down like flies with malaria, dysentery and other fevers and the death rate went up. The medical officers advised leaving the scene of battle. Calvert ordered his radios to be shut down and sent the weary survivors of his brigade down the road towards Kamaing. With hindsight they should have marched out via Myitkyina because the trek to Kamaing was a nightmare. It took a fortnight of marching through mud and water, of crossing deep and fast-flowing rivers, and of miserably damp nights. Two more men gave up and died on the journey.

Stilwell summoned Calvert to his headquarters, together with Lentaigne. Stilwell began: 'You sent some very strong signals.' Calvert replied: 'You should have seen the ones my Brigade Major wouldn't let me send!' Much to his amazement, Stilwell roared with laughter and informed Calvert that he had just the same trouble with his own staff officers. From then on the atmosphere changed and when Calvert told Stilwell about the achievements and sacrifices of his brigade, the American seemed amazed, as though he did not know that 77 Brigade was the original unit that flew in four months before. He interrupted Calvert's story with questions to his aides: 'Check that. Is it correct? Why wasn't I told?' Stilwell may or may not have been completely honest in his conversation with Calvert, but the interview ended with the award of five Silver Stars to officers in the brigade, including one for Calvert. To the disgust of all in 77 Brigade it was the only award given to the Brigadier. The officers of the brigade put his name forward for a Victoria Cross, but it was not approved. Perhaps Lentaigne, Slim and Mountbatten considered Calvert had walked too long in Wingate's shadow? At any rate, the men of 77 Brigade thought the world of him, and fifty years later they still do. Captain Fred Freeman:

'Those of us who were still with the brigade were at Kamaing at the edge of the Mogaung River at the time Stilwell sent for Calvert. We knew what was in the wind and that there was a possibility of him being court-martialled. Instead, Mike Calvert returned in a light aircraft which had been fitted with floats and landed on the Mogaung River. A smiling Mike Calvert quickly came ashore and he was seen to be wearing an American Silver Star medal. It was a real moment of triumph for Mike, everyone cheered and was delighted.'

Fred Freeman was made animal transport officer for the brigade and was in charge of a party of Chindits taking their last mules to Shadazup for handing over to 36 Division. On the way they bivouacked near Stilwell's headquarters. An American Colonel and some of his officers arrived and invited the men to visit the camp cinema. Freeman found himself in the officers' mess tent enjoying his first good meal for many months:

'There was a sudden silence at our round table, with eight officers present. A bottle of Haig whisky was produced and the Colonel said: "Capt'n, I want to ask you a straight question and I want a straight answer. Tell me what is your frank opinion of General Stilwell?" I feared at the time perhaps he was the hero the Americans were said to think of him as, so I replied to the effect that I imagined he had good qualities which had been concealed from us in the Chindits. That seemed to satisfy the Colonel, who said, "Well, if you want to know our opinion, we think he's a lump of crap!"'

An Air Commando C-47 practises towing a glider before Operation 'Thursday'. On invasion day the C-47s tried to tow two gliders each, and many came to grief.

Men of the 1st Battalion, King's Liverpool Regiment. *(Front, left to right)* Roland Evans, Arthur Hoose, 'Bimbo' Forrester, George Heywood. *(Rear)* George Hodson, Sgt Fallon, Bob Corrington.

Captain Denis Arnold of 29 Column, 7th Battalion, Nigeria Regiment, inspects two of the lorries ambushed by the Africans outside White City.

A few hours before Operation 'Thursday' was due to commence, an Air Commando reconnaissance plane brought back photographs which showed that the Piccadilly landing area was covered with logs.

BELOW: Chindits loading an obstinate mule into an Air Commando C-47 transport plane. If a mule became too distressed in flight, it was sometimes necessary to shoot it before it got loose or damaged the aircraft.

David Rowlands' painting of the 1st Battalion, King's Liverpool Regiment landing by glider at Broadway on the night of 5 March 1944. Lt-Col Walter Scott stands in the foreground, *(without hat)*, directing his men.

The morning after. Air Commando glider pilots and US Army engineers sit with Chindits amongst the wreckage of the gliders at Broadway.

An extremely rare photograph of men of the 1st Bedfordshire and Hertfordshire Regiment in the jungle. Platoon commander Lieutenant John Salazar sits in the second row, third from right. Private Bob Boyd MM, sits three rows directly behind Salazar.

ABOVE: Brigadier Tom Brodie *(centre)* and an American Air Commando sergeant pilot discuss the evacuation of wounded.

On 30 April 1944, the CO of 2nd York and Lancs, Lt-Col Graves-Morris is given his birthday present in the jungle by Sergeant-Major Jones; a bottle of beer which he had carried in his pack for a month.

Chapter 15

Fight to the Last Chindit

N ew orders came for the three brigades around Indawgyi Lake. They were to move north and operate against the Japanese west of Mogaung. At that time 77 Brigade was still locked in a bloody battle to take the town. On 9 June, Jack Masters started his brigade northwards, together with half a dozen elephants which his Burrifs had acquired, complete with their mahouts. The first night of the march they slept soaking wet, in muddy pools, attacked by large, vicious, striped mosquitoes, biting flies, eye-flies and leeches. Condoms had been issued earlier in the campaign, to the chortles of the men who wondered what they were to do with them. As time went by, they discovered they were ideal for keeping maps and matches dry, for keeping rain out of their rifle barrels, and now, ironically, for keeping leeches away from their private parts. Such was the lot of the Chindits of these three brigades over the next couple of months. They fought skirmishes and platoon-sized fire fights and men died and were wounded. However, the weather and sickness now became their worst enemies and many more would succumb to those two evils than to Japanese bullets.

From 20 June to 9 July, 111 Brigade fought to take Point 2171, a high point on the crest line of the mountains, in order to push down on to the Japanese lines of communication in the railway valley below to the east. 14 Brigade, marching a week behind them, would reinforce them later. The fighting was as hard as anything Masters had experienced before and culminated in an attack by the Gurkhas which would take the summit at the cost of many brave men and lead to a posthumous award of the Victoria Cross to one of their officers. The official citation described the action:

'On 5 July, 3rd Battalion, 9th Gurkha Rifles advanced along the Salman Chaung under the western slopes of Hill 2171, a jungle-covered spur which stood above Taunghi. Here the Japanese were determined to make a stand. By 6 July a path had been cleared to the summit and on 9 July "B" and "C" Companies were entrusted with the task of taking the crest of the hill.

'The plan was that "B" Company would attack frontally up the southern face of the feature and "C" Company, under command of

221

Major Blaker, would encircle the spur and attack from the other side. Twenty-four years old, Captain Blaker held the temporary rank of Major and had already won the Military Cross in the Arakan the previous July. It was the intention that "B" Company would commence their attack when firing was heard from the other side of the spur. Unfortunately, "B" Company closed up on the Japanese outposts too soon and lost thirty men in a short space of time. Meanwhile, "C" Company, who had heard the firing, quickened their pace and, almost at the top of Hill 2171, ran into heavy Japanese machine-gun fire.

'Having gone to ground and without room to manoeuvre, Blaker sprang to his feet and shouted for his men to charge. As he charged, Blaker fired at the machine-gun and received a grenade wound in his left wrist. When he was seven yards from the gun, he was fatally wounded by a long burst of fire. The men following pressed on, some Japanese were cut down and the rest fled. Resistance on Hill 2171 then weakened, enabling the front and rear companies to link up and the hill to be captured.

'Captain Sweetman, who had taken over the company when Blaker was wounded, found him forty yards in rear with bullet holes in his stomach, chest and shoulder. Blaker, who knew he was going to die, ordered Sweetman to return to "C" Company, but the latter ordered the Havildar Major to stay with Blaker. Soon after, Blaker told the Havildar Major that he was dying and asked that the names of two men he wished to be recommended for gallantry should be passed to Captain Sweetman. His last words, relayed to Captain Sweetman by the Havildar Major, were "Thank 'C' Company for all they have done for me. Tell them that I have gone from them, but they must go on fighting to the end."' '

In 1945 a graves registration unit recovered the remains of Blaker and the others who fell in the fight for Hill 2171. He is now buried at the Taukkyan Military Cemetery on the outskirts of Rangoon.

The men were now worn out. Masters describes how he sent out a patrol of sixty-three Cameronians, all the 'fit' men from two rifle companies. The next day only four were able to move. Maubahadur Rai was a medical orderly with the Gurkhas and described their condition after the hill was taken:

'The men were exhausted and sick from malaria, dysentery, typhus and other diseases. They gallantly held the hill against numerous counter-attacks by the fanatical Japanese. Their condition deteriorated as the torrential monsoon rain continued without a break for several weeks. Fatigue became so serious that several men fell asleep while actually firing their guns. Once, when our medical unit was searching for casualties in the thick brush around the hillside, we came upon three

Japanese in deep sleep, only a few feet away from two Gurkhas who were also sleeping. At another time, we found two Japanese and a Gurkha sleeping in the same foxhole, all half-buried in mud. They were too weak and sick to try to kill each other.

'On 17 July, in order to persuade Stilwell that we were not malingering, Jack Masters ordered us to construct a medical examination centre a few miles away from Pahok, where an American field hospital had been established. An Allied Medical Commission made up of two English and two American doctors and six nurses conducted a thorough medical examination of every man still with the brigade. They discovered that all of them were suffering from malarial fever and amoebic dysentery. Their weight loss averaged between thirty-five and forty pounds. Many had typhus, foot rot, tooth rot, septic sores, dengue fever, fungi, yaws, scabies, leech ulcers, insect bites and blisters. There were also a dozen psychiatric disorders. The Commission concluded that only 120 out of the 2,200 men were fit for further duty – seven British officers, twenty-two British soldiers and ninety Gurkhas. The rest of the brigade was evacuated for hospitalization in India. Masters took his name from the sick list and made the number of officers up to eight. Bill Towill was one of the officers passed as fit, but when he finally reached India he spent five weeks in hospital with a fever that would not respond to treatment.'

As the bulk of 111 Brigade made their way to Kamaing for evacuation, Masters sarcastically asked for orders for the remaining fit men of '111 Company'. Stilwell ordered them to guard a Chinese artillery position near Pahok. Ten days later they were allowed to leave and they marched the ten miles on to Mogaung and entrained for Myitkyina. It was 1 August 1944, the day that Stilwell was promoted to full General, two days before Myitkyina at last fell.

Often neglected by historians, 23 Brigade was taken away from Wingate's control and used by Slim in the rear of the Japanese divisions attacking 14th Army. Their task was twofold: firstly to threaten and cut the Japanese lines of communication, thereby forcing them to withdraw; and secondly to protect the left flank of Lieutenant-General Stopford's 33rd Indian Corps as it advanced. Under the command of Brigadier Lance Perowne, the four battalions provided sterling service, ambushing the Japanese on the jungle tracks and destroying their supplies wherever they found them. Three of the men describe their various experiences as they fought behind the lines in the true Chindit way.

Stan Hutson, 60th Field Regiment, Royal Artillery:

'We handed our guns over to an Indian regiment and split into two columns. With an influx of Gurkhas for recce platoon and some men from the 1st Essex and 4th Borders the 60th Field Regiment became known throughout the brigade as 60 and 68 Columns, Royal Artillery. When we came under Slim's control there were three Japanese divisions attacking Kohima and Imphal. The Japanese High Command did not believe in feeding their troops, so much better to make them fight harder to take the enemy's food. This "cleverness" of the Japanese was to be part of their undoing, for when 23 Brigade got into the rear of them, across their supply route, our lightning raids and ambushes cut supplies of ammunition, medical supplies and reinforcements down to a trickle. Matters got worse when the monsoon started. Saito's 31st Division was bogged down in the mud of Kohima. He had been ordered by General Mutaguchi to take the place in a maximum of ten days, yet here he was over a month later with very little ammunition, no medical supplies and no food, because he could not get into Kohima. In desperation he sent out foraging parties to the Naga and Manipuri villages to steal their rice and pigs, but very few ever got back – we were waiting for them. Mutaguchi refused to allow Saito to pull out, but Saito ignored the order, but by then it was too late. The attack route used by the three main divisions was now their escape route, but now it was ankle deep in mud with the torrential monsoon rain slowly turning the tracks into quagmires.

'As the two gunner columns put down ambush after ambush we were finding more and more dead bodies where they had collapsed into the muddy slush. On slightly higher ground we found stretchers with Jap soldiers on them that had been dumped because the carriers could take them no further. When the 60th had been fighting in France, Belgium, Syria and the Western Desert we had always had a certain amount of compassion for the enemy, but for these people – none! During a battle between both of our columns and a large group of Japanese Imperial Guards at the village of Nhum Phung, one of our men was captured. When the battle was over we found him. They had just cut both his hands off and left him to bleed to death. Possibly this was in the mind of the gunners when the following episode happened.

'13 Platoon, of which I was a part, had discovered a fairly wide track with lots of Japanese footprints on it. The track went gradually downhill to a bend where it went out of sight. Our Captain decided it was ideal for an ambush, so the Bren gun was set up behind some bushes near the top of the track and we waited. The rain poured down and the two men with the Bren gun were fed up with the waiting, when suddenly a lone Jap came around the bend and just stood there, looking up the track. Nothing moved, so three or four minutes later he waved about ten of his compatriots to follow him up the track. The soldier behind the Bren gun let them come to within about twenty-five yards of him, then opened up, killing all of them. The rest of the platoon rushed forward to push the bodies off the track down the steep slope into a small hollow. The scenario was repeated at long intervals throughout the day, when groups of Japs would appear to slip and slide on the now rain-sodden track. They all finished ignominiously in the small hollow. The following morning, around midday, a lone Jap soldier appeared round the bend and began to ascend the track. He had a rifle slung over his shoulder as though he had no intention of using it (perhaps he had no bullets). He appeared to have no shoes on and his feet and legs were covered in old sacking. When he reached the part of the track where his compatriots' bodies had been rolled down into the hollow he looked down and saw them. The gunner behind the Bren watched him as he hesitated for a few moments, then climbed over the edge and descended into the hollow. The second gunner wormed his way to the edge to look down. The Jap was searching among the bodies and after a few minutes he found what he was looking for, a pair of shoes that would fit him. After about ten minutes the Jap climbed laboriously out of the hollow on to the path, now wearing the shoes he had found. That's when the gunner shot him and he went crashing down to join the others, taking his newly acquired shoes with him.

'It was a recognised thing in the Chindits that if you could not keep up with the column you were left behind to fend for yourself. I had malaria and dysentery and was feeling quite weak. I kept falling back and eventually the column was gone and I was left alone. That didn't bother me for I had seen the map and knew we were heading for a village on top of the next hill. This entailed going down the winding track into the valley, across a fairly wide river then a climb up the hill to the top where we were to take an air drop the next morning. My first mistake was that I decided to take a short cut, straight down the hillside to reach the river. The going got harder and harder and I was soon held up by thick bamboo laced with fantastically strong bamboo creeper. When night fell I was only about a quarter of the way down the hill. That night I ate my last piece of cheese and two small biscuits and went to sleep by the side of a waterfall. It took me the whole of the next day to reach the river which was so swift running it cut a groove in the side of the hills it went through, so that at each bend I had to climb up some way and then down on the other side of the bend. As this was so slow I decided to make my second mistake.

'When crossing a river the Chindits had been taught to make a "sausage". A groundsheet would be laid on the floor with all one's possessions on it. The groundsheet was then laced with rope or bamboo creeper. The second man's groundsheet was put over the lacing and that laced up on the other side, making a water-tight "sausage". Fortunately I had acquired a second groundsheet, so having made my "sausage" I entered the fast-flowing river which fortunately was flowing in the right direction. Everything went well for about fifteen minutes as I swirled down the river at great speed, then suddenly, calamity! I hit a waterfall, the edge of which was lined with huge jagged rocks. My "sausage" was dragged out of my hands and disappeared over the waterfall. I watched in dismay as it went off down the river and

225

round the next bend. I climbed on to the bank and took stock. I was virtually trapped in dense virgin jungle, as naked as the day I was born, suffering from malaria and dysentery and desperately hungry. This was when the arduous training we had done back in India proved its worth. Being a good swimmer I decided my best chance was to continue swimming down the river until I came to the "Burma Rope Bridge" then take the track to the nearest village. As I swam down the river my luck suddenly changed – I found my "sausage" half submerged in a quiet backwater of the river. I dragged it out on to the bank, dried my clothes and equipment then carried on with my journey. The next day I met recce platoon who were able to tell me where I could find the column. When I walked up to 13 Platoon, very hungry and weak, I had been missing for four days with no food. When I reported to the platoon officer he said: "Ah, you've caught us up then. Good show!" '

Charles Tinsley, 4th Battalion, Border Regiment:

'I was a Lance-Corporal muleteer in Major Geoffrey Harker's 55 Column. The other column was number 34 and was commanded by Lieutenant-Colonel John Burgess. We thought we were going to join other Chindits, but I think orders changed and we headed south to a place called Mariana Fortress. We camped under the Sago plantations and had our first meeting with the leeches that would be with us throughout the campaign. Lord Mountbatten visited us there and wished us good luck. We were going into the land of the Naga headhunters, high mountains and dense valleys. One of our first stops was at Mokachung where we met the village chief, who carried a large spear, and the only white man there, the district commissioner. We took our first supply drop there of K rations, which soon became very boring. After about ten weeks we occasionally had a "luxury drop" which consisted mainly of a mildewed loaf and a two-pound tin of Australian jam between ten men. We were told on no account to try to have a relationship with the Naga women. Married women had long hair, but maidens had theirs cropped and were quite pretty. Older women had wood like skewers in their noses, protruding either side. Many of the villages had never seen a white man before and we had to try to get interpreters. We started with a near disaster – our interpreter on an ambush was the son of a chieftain and he was the only one killed.

'Although it rained in bucketfuls we never stayed in villages more than necessary, because the Japs shelled them if we were in them and many villagers were killed or maimed. The few times we slept in bamboo huts the fleas would take off with you. Our main objective was stopping supplies getting to the Japs at Kohima and Imphal. We had amazing success; at the final reckoning their casualties were more than 25–1. Nothing escaped our ambushes; our lads would wait days and nights without a fire or hot drink, maybe a cigarette at night with a blanket over your head so it would not give your position away. When you went to the toilet you always took someone with you to keep watch. One man in my section went out alone and came back quite shaken. He said a large Jap patrol had passed him, so close he could nearly touch them. He said it was the fastest shit he had ever had!

'Early on when everyone was a bit green, one of our Sergeants and a Gurkha went to the aid of a badly wounded Jap and the Jap shot them both. After that there were no more wounded, you finished the job. There were some terrible things out there; if you went down a track where there'd been an ambush you would think someone had been fishing and dropped their maggots, but it was Jap brains on the track. We once went along a track where the Nagas had buried some Japanese. There must have been quite a lot – all the arms were sticking out of the grave straight up, they could not have been dead long or buried deep. Some Nagas were given twelve-bore shotguns with large shot, which made a terrible wound.

'Eventually we joined up with the rest of 14th Army at Ukral. A Pathan officer asked our wireless operator to talk his supplies down and our Corporal Fergusson, who had been right through with us, was killed by a chute that did not open.'

Private Frank Billyeald, 1st Battalion, Essex Regiment:

'I was a muleteer in forward column HQ, 44 Column. My mule, who I called Brandy, carried the wireless batteries for the RAF, who dealt with supply drops. On our way into Burma we had two supply drops, the first being K Rations and the second new light carbines. Our Indian coolies dug a large hole and we threw in our old rifles and ammunition. We then went over Border Hill into Burma, heading for Fort White. We took a supply drop when we arrived and one of the men shot himself in the foot. We first made contact with the enemy at Phekekruma, a strongly held town fewer than twenty miles east of Dimapur. After it was taken from the Japs, the Recce platoon carried on through the village and down the hill, where the Japs were waiting. Two of our lads were taken prisoner and when we found them they had been bayoneted God knows how many times and decapitated. We took a supply drop one afternoon, but the column had to move on, leaving a small party of us to collect the supplies. We rejoined the column the next morning and unloaded, then returned to the area of the supply drop. On the way we got fired on by our sister column, number 56, who had mistaken us for Japs.

'Our next trek was to Fort Keary on the Assam–Burma border. God, what a stench of rotting animal carcasses; we had to burn everything before we could get a supply drop. There must have been a battle there of some sort. One of the muleteers had been saving the silk map sections which he got from the admin officer. He and another muleteer went AWOL (absent without leave) during the night. They got fed up with the conditions we were going through and decided to make their own way out. However, they went on the wrong track and into the direction where the Japs were. We never heard from them again, but I hope they made it.

'I only saw one snake during the campaign. We had just completed a march of one night and a day and it was going dark when we halted. I propped myself up against a tree trunk and looked up and saw this snake coming down the tree. It was about a yard in length and I watched it go into a hole in the tree about twenty feet up. I just thought "bugger you" and drifted into a deep sleep.

'Finally, from Fort Keary we went north to Ukhrul, where we were met by the catering corps boys who gave us a hot meal. We then boarded the lorries and drove back to Kohima. We had not had a shave or wash for three months. I went into hospital with sprue and dysentery and my weight was only six stones. I was later invalided home.'

Brigadier Perowne summed up the results of his brigade's operations between April and July 1944 thus:

'For nearly four months the brigade has been in action at once against nature and the enemy without rest or relief. In that time it had contributed to a major defeat of the Japanese Army, and killed, wounded and taken prisoner 854 of them, for a total loss to themselves of seventy-four killed and eighty-eight wounded. The figures quoted for the Japanese casualties include only those actually seen and takes no account of the effect of mortar and machine-gun fire or of the several occasions on which air bombardment was directed by our columns. The number of sick evacuated by the brigade was considerable and was much increased immediately once relaxation set in at Dimapur.'

One of the more harrowing stories to emerge from the second Chindit campaign concerns the evacuation of sick and wounded during the last couple of months. The flying boats had ceased their mercy flights to Indawgyi Lake and the river route to Kamaing was not available to all Chindit battalions. The air commando light planes had ceased to fly as their airstrips in India came under water and in any case there were few places where landing strips could be prepared. The only choice for the sick and wounded was to walk out to the nearest Allied position, to march or die.

The author found two written references to such walk outs; both referred to 14 Brigade. The first was in the history of the 2nd Battalion York and Lancaster Regiment, written by its commander, Lieutenant-Colonel P. H. Graves-Morris DSO MC. On page 89, after the capture of Labu on 7 August, he writes:

'The evacuation of sick and wounded was made easy by access to the road. It was a sorry sight to see these columns of diseased and dying men dragging themselves along, or being helped by their less sick comrades.

Most were unrecognisable, being shadows of their former selves – twelve-stone men now only weighing seven stone or eight stone, and their sunken faces and hollow staring eyes gave signs of their condition. The Army photographer who took photographs of them said he had to take them "for nobody would believe it, without the evidence of these!" Those left with the columns were little better, as all were half-starved, emaciated and racked with dysentery, malaria and jungle sores. Only the will to live had kept many going, once the end was in sight.'

The second account appeared in the book *The Black Watch and the King's Enemies* (Collins, 1950) written by none other than Bernard Fergusson, the former commander of 16 Brigade. Both columns of the 2nd Black Watch rested in the Pungan area for the last ten days of July 1944. Fergusson wrote:

'The days at Pungan were sad ones. There seemed so little to show for all the miseries that had been undergone; there seemed no prospect of either the campaign or the monsoon ever coming to an end; men had died from sheer exhaustion on the way over the hills; and now typhus broke out. Seventy men of the regiment died from this disease in July and August. Special Force HQ called for a special confidential medical report on how many officers and men would be physically fit to carry on fighting for another month; the figure for the two columns was two officers and forty-eight other ranks. No column of the brigade was in any better shape, and convoys of sick were formed at an improvised jungle hospital to march northward in their own time by a comparatively easy route, to join the nearing Allied forces. The first such convoy passed through the regiment's area on 28 July. An officer wrote: "The sight of this column starting off was the worst thing I have ever seen. The just living were astride the mules and ponies, while on either side those that could still totter and stumble along held on to the stirrup-leathers. The whole was in charge of an MO with a Sergeant to help him and as escort he had those sick who still had strength to hold a rifle and stumble unassisted. That the majority reached their destination is the highest tribute that could be paid to that MO."'

Not all of the columns of sick men had such success in reaching their destination. One party lost two thirds of its strength on the way to Shadazup. Colonel Eason, the commander of the 1st Battalion, Bedfordshire and Hertfordshire Regiment, also succumbed to disease, dying shortly after evacuation. Private Jim Perry, also of the Bedfordshire and Hertfordshire Regiment, was suffering from malaria when he was told to help escort a party of sick men. He told the author:

'The "walking wounded" were assembled in a village and all rifles were taken to a basha to be stacked. Heavy packs were taken away from the figures that were like the dead. The stench of filth and excreta stained their green uniforms, some were without boots, with ammo pouches on their feet. Burmese villagers cut bamboo sticks to enable the worst cases to support themselves. An elephant was hired for one day to carry the human bundles, ragged and forlorn in the tropical sun.

'The order of the day was, "Any man that falls out of line will be left to die." I see that few of the sick will travel far . . . these teenagers are aged before their time. I see a teenager walk into a tree, he falls to the ground. I help him up and give a drink. He vomits and sobs. I find a letter in his haversack and read it to him; from a mother to her son, looking forward to his homecoming. He does not understand. I leave him and move on. Another makes a run into the jungle; I follow to bring him back. He pleads to be left behind; I give him a cigarette and wait until he has smoked it. As I left him I looked back – my thoughts: I have left a man to die.

'There are no medics with our party. It is a desperate aim to reach the Meza River, where small canvas boats will take us to the American base at Shadazup. I see escorts with long bamboo canes strike the backs of the slow moving, it is like driving cattle with shouts of "Keep 'em moving." We were informed that Red Cross parcels would be distributed at the first halt. It was a lie.

'We emerged on to a vast area of charpois; white and black Chindits resting on bamboo frame beds. A bearded face looked up to me with an appeal for water. I stooped down to give a drink from my water bottle. The next second a shot made me turn in the direction of the sound. A figure waving a revolver shouted, "Keep away from them. They are contagious cases." I replied, "Does not a dying man have a right to a drink of water?" He replied, "This is an order – keep away," and took aim to indicate he would fire. I shouted, "Where are the Red Cross parcels?" His laughter told me that we had been told a lie as a means of encouragement. We boiled grass and bark to help appease hunger. Later four of us crawled along the long lines of charpois to water the sick, just like plant pots. At daybreak I tried to waken the men on either side of me; they were both dead. Last night I had spoken to both.

'We leave this death camp and start walking again towards the Meza River. We find our boats and finally reach Shadazup. We fall in outside an American mess tent, the cook shouts: "Why are you waiting? I was informed that ninety-two starving Chindits were on the move and to prepare food. Come and get it." There were only thirty of us left.'

This pony gave birth on the march in the middle of April 1944 and the one-day-old foal is loaded onto the back of its mother for transporting by Alf Prince and Dickenson of the 2nd York and Lancs. Sadly it did not survive to the end of the campaign.

Chindits loading a sick comrade into an Air Commando light plane for evacuation. The brave American pilots saved hundreds of lives during the 1944 campaign.

Padre Bob Bellfield from the 2nd Battalion, York and Lancs having tea with friendly Kachin villagers.

A casualty is evacuated by Sunderland flying boat from 14 Brigade's 'Plymouth' station on Indawgyi Lake. Without the two flying boats, many hundreds of Chindits would have died.

Men of the 2nd Battalion, York and Lancaster Regiment warily negotiate 'snipers corner' where four men were wounded.

Men of 51 and 69 Columns, who left 16 Brigade during the march-in to take the town of Lonkin. American General Stilwell insisted the town be taken to repay his assistance in moving the brigade up to their start line.

An unidentified Chindit column crossing the Meza River. The photograph illustrates the length of a 400-man column 'snake' which stretches into the distance.

Lieutenant Roddy Wilkins of the 45th Reconnaissance Regiment was hit in the shoulder by a machine-gun bullets during the fighting outside White City. He willed himself to live and is now retired in Northern Ireland.

Captain Robert St John Walsh of the 6th Battalion, Nigeria Regiment, Royal West African Frontier Force, wearing the Chindit flash.

Chapter 16

End of the Road

P iper Bill Lark's thoughts wandered back to 21 November 1941, when the 2nd Battalion Black Watch was on the start line ready to break out of Tobruk and meet the Eighth Army. His stomach was churning as he waited for the dawn barrage from the artillery which would soften up the Germans. As he tuned his pipes the voice of Captain Boyle barked, 'Lark, what are you doing with those bagpipes? This is not 1914. Get them on the truck and take a rifle.' Disappointed, he threw them on the truck, hoping they would break, although they didn't.

Early 1944 saw the battalion preparing to fly into Burma as Chindits. The pipe band decided to become muleteers rather than going back to the ranks, but this time Bill decided to wrap his pipes in towels and shirts for protection and stuff them into a kit bag with a tin of syrup for seasoning them. He gave them to Jackson the storeman with instructions that if needed they were ready to send in. That time had come. Bill's pipes were mentioned to Colonel Green who sent for them straight away. A supply drop was made at Pungan and one of the items to float down from the sky was Bill's bagpipes. A number of men came down with typhus and a separate place was provided for them, with tents made out of parachutes from the supply drop. The MO requested that the piper come and play for them and this Bill did. There seemed to be a marked improvement, so every day he had a piping session for the sick. One soldier, when he finally returned to the battalion on his recovery, said that hearing the pipes had given him the will to live.

Seventy men of the Black Watch died from disease in July and August. Those men who were still on their feet were asked to make one more effort before they were flown out. They were to attack the village of Labu, which was located four miles from the railway. The attack went in on 5 August and the three weak platoons of 42 Column managed to get to the enemy forward positions, but had to withdraw with the loss of their sole platoon officer, Lieutenant Wynne. The next day 73 Column would join them, together with Corporal Bill Lark and his pipes.

Sergeant Major Gibb, recently commissioned in the field as a Lieutenant, together with his batman, carried out an early morning reconnaissance along the ridge and reported that the enemy had withdrawn from his forward positions. As 73 Column moved up they found the enemy in new positions further along the ridge and during the morning, by using mortar fire and manoeuvre, drove them out and into their last line of defence, a series of well prepared dug-outs immediately in front of the village. The mortars could not shift them and as evening approached a final effort was ordered. Gibb's men engaged the enemy with fire from the right flank and the mortar crews threw their last bombs down their tubes and watched them arc skywards towards the village. With one last look at the Jocks fixing bayonets around him, Piper Lark puffed out his chest and began to play his bagpipes. With the sound of the pipes ringing in their ears the riflemen ran screaming towards the enemy. The Japanese took to their heels and fled.

The campaign was over at last. On 9 August a patrol from the battalion went down into the railway valley and met the first troops from the 36th British Division, who were heading towards White City and Indaw, over a hundred miles to the south. The next day an enormous supply drop arrived. A week later, on 17 August, the Black Watch came out of the jungle. Bill Lark recalls:

> 'Possibly my greatest honour was to play at the head of the two columns as they came out of the jungle and marched along a main road leading to Mogaung, passing men of the 36th Division going in the opposite direction. It was a joy to play with each company in turn, standing beside Colonel Green as the men marched past into Mogaung. I played each company's march past, including my own "C" Company's tune "Lawson's Men".'

On 18 August they travelled by train, in jeeps modified for the railway, from Mogaung to Myitkyina and the following day flew home to Assam, hot showers, clean clothing and fresh cheese sandwiches. Captain Shadbolt recalled the end of the campaign:

> 'It is interesting, to me anyway, there appeared to be more suicides on the way out than at any other time. I simply cannot understand this. So we arrived in India and as I weighed only 100 pounds sprue was diagnosed. Straight into hospital on a diet of raw liver and bananas for three months. Fed up I discharged myself, returned to my unit to walk into a cocktail party. While talking to three lovely young ladies I filled my boots. Immediately to Bombay and a ship. Within twelve hours of sailing I was back to normal.'

The 3rd West African Brigade also came out of the jungle and moved slowly down to Myitkina for evacuation. It was 15 August when the 12th Nigeria Battalion walked into Mogaung, looking for their train ride to Myitkina. Less than half of the Africans who had marched out of White City on 10 May were still left and of the forty white men with the battalion only six remained.

Probably the last Chindit unit to return, the 2nd Battalion, York and Lancaster Regiment, was evacuated by air from Myitkyina to Assam on 25 and 26 August. Of the 900 of all ranks who had landed at Aberdeen on 2 and 3 April, only eighteen officers and 300 other ranks marched into the reception camp at Tinsukia. The remainder had either been killed in action, succumbed to the rigours of the campaign, or been evacuated as so sick they would have been unlikely to survive if they had stayed.

As the sick, exhausted Chindits returned from leave or hospital and travelled back to their barracks, plans were made for another campaign in support of 14th Army which was about to cross the Chindwin and pursue the Japanese through central and southern Burma. Perhaps they would be used in the invasion of Malaya or Siam, or maybe even in China?

Colonel Wilkinson of the Leicesters was given command of 77 Brigade when Mike Calvert departed for England after damaging a tendon playing football. He was later given command of the Special Air Service Brigade and went on to fight in Holland. The survivors of the 1st South Staffords and the 45th Reconnaissance Regiment were amalgamated and became a parachute battalion. They were training to drop into Singapore when the war came to an end.

Brigadier Jumbo Morris was given command of 62 Brigade in 19th Indian Infantry Division. Jack Masters had originally rejoined 111 Brigade as a Lieutenant-Colonel commanding the 3rd Battalion, 4th Gurkhas, a job to which he had officially succeeded after the death of Ian Monteith. He was later sent to 19th Division as a general staff officer.

General 'Vinegar Joe' Stilwell was not around to see the recapture of Burma. On 19 October 1944, on the express demand of General Chiang Kai-shek, he was recalled to the United States by President Roosevelt. He died of cancer on 12 October 1946.

Claude Fairweather stayed on at Special Force Headquarters as chief signal officer after Wingate's death. He knew Joe Lentaigne well:

> 'There is no truth that Joe was responsible for keeping his exhausted 111 Brigade in the jungle after Blackpool. It was Vinegar Joe Stilwell who kept them there. With the help of Lord Mountbatten, Joe Lentaigne got them out. Joe was a very likeable man, a very gallant commander of his splendid Gurkha brigade and well supported by his Brigade Major Jack Masters with whom I went on leave to Kashmir after the expedition. He was a very popular commander with all those in headquarters and, to be honest, being a well-groomed regular soldier, he never really understood Wingate. After the force was withdrawn Joe and I were instructed to leave for England to attend conferences, Joe to give an account of the whole affair and I was summoned to discuss with Signals in the War Office the matter of WT sets in the jungle, which were not a great success. It was a hair-raising trip home in a York aircraft. We had a forced landing in Malta

where Joe and I stayed in the club there for a week, waiting for the plane to be repaired. When we eventually set off and were over the Med the captain of the aircraft came to Joe and said, "General, we must get down again and the only place is Sardinia, which only has a small fighter strip." We put on our lifebelts and waited and watched the water flash past the windows and we stopped at the end of the runway with the nose of the aircraft over the water! The York had to be dismantled and we finished up in a DC-3 sitting on packing cases all the way to Northolt.'

Brigadier Fergusson was given a job running courses in jungle warfare and setting exercises for newly arrived formations. He went back to England in January 1945 for a job at Combined Operations Headquarters.

Brigadier Abdy Ricketts was appointed commander of the 4th West African Brigade in the Arakan. He later became a Major-General and lived to the ripe old age of eighty-seven.

On 1 February 1945 all battalion commanders were summoned to meet General Oliver Leese, of Allied Land Forces, South-East Asia Command. He announced that Special Force was to be broken up and the battalions were dispersed all over SEAC and India Command.

After the last Chindits came out of the jungle in August 1944 and Special Force was disbanded in February 1945, there still remained a small number of Chindits who had yet to find their way home. The majority of these were in Rangoon jail. Allen Wilding recalls their last, long march to freedom:

'Towards the end of April 1945, various reports of the Japs burning documents etc. began to circulate. This was both good and bad news. From past experience it was, we thought, unlikely that we should be left alive if and when they left. On the other hand, it pointed to their acceptance of defeat, and we might, just perhaps, get away with it.

'On 25 April, we were issued with some cotton "long-johns" and very small plimsoles and told that all "fit" men were to march out that evening.*

'Around 1300 hours we finally set off. John Wild and I slung our small bundles on a bamboo pole and carried it between us. Some of the men had been in solitary up to the start of the march. They were wonderfully brave and with one tragic exception managed to keep up, although they had had no exercise for months. None of us was exactly fit – at the time I weighed about seven stone. That day we marched about fifteen miles. We set off again at dusk on 26 April and marched for twenty miles. By now our feet were getting really sore. One officer could go no further and I am afraid he was bayoneted by a rather horrible guard we called "the Jockey".

---

* In the event, all those who were left behind were alive when the relieving troops arrived, including Lieutenant John Kerr (5 Column, 8 Plt Commander) with his wounded leg.

The next march, from the evening of 27 April, was fairly horrible. It was perhaps eighteen or nineteen miles and we finished up just south of Pegu. All day Allied planes flew over our position. While it was wonderful to see a Spitfire again it was a bit alarming. I found myself a nice deep rut made by a bullock cart into which I fitted nicely. During the day Ken Spurlock and Johnnie Nealon (1 Column commando platoon), together with a number of Australian NCOs, pushed off. Their slightly hilarious adventures may some time be told.

'The next night we passed through Pegu and were cheered by the signs of panic there. A Jap staff car came along and the occupants had a chat with the commandant. Shortly after this we left the road and proceeded across country. I had about "had it" by now. At all halts I just curled up and went to sleep. I thought I might be able to manage another night's march but that was all. Alas, another poor chap fell out and was murdered by one of the guards. He had come out of solitary just before the march.

'Just after dawn on 29 April we halted in a deserted village. I spread out my half blanket and went to sleep only to be roused by a lot of semi-hysterical shouting – the Japs had left us! On the orders of the senior officers a very long message was laid out using our long-johns, together with a Union Jack made using a red "hospital" blanket as a base. Then our RAF types proceeded to flash mirrors at passing planes to attract their attention. In this they succeeded only too well. A flight of "Hurribombers" of the Indian Air Force bombed and strafed us. The trees seemed to bow under the weight of the cannon shells and the stout tree behind which I sheltered seemed to grow thinner by the minute. My mess tin, containing my pipe and my emergency ration, an onion and a small lump of jagri, just vanished. It must have taken a direct hit. When the planes had gone, we discovered there was only one casualty out of the 400 prisoners, Brigadier Hobson, the senior officer in the jail. A few hours previously he had announced to us all, "At last I can tell you something that you have been waiting to hear for years: we are all free men." He had been killed outright. That night, two of the American prisoners made contact with the Burmese and with the Army. They returned with instructions that we were to wait until moonrise, then cross the paddy fields where we would be met by our own troops. We owe a lot to those two Americans.

'Joe Edmunds (RAF, 1 Column) and I set out with some others. At length we came upon a very efficient looking, very well organised company of Pathans, who guided us very gently on to trucks. We were officially greeted by an enormous Sikh medical officer who shook us each by the hand and said, "Thank you, thank you!" I should have thought that we should have thanked him. A short run in the vehicles and we were in the West Yorks lines.'

On 15 August 1945, following the detonation of two atomic bombs over Hiroshima and Nagasaki, Emperor Hirohito signed an Imperial Rescript, telling his people that they must 'endure the unendurable' and surrender. On 18 August all remaining Japanese troops in Burma were instructed to lay down their arms and on the twenty-second the first formal surrenders began.

'Too many damn books!' wrote Brigadier Jack Wilkinson, former CO of the 2nd Leicesters, to the author one day in 1995. And as the bibliography shows, there have indeed been many books written about Wingate and his Chindits. As the author typed these words in April 1996 he looked at his bookshelf and counted twenty-one of them. How many have been written about Slim, Mountbatten or Stilwell? Wingate was a dyed in the wool, slightly eccentric British hero, the Burma equivalent of Lawrence of Arabia, and he will be remembered and written about for a long while yet. Unlike many of his contemporaries and detractors, he wanted to get to grips with the Japanese and fight. Not for him the clubs and mess nights back in Delhi. He led from the front, and when he was unable to be there, he made sure that his men were trained and supplied to the best of his ability. What footslogger could ask for more?

What did Wingate and his Chindits achieve? Although the Chindits' main role was to help the American-Chinese force forward to Mogaung and Myitkyina and open the overland route to China, their operations also greatly assisted Slim's IV Corps. 111 Brigade and 14 Brigade had between them cut the land communications of the Japanese 15th and 31st Divisions attacking Kohima. They had also destroyed supply dumps east of the Chindwin and drawn off half of the effort of the Japanese 5th Air Division, which reduced support to the troops attacking across the Chindwin. In April, the Chindit invasion caused General Mutaguchi to divert the newly arrived 53rd Division to clear up the airborne forces. They had in fact been earmarked as a reserve to help him take Imphal, and he later complained that 'if I had had only one regiment of 53rd Division, I could have taken Imphal and opened the route to the Assam Valley'. With Mogaung and Myitkyina now in Allied hands, the oil pipeline and road to China was now open. The British 36th Division flew into Myitkyina airfield and began to make its way south towards Indaw. Mutaguchi's right flank and rear were being threatened long before 14th Army crossed the Chindwin in pursuit. With them went the RAF detachments who had served with the Chindits. They were required to call in air support and supply drops, an idea patented by Wingate and now adopted by the whole Army.

As for the decision to disband the Chindits, Lord Louis Mountbatten later wrote to Mike Calvert and informed him that: 'It was the most distasteful job of my career to agree to your disbandment. I only agreed because by that time the whole Army was Chindit-minded.' Wingate would have appreciated the compliment.

The last word on Wingate, in this book at any rate, will go to Major J. C. Long, who wrote the following in 1980 for an Appreciation of Wingate compiled by the Chindits Old Comrades Association, and it is reproduced here with his permission. John Long marched with Wingate in 1943 as a demolitions officer with the 3rd Battalion, 2nd Gurkhas and again in 1944 as a column 2ic with the 1st Battalion, King's (Liverpool) Regiment. He carried his pack, walked the miles and fought the fight and earned his right to pass comment on Wingate:

'I was privileged to take part in both of General Wingate's campaigns, though I need not have participated in either. That I did so does not presuppose any undue hankering after adventure on my part, nor was I too witless to find an easier job. It was simply that I was convinced, as I remain convinced today, of the integrity and ability of that great man Orde Wingate.

'Due to a quirk in military postings I, together with other officers in our particular draft, found myself unemployed in India during the spring of 1942. Our host unit, a regular British battalion, was kindness itself, but not unnaturally looked forward to a return to their normal regimental life on our departure. They were, therefore, not displeased to announce, one day, that there was an odd character called Wingate in the jungle near Saugor who might find jobs for some of us. Accordingly, we repaired to Patheria, near Saugor, where we disturbed Brigadier (as he then was) Wingate addressing an audience seated in a four-sided amphitheatre formed by steps leading down to a well. Clearly annoyed at the interruption, he bade us be seated, and continued with his exposition on long-range penetration groups. It was then that I, and indeed the majority of our particular draft, decided that Orde Wingate was the man for us – as I still feel thirty-eight years later.

'Why? It was certainly not any kind of charisma on his part, – for even on further acquaintance I found him a prickly, rather than easy, individual. It was not purely his eloquence, for oratory alone, albeit helpful, does not win over the wide cross-section of people who believed so implicitly in Wingate. It was, I am convinced, the way his undoubted ability came over, and the feeling he gave that here was an honest man whom one could trust, and who would not let one down if one threw one's lot in with him. Such proved to be the case.

'The word "leadership", or lack of it, is in the 1980s a much overused word, whether applied to the Church, the state, industry, the armed forces, the police or other facets of national life. It seems almost trite to say that Orde Wingate was a great and natural leader, but such he was. His leadership, or "power of communication", was not confined to any particular group of followers. He came across to officers and soldiers alike, no matter how diverse their backgrounds, or whether their skins were coloured black, white, brown or yellow. Each of us felt that any communication from Orde Wingate, whether verbal or written, was addressed to us personally. He behaved as senior officers, i.e. leaders, are meant to behave, but sometimes don't. As the senior officer present, he took the rap from higher authority when something went wrong, even though the fault was that of a subordinate (the subordinate would not, of course, escape unscathed). He never asked anybody to do something he couldn't do himself, or have a damned good try at doing himself. This, in many cases, involved tremendous mental guts on his part, for his physique, *per se*, was certainly not robust enough to match the immense physical demands he made upon it. His physical presence, in any given situation, even a brief visit, was always an inspiration to all ranks present, any language barrier notwithstanding.

'To revert to that overused word "leadership". In a lifetime, one is lucky to meet but one or two great leaders of men, and Orde Wingate was one such. Of those who served with him in Burma, of whatever rank, race, colour or creed, there can be few who would not follow him again. I certainly would, either on or off the battlefield.'

Appendix One

Chindit Awards

VC

Captain George Cairns, Somerset Light
  Inf, attd South Staffords (*posthumous*)
Maj F. G. Blaker, MC., 9 GR (*posthumous*)
Rfn Tul Bahadur Pun, 6 GR
Captain Michael Allmand, 6th Duke of
  Connaught's Own Lancers, attd 6 GR
  (*posthumous*)

CBE

Maj-Gen W. D. A. Lentaigne, DSO.,
  4 GR–*Comd Special Force*
Brig L. E. C. M. Perowne, *Comd Inf Bde*
Brig J. M. Calvert DSO, *Comd Ind Inf Bde*

Bar to DSO

Brig J. R. Morris, DSO., *9 GR Comd Ind
  Inf Bde*

DSO

Lt-Col C. J. Wilkinson, *Leicesters*
Brig D. C. C. Tulloch, MC., *RA HQ
  Special Force*
Lt-Col W. P. Scott, MC., *Kings*
Maj D. G. C. Whyte, *RAMC*
Lt-Col J. Masters, *4 GR*
W/Cdr R. G. K. Thompson, MC., *RAF*
Col F. D. Rome, *RF*
Lt-Col G. G. Green, *BW*
Lt-Col R. Degg, *S. Staffords*
Lt-Col N. F. B. Shaw, *6 GR*
Lt-Col T. J. Barrow, *Beds and Herts*
Lt-Col P. H. Graves-Morris, MC., *Worc R
  attd Y and L*
Lt-Col J. N. Dainiels, *Leicesters*
Lt-Col T. V. Close, *Queens*
Lt-Col C. P. Vaughan, *WG attd 7 NR*
Lt J. E. D. Wilcox, *S. Staffords*
Maj. J. G. Lockett, MC., *Seaforths, attd
  Leicesters*
Maj. T. D. Ross, *BW*

OBE

Col C. C. Fairweather, *R Sigs HQ Special
  Force*
Lt-Col R. Chalkley, GM., *RAOC HQ
  Special Force*

MBE

Maj F. B. Ledlie, *RIASC*
Maj R. H. R. Stainton, *King's Own*
Lt-Col E. F. Kyte, *RE HQ Special
  Force*
Maj P. Hothersall, *REME HQ Special
  Force*
Capt L. Lazum Tang, *Burma Rifles*
Lt J. G. Crowne, *NR*
Capt A. A. Tuck, *King's Own*
Maj J. J. Elbert, *RAMC*
Capt M. M. Campbell *RAMC*
Maj J. W. Robinson, *RE*
Capt (QM) R. Abbott, *Border Regt*

IOM

Sub Tika Bahadur Khattri, 9 GR
Jem Lalbir Gurung, 6 GR
Jem Riki Ramiale, 6 GR

DCM

Sjt J. Donald, *Cameronians*
Sjt W. Bolton, *King's Own*
Sjt J. T. Chandler, *Leicesters*
Sjt J. Perry, *S. Staffords*
L/Cpl J. Young, *S. Staffords*
Pte J. Levene, *King's Own*
CSM W. Cargill, *Black Watch*
Sjt Alhassan Geiri, *7 NR*
Sjt A. Hough, *Beds and Herts*

IDSM

Hav Tilak Bahadur Khattri, 9 GR
Hav Chakra Bahadur Mall, 9 GR
Hav Top Bahadur Gurung, 6 GR
Nk Patti Thapa, 6 GR
Nk Chaman Sing Thapa, 6 GR
Nk Moti Lal Thapa, 6 GR
Rfn Nar Bahadur Khattri, 9 GR
Hav Chakra Bahadur Mall, 9 GR

Bar to MC

Maj J. C. Bruce, MC., *Burma Rifles*
Maj E. M. D. Vanderspar, MC., *Leicesters*
Capt C. V. E. Gordon, MC., *RE*

MC

Maj B. J. Brennan, Cameronians *(SR)*
Lt-Col G. H. Astell, *Recce*
Lt-Col P. G. Cane, *9 GR*
Maj J. C. White, *Recce*
Maj G. M. K. Hall, *7 NR*
Maj D. M. Scott, *Border*
Capt (Rev) T. Hawthorn, *RACHD attd.*
  Cameronians (SR)
Capt W. A. Anderson, *BW*
Capt J. S. Ross, *Beds and Herts*
Capt A. B. Whitehead, *King's Own*
Capt D. M. E. McGillycuddy, *4 GR*
Lt B. S. Burns, *6 GR*
Lt D. L. G. Scholey, *S. Staffords*
Lt S. J. Smith, *Leicesters*
Lt W. D. Hardless, *RIASC attd Burma*
  Rifles
Lt G. F. Anderson, *Black Watch*
Lt T. A. Riley, *King's Own*
Lt J. C. Salazar, *Beds and Herts*
Lt D. E. Arnold, *RWF attd 7 NR*
Lt P. B. Chambers, *Cameronians(SR)*
Lt E. Brain, *Border*
Lt H. C. Marshall, *Border*
Maj E. F. O. Stuart, *1 Punjab*
Maj P. Cox, *RA*
Capt T. C. Thorne, *R.A.M.C.*
Jem Digbahadur Gurung, *6 GR*
Sub La Raw, *Burma Rifles*
Sub Khama, *Burma Rifles*
Sub Kara Nand Surma, *Burma Rifles*
Sub Agu Di, *Burma Rifles*
Jem Lian Nawn, *Burma Rifles*
Jem John Hla Shein, *Burma Rifles*
Jem Bu Gyan, *Burma Rifles*
Lt R. D. Stevenson, *Borders*
S/Ldr R. J. Jennings, *RAF*
F/Lt J. Gillies, DFM, *RAF (missing)*
F/Lt G. Allan, *RAF*
F/Lt B. J. V. Young, *RAF*
Sub Indra Bahadur Khattri, *9 GR*
Sub Saw Min Maung, *Burma Rifles*
Sub La Bang La, *Burma Rifles*
Sub Karna Bahadur Khattri *9 GR*
Jem Yembahadur Sahi, *9 GR*
Jem Bhagtbir Gurung, *6 GR*

Jem Digbahadur Gurung, *6 GR*
Jem Keshbahadur Khattri, IDSM, *9 GR*
Maj J. C. K. Harrington, *LF*
Lt J. Devlin, *Beds and Herts*
Maj F. Hilton, *S. Staffords*
Capt J. S. I. Chesshire, *RAMC*
Lt A. D. Pond, *Beds and Herts*
Capt G. W. F. Smith, *6 GR*
Capt H. P. N. Benson, *S. Staffords*
Maj A. S. Gurling, *RIASC*
Sub Yem Bahadur Khattri, *9 GR*
Maj J. M. Ritchie, *6 GR*
Capt M. E. Busk, *Burma Rifles*
Lt F. H. Luxa, *York and Lancs*
Capt L. J. Stevens, *Beds and Herts*
Lt N. Durrant, *S. Staffords*
Lt A. S. Binnie, *DWR*
Maj C. C. A. Carfrae, *NR*
Capt G. V. Faulkner, *IMS/1AMC*
Lt F. Halliwell, *S. Staffords*
Capt R. A. B. Kinloch, *RAMC*
Lt E. R. Macaulay, *NR*
Lt G. B. Down, *Burma Rifles*
Capt W. E. G. Butler, *Lancs Fus*
Maj E. C. Booth, *Leicesters*
2/Lt Saw Lader, *Burma Rifles*
Capt F. B. Newbould, *Burma Rifles*
Lt J. W. Passmore, *9 GR*
Capt O. P. Llewellyn, *RAMC*
Capt W. A. Johnston, *York and Lancs*
Lt A. B. B. Woodburn, *King's Own*
Lt G. S. Pearce, *York and Lancs.*
Capt W. M. Park, *R Sigs*
Lt C. K. Rooke, *6 GR*
Capt H. W. Swannell, *BW*
Lt J. C. Finlay, *Queens*

Bar to MM

Tpr M. J. Flynn, MM., *Recce*
Sjt G. Smith, MM., *Essex*

MM

CSM S. Robson, *King's Own*
Sjt R. C. Newton, *Recce*
Sjt R. A. Ross, *Leicesters*
Sjt H. Cropper, *Lancs Fus*
Sjt W. H. Haynes, *Lancs Fus*
Sjt K. E. Crute, *Lancs Fus*
Sjt J. J. Gibson, *Lancs Fus*
Sjt B. Lowton, *Lancs Fus*
Sjt W. Bartlam, *S. Staffords*
Sjt C. McCluskey, *Black Watch*

Sjt C. C. Perkins, 7 NR
Sjt H. Steen, *York and Lancs*
Sjt J. J. McQuillam, *King's Own*
Sjt W. H. Boon, *King's Own*
Sjt F. Pratt, *RA attd King's Own*
Sjt H. Eden, *Leicesters*
Sjt W. Clift, *S. Staffords*
L/Sjt L. Rogerson, *Border Regt*
Sjt A. M. Fraser, *RAF*
L/Sjt J. C. Jenkins, *S. Staffords*
Cpl. G. Farrand, *S. Staffords*
Bdr L. J. Summers, *RA*
Cpl W. J. Conkey, *Border Regt*
Cpl J. F. Evans, *Beds and Herts*
Cpl F. Fox, *Leicesters*
Cpl H. W. Smith, *Lancs Fus*
L/Sjt L. Mahon, *King's Own*
L/Cpl A. Halsall, *King's Own*
L/Cpl W. Wedgewood, *Lancs Fus*
L/Cpl V. J. Higgins, *S. Stafford*
L/Cpl D. McLellan, *Black Watch*
Tpr M. J. Flynn, *Recce*
Gnr W. Sawyer, *RA*
Gnr T. Condon, *RA*
Gnr L. Turner, *RA*
Pte A. Bristow, *S. Staffords*
Pte J. M. Bailey, *Border Regt*
Pte S. Cottle, *Essex Regt*
Cpl S. Henshaw, *Border Regt*
Pte W. Ironside, *Border Regt*
Pte S. J. C. Danks, *S. Staffords*
Pte J. Munt, *RAMC*
Pte D. Brown, *King's Own*
Hav Shib Jang Gurung, *4 GR*
Hav Tilbur Gurung, *6 GR*
Hav Bal Bahadur Pun, *6 GR*
Hav Tirth Bahadur Thapa, *9 GR*
Hav Bhimlai Gurung, *6 GR*
L/Hav Pahalsing Thapa, *6 GR*
Nk Tikaram Thapa, *6 GR*
Nk Khalbahadur Khattri, *9 GR*
L/Nk Thamansing Thapa, *6 GR*
L/Nk Tek Bahadur Khattri, *9 GR*
L/Nk Lal Bahadur Gharti, *9 GR*
L/Nk Tula Ram Gurung, *6 GR*
Rfn Chhiring Lana, *6 GR*
Rfn Bahadur Thapa, *6 GR*
Rfn Gupta Bahadur Khandka, *9 GR*
Rfn Dilli Bahadur, *9 GR*
Rfn Bhairab Bahadur Thapa, *6 GR*
Sjt Abdulla Banana, *NR*
Cpl Adamu Gafasa, *NR*

Cpl Ibrahim Mansu, *NR*
Cpl Audu Tuberi, *NR*
Pte Mailafu Shangev, *7 NR*
Pte Umoru Malanawa, *7 NR*
CSM A. Kitt, *7 NR*
Sgt H. Bottomley, *Lancs Fus*
Hav Tirth Bahadur Thapa, *9GR*
Hav Kul Bahadur Gurung, *6 GR*
Nk Chandra Prasad Rana, *6 GR*
Sjt S. D. McFall, *King's Own*
Pte W. Muggleton, *S. Staffords*
Pte R. Boyd, *Beds and Herts*
Cpl Adamu Bauchi, *7NR*
Pte J. Welsh, *Black Watch*
Sjt R. L. M. Waters, *RAMC*
Pte T. B. Bramble, *Queens*
Cpl S. Priestley, *York and Lancs*
Gnr G. W. Parchment, *RA attd*
    Cameronians (SR)
Sjt Umoru Numan, *7NR*
Sjt H. Dodd, *R. Sigs*
Sigmn J. H. Charleston, *R. Sigs*
Sigmn A. E. Ward, *R. Sigs*

BGM
Nk Lazang Tu, *Burma Rifles*
Nk Kya Lin, *Burma Rifles*
Hav Hla Maung, *Burma Rifles*
Sub La Bang La, *Burma Rifles*
Hav Lauk Kunga, *Burma Rifles*

BEM
Sjt T. Collins, *Border Regt*
L/Sjt S. Oliver, *RE*
Pte D. Irving, *Border Regt*
Pte R. French, *Beds and Herts*
Sigmn H. E. Froom, *R. Sigs*
L/Sjt J. C. Grummitt, *Beds and Herts*
Cpl C. A. Ralph, *R. Sigs*
Sjt J. R. Roberts, *RAMC*

Certificates of Gallantry
Sjt T. Temple, *Cameronians (SR)*
Sjt W.W. Trott, *Recce*
Sjt J. A. Chaplin, *King's Own*
Sjt P. O'Connor, *Lancs Fus*
Sjt C. W. J. Hart, *York and Lancs*
Cpl G. Fletcher, *King's Own*
Cpl L. Shepherd, *Cameronians (SR)*
Cpl L. E. Muggleton, *Leicesters*
L/Sjt T. Pickering, *King's Own*
Cpl G. Ewens, *R. Sigs*

Cpl A. M. Yuille, *R. Sigs*
L/Cpl F. C. Brown, *Recce*
L/Cpl R. Williams, *King's Own*
L/Cpl J. A. Holden, *S. Staffords*
Cpl J. Worsley, *Lancs Fus*
L/Cpl F. C. Brown, *Recce*
L/Cpl J. E. Kirke, *R. Sigs*
Pte R. Tucker, *Border Regt*
Pte C. T. J. Dunford, *Border Regt*
Cpl H. M. Jones, *R. Sigs*
Pte A. Tomlinson, *DWR*
Pte T. Jones, *Leicesters*
Pte A. Reid, *King's Own*
Pte A. H. Spark, *York and Lancs*
Pte D. W. Thompson, *King's Own*
Pte J. Cramp, *King's Own*
Gnr W. H. C. Wales, *RA*
Spr R. Theobold, *RE*
Spr W. J. Terry, *RE*
Jem Chhabi Lal Thapa, *6 GR*
Hav U Byit Tu, *Burma Rifles*
Hav Bahadur Gurung, *4 GR*
Hav Dila Sing Gurung, *4 GR*
Nk Sher Bahadur Thapa, *6 GR*
Nk Moti Ram Thapa, *6 GR*
Nk Balbir Pun, *6 GR*
L/Nk Rabi Lal Thapa, *6 GR*
L/Nk Gyan Bahadur Karki, *9 GR*
L/Nk Aitbur Pana, *4 GR*
Rfn Damar Bahadur Gurung, *4 GR*
Rfn Jagat Bahadur Khattri, *9 GR*
Rfn Jit Bahadur Thapa, *4 GR*
Sjt Shaibu Godabawa, *NR*
Sjt Garaba Gombe, *NR*
Cpl Buba Biu, *NR*
Cpl Jemo Maidoba, *NR*

Pte Yando Audu, *NR*
Pte Baba Bruce, *WAAMC*

Mentions in Despatches
F/Lt L. Hart, *RAF*
F/Sjt J. F. Bishop, *RAF*
F/SJt A. C. A. Thompson, *RAF*
Sjt J. F. Kelsall, *RAF*
Sjt E. J. Horton, *RAF*

American Awards
Silver Star
Brig J. M. Calvert, DSO., *late RE Comd
Ind Inf Bde*
Lt J. E. D. Wilcox, *S. Staffords*
Jem Riki Ramiale, *6 GR*
L/Nk Balbir Pun, *6 GR*

Soldiers' Medal
Maj K. I. Barlow, *RAVC*

Awards to Allied Personnel
DSO
Brig/Gen W. D. Old, *Troop Carrier Comd*
Col P. J. Cochran, *No. 1 Air Commando
USAAF*

OBE
Col Li Hung, *Chinese Army*

MC
Maj Pang Hak Lup, *Chinese Army*
Capt Su, *Chinese Army*

MM
S/Sjt R. S. Eudy, *No. 1 Air Commando*

Appendix Two

Chindit Doctor

Men wounded or taken ill during the first Wingate expedition had no
chance of evacuation to India. If a friendly village was near, they might
be entrusted to the care of the headman, and indeed one or two 'Ben
Gunn' types were found the following year living with villagers. On the
other hand, many villagers were not friendly, especially when threatened
with reprisals for helping the British. Some men were killed or literally
'sold down the river' by villagers, particularly after Wingate had
dispersed his brigade. The sick and wounded who could still stand
had one simple choice, to keep up with one's comrades or fall by the
wayside. Some were left, sitting against a tree, to wait for the Japanese, or
death itself, to find them.

Wingate tried to rectify the problem for the second campaign in 1944.
The Americans would supply light planes to take out the wounded from
short strips hacked out of paddy fields or from airstrips at established
strongholds. However, they were largely withdrawn in May with the
onset of the monsoon rains and it was up to the ingenuity and fortitude
of the Chindits to get their casualties out as best they could. In the latter
stages of the campaign men had no choice but to march or die. It fell to
the Chindit doctors to try to keep the men fit and healthy. It was easier
said than done. The men were living on K rations, designed for short-
term operations only; they were behind the Japanese lines for months,
with all the stress that entails: carrying heavy packs and sleeping on the
wet jungle floor did little to enhance fitness, and then there was the
jungle itself. Leeches were everywhere and disease was rife. Two Chindit
doctors described some of the problems to the author:

Captain John Chesshire, RAMC, attached to the South Staffords:

'Mepacrine tablets were given to suppress malaria, but the supply of them
was linked to food rations. If we were fighting hard, which we were most
of the time, we left out food in supply drops in favour of ammunition and
it took a little time for the supply people to catch up with this. Also there
was a rumour that mepacrine would render you impotent. It is impossible
to know how much influence this had. I got malaria myself and I was fairly
good at taking mepacrine. We had little confidence in mepacrine for

treatment and used quinine, usually the first dose intravenously. I was unconscious with malaria, had intravenous quinine at sundown and was fit for work the next day. We had so much cerebral malaria and so much relapsing malaria that I feel sure that malaria did break through the mepacrine barrier.

'Many of us had an intestinal sprue-type diarrhoea, which often did not even give time to get one's trousers down. We had difficulty in effective disposal of faeces, especially in White City where we were stuck in trenches for days on end and at Mogaung where we were in several inches of water and latrines could only be built up above the flood water – not very practical. Water sterilising could be done with tablets. However, many times men were too thirsty to wait, but were well aware of the need. A water point was always dangerous, so the men went down in small parties, drank as much as they could, then filled everything they could and put in the tablets.

'Vasovagal attacks could have a devastating effect on the column, because they occurred in epidemics. You might have six men go down at a time, white, unconscious, sweaty. The causes were salt deficiency, fall of blood pressure, fear of failure, lack of interest. The only treatment was brutality with verbal or more often physical provocation. If I saw it likely, I gave the man a particular job to do, like cleaning his rifle, either on the march or more often at the ten-minute halt which was when the attacks most often occurred. They did not happen when bullets were flying about. It was sometimes difficult to distinguish from cerebral malaria, which can be quite sudden.

'Cutaneous diphtheria. I suspected this and wrote to medical branch. I was told "nonsense"; this only occurs in parts of the Middle East. However, there were some unexplained deaths, even in those evacuated with only moderate wounds. I travelled on the train across India with the men after the second campaign and some found they could not read the newspaper. Later, when we got to Dehra Dun, there were cases of food drop and clumsiness. One Sergeant died in Dehra Dun hospital of intercostal paralysis and a Captain Lawrence was in the same hospital with sores and paralysis of some sort.

'Evacuation of wounded. It really needs eight men to carry one through hilly jungle. Four are resting and carrying the equipment of the four with the stretcher. So in theory, with fifty stretcher cases the whole column would become a stretcher party. Until we got to Loihinche we never had more than twelve stretcher cases, but thereafter we started hiding dumps of wounded until we could collect them.

'After the Mogaung battle, while we were marching to Shadazup, morale did fall off and I had several times to use verbal and sometimes physical violence to make men get up and walk. I hope they forgive me! I was the last to leave Mogaung and after I crossed the bridge, which was only two planks wide, I passed out for the first time. Later my batman started to collapse and I had to use force to keep him going. I was rebuked by some NCOs for being rough with him, but he got home.

'In Slim's book *Defeat into Victory*, he quotes the ratio of sickness to battle casualties as 100 sick for every one battle casualty. That may have applied to his men fighting at Imphal, but it did not apply to the Chindits. I kept records for the South Staffords which showed that, including those who went into hospital after we came out, our rate was one sick to one battle casualty.'

Major Desmond Whyte, senior medical officer, 111 Brigade:

'In addition to battle casualties and accidents, we doctors had in mind malaria, dysentery, hepatitis, scrub typhus, helminthic infections and skin problems. Each column would have 100 pounds of medical supplies, one side of a mule being allotted for the doctor's pannier, designed to give ready access to all items without unloading the animal. Three ponies with convertible saddles were assigned for casualties and there were four medical orderlies. Each soldier carried his first field dressing in his seventy-pound pack.

'A Gurkha could construct a stretcher from bamboo in a short time which could be dragged behind a mule or pony. One end rested on the saddle of the mule and the other end was dragged along the ground, with four men in attendance to push the ensemble up steep or slippery slopes. One early casualty – a skull injury – was transported for several days, unconscious but kept alive by fluid, brandy and sugar, plus intravenous drip. Catheterisation and the penetrating heat of the sun were problems. Eventually he was flown out and survived. Casualty evacuation by air often entailed lengthy and isolated journeys by the medical team and casualties to find a suitable strip, with enemy attention never far away. One day a light plane landed and seeing my party of several casualties said, "I'll take two." We pointed out that his plane could only take one, the patient almost literally being wound around the pilot's waist. He said, "We can't leave these dying men here" loaded up and sped across the open paddy. The plane was too heavy to take off and he hit the trees at the far end. The pilot climbed out of the wreckage and said, "Aw shit, I ought to be shot," to which I replied, "We will be if we don't scarper." We loaded the casualties on to the mules, set the plane alight and slipped into the jungle to the sound of ranging mortar fire. One man was dead, the other died soon after. I read a short prayer from a cellulose-covered card as we buried them, placing a small bamboo cross over the site. We knew that the jackal, ever present in the jungle, would find the shallow grave.

'We were greatly concerned about the increasing incidence of sepsis, particularly from leech bite, which resulted in a chronically indurated ulcer (jungle sores), a cause of increasing disability. Infectious hepatitis also spread slowly through the formations. Treating surgical emergencies, particularly in view of our circumstances, taught us the importance of conservation of tissue with minimal interference. When we were static, immediate debridement, using sodium pentothal as the only anaesthetic, and treating shock by conservation of heat and intravenous transfusion, were our mainstays. Splinting and delayed primary suture of wounds were routine. Serious leg injuries were often disastrous, although we later received considerable help transporting these from a team of mahouts and elephants who had been employed on teak forestry before the Japanese invasion.'

The doctors were the unsung heroes of the campaign. Readers have already noted the descriptions of the casualties at White City and particularly Blackpool. At the end of the campaign Doc Whyte was awarded the Distinguished Service Order and John Chesshire the Military Cross.

Bibliography

Allen, Louis, *Burma – The Longest War 1941–45*, J. M. Dent and Sons, 1984. A very well researched book on the whole war in Burma, including the part played by the Chindits. Includes much material from Japanese sources.

Bidwell, Brigadier Shelford, *The Chindit War – The Campaign in Burma 1944*, Hodder and Stoughton, 1979. Very good analytical account of the 1944 Chindit campaign.

Biggs, Maurice, *The Story Of The Gurkha VCs*, Southern Press 1993. An account of each Gurkha Victoria Cross winner from 1858 to 1965. Includes the three Chindit Gurkha VCs. Available from the Gurkha Museum, Winchester.

Calvert, Mike, *Fighting Mad*, Airlife, 1996. An excellent autobiography of a fearless warrior who became Wingate's right-hand man and led 77 Brigade, the most successful Chindit unit, in the 1944 campaign. Calvert went on to command the SAS Brigade in Europe and refounded the regiment in Malaya during the communist insurgency.

Calvert, Mike, *Prisoners Of Hope*, Leo Cooper 1996. Brigadier Mike Calvert's own description of the activities of 77 Brigade, from its fly in by glider in March 1944 to the walk out of its survivors after the battle for Mogaung four months later.

Cane, Peter, *Chinese Chindits*, Gale and Polden, 1948. Written by a column commander in 4th Battalion, 9th Gurkhas who was part of Morris Force. A brave Chindit describes the attempts by his column to kill as many Japanese as possible, despite the squandering of the force by Stilwell and mishandling by Morris.

Carfrae, Charles, *Chindit Column*, William Kimber, 1985. Written by one of the column commanders of 7th Battalion, Nigeria Regiment. A very interesting account of an African Chindit battalion.

Fergusson, Bernard, *Beyond The Chindwin*, Anthony Mott Ltd., 1983. An updated version of the 1945 edition. Describes the adventures of 5 Column during the first Wingate expedition. Only one in five made it back to India. Updated with notes on fates of members of column.

Fergusson, Bernard, *The Wild Green Earth*, Collins, 1952. An account by a master of words of his 16 Brigade, the only Chindit brigade to walk into Burma in 1944.

Hawley, Dennis, *The Death Of Wingate*, Well researched book covering all aspects of the tragic death of the Chindit leader, whose remains are now buried in Washington. Available from the author at Yew Tree Cottage, Yew Tree Lane, Slaithwaite, Huddersfield HD7 5UD.

James, Harold, *Across The Threshold Of Battle*, Book Guild, 1993. The story of nineteen-year-old Second Lieutenant Harold James and his adventures with Mike Calvert's 3 Column during the first Chindit expedition in 1943. A good insight into the lot of the Gurkha Chindits.

James, Richard Rhodes, *Chindit*, John Murray Ltd., 1980. Cipher officer on the staff of 111 Brigade, Rhodes James was in a good position to know what was going on, particularly during the fighting at Blackpool and afterwards.

MacHorton, Ian, *Safer Than A Known Way*, Odhams Press, 1958. A dramatised account of the nineteen-year-old Lieutenant's journey back to India after being wounded during the ambush of his column deep inside Burma.

Masters, Jack, *The Road Past Mandalay*, Michael Joseph, 1961. A fine account of the activities of 111 Brigade by the Brigade Major who became its commander, if only temporarily. A good account of the fighting at Blackpool.

Milner, Joe, *To Blazes With Glory – A Chindit's war*, Gaskell, 1995. 450 pages. Excellent fictionalised account of a Chindit NCO and his experiences as he fights at White City, Broadway and Blackpool. Written by a former member of the King's Own.

O'Brien, Terence, *Out Of The Blue*, Collins, 1984. An Australian RAF officer serving with Morris Force describes their trials and tribulations and the lost opportunities of the force led by the controversial Brigadier 'Jumbo' Morris.

Rolo, Charles, *Wingate's Raiders*, George Harrap and Co., 1944. An excellent contemporary account of the first Wingate expedition, with much material from Major John Jefferies and Squadron Leader Robert Thompson.

Sharpe, Philip, *To Be A Chindit*, Book Guild, 1995. A signaller NCO with the 45th Reconnaissance Regiment tells of his time with the unit, which was destroyed fighting the Japanese at Thetkegyin and outside White City.

Shaw, James, *The March Out*, Rupert Hart-Davis, 1953. Life in the 12th Battalion, Nigeria Regiment during the 1944 campaign, by one of its European sergeants. He was one of only six out of the forty Europeans with the battalion to walk out at the end.

Stevens, Lieutenant-Colonel G. R. OBE. *History Of The 2nd King Edward's Own Goorkhas Vol 3. 1921–48*, Gale and Polden, 1952. A very detailed record of the activities of the 3rd Battalion, 2nd Gurkha Rifles during the first Wingate expedition. Not very flattering towards Wingate. Available from the Gurkha Museum in Winchester.

Stibbe, Philip, *Return via Rangoon*, Leo Cooper, 1994. The story of a platoon commander in Major Bernard Fergusson's 5 Column during the 1943 expedition. Wounded at Hintha and incarcerated in Rangoon jail, he was one of the few Chindits to survive two years of captivity.

Towill, Bill, *A Chindit's Chronicle*. A very good account of the activities of all of the Gurkhas battalions who served with the Chindits, by a former officer with 3rd Battalion, 9th Gurkhas. Self-published and available from the author at Wildwoods, Motts Hill Lane, Tadworth, Surrey KT20 5BH.

Tulloch, Major-General Derek, *Wingate In Peace and War*, MacDonald, 1972. A unique insight into Wingate by his chief of staff and friend. Goes a long way to right the wrongs perpetrated against Wingate's memory by his critics.

Index